D0650690

# CHUCK BERRY

John Collis is a music journalist and
author, and a life-long fan of Chuck Berry.
His previous books include The Rock Primer,
The Story of Chess Records and biographies
of Ike Turner and Van Morrison.
He also covers cricket for the Guardian.
He lives in London.

# CHUCK BERRY

## The Biography

## John Collis

AURUM PRESS

First published in Great Britain
2002 by Aurum Press Ltd
25 Bedford Avenue, London WC1B 3AT

This paperback edition published 2004

Copyright © John Collis 2002

John Collis has asserted his moral right to be identified as the Author
of this Work in accordance with the Copyright, Designs
and Patents Act 1988.

All rights reserved. No part of this book may be reproduced or
utilised in any form or by any means, electronic or mechanical,
including photocopying, recording or by any information storage
and retrieval system, without permission in writing from
Aurum Press Ltd.

Every effort has been made to trace the copyright holders of material
quoted in this book. If application is made in writing to the publisher,
any omissions will be included in future editions.

A catalogue record for this book is available from the British Library.

ISBN 1 85410 965 0

1  3  5  7  9  10  8  6  4  2
2004  2006  2008  2007  2005

Design by Roger Hammond
Typeset in Perpetua by M Rules
Printed by Bookmarque, Croydon, Surrey

This book is dedicated
to my wife Anne

# contents

# rock 'n'
# roll music

**I**T'S HIS HANDS that leap out of the on-stage photographs, when you get beyond the calculating eyes. Once you've noticed them your own eyes are drawn enviously to these supernatural digits. Chuck Berry has inherited his hands from Robert Johnson. While we mortals struggle to find our way around a Gibson fretboard, to produce a simplified version of our mental lick, these geniuses – Jimi Hendrix was another – have freakishly long, slender fingers, casually covering an octave, crushing two strings together for a chicken-scratch double note, caressing the maplewood, persuading out of the strings the perfect sounds in their head. That's all it takes for them, the gifted ones.

'They look like baseball gloves hanging off his arms,' says Johnnie Johnson. This is clearly a case of the pot calling the kettle black – Johnson's own hands are like bunches of overripe bananas, swallowing up the keyboard. But somehow his fingers are still sensitive, magically free from arthritis except for a little stiffness in one thumb, and capable of those machine-gun bursts of crazy notes that characterize his style, whereas when Berry tried to play piano, according to Johnson, he would often hit two notes at a time.

On stage, when the mood and the money were right, Berry in his prime was the most exciting of all the rock 'n' roll performers, no less of a showman than Little Richard but more subtle, more in control. He started with the advantage of having created the biggest catalogue of instantly recognizable rock 'n' roll classics, each guitar introduction triggering a roar of recognition in the audience to get the song under way. He was – and remains – a commanding physical presence. His ascetic leanness makes his 6ft 3in look even taller, and his high cheek-bones and flawless ebony skin give him a remarkable physical charisma, something he has made tireless use of in his leisure hours. He developed the sexual symbolism of man-and-guitar to its highest degree, caressing the strings, stopping and starting, strutting one minute, gradually widening his legs the next, his guitar pointing out from his groin towards the audience. And at a perfectly timed moment came the duck walk, knees bent, head pecking back and forth, guitar at his side, drape jacket brushing the floor as he waddled across the boards.

Add to his control of the guitar fretboard a perfect musical memory for mimicry, and Chuck Berry at the height of his powers felt that he could have been anyone he wanted to be – downhome bluesman, Hawaiian serenader, latter-day Les Paul instrumentalist, calypso king even before Harry Belafonte's debut hit 'Jamaica Farewell', smooth Nat 'King' Cole imitator or, above all, rock 'n' roll revolutionary. And yet he has always had a remarkably dismissive stance towards his talent – justified in all cases except the last. One sometimes feels that it needed his audience to point out to him the qualitative difference between, say, 'Havana Moon' and 'Johnny B Goode'.

At the age of thirty he invented popular music for teenagers. So wonderful was this invention that it was always a disappointment when he adopted one of those other musical hats in the recording studio – however proudly he wore it, it hid his uniqueness. And, try as he might, he was never very good at Nat 'King' Cole impersonations anyway.

He did not invent his sound on his own, of course. At the root of Berry's rock 'n' roll style is Johnson's left hand, a boogie-based rhythm propelling the music forward. This was a partnership, where songs started with Berry's intricate words on paper, sometimes a paper bag, to be transformed and given shape by Johnson's intuitive genius. Berry's greed for money and fame has tended to mask the collaborative nature of these songs, as has the Chess Records preference for miking up

Johnson's right-hand decorations, those unique flights of keyboard fancy that are the perfect complement to Berry's guitar. It was only recently, in his old age, that the trusting, easy-going Johnson asked the American courts to recognize this contribution to rock 'n' roll history.

'I'm not after anything,' he says. We are eating soul food at Sweetie Pie's, a cafeteria owned by ex-Ikette Robbie Montgomery in Dellwood, an anonymous strip of north St Louis, where Johnnie and his wife Frances are regulars. 'Only to get recognition of recording all those songs we did together. That's all I'm really interested in.' I ask Johnnie how he feels about Chuck, now that they are officially in dispute. 'I feel the same that I did before,' he replies. 'Like I say, I'm after recognition, that's all. I mean, I don't dislike him or anything. In fact we have played together since this thing started and been unaffected, you know. I have no animosity towards him whatsoever. We never had no disagreement all the times we played together. We've seen each other lately and there hasn't been no argument or anything. We played together at the beginning of the year [2001]. Of course, he always has me contacted through his secretary. He always did that, you know? He'd never phone. He'd call his booking agent or something, but he'd never call me. You got to come to Chuck, he ain't gonna come to you.'

Berry's prudence with money, his fascination with its accumulation, is legendary. He loves it more than he loves rock 'n' roll. The deal is what matters to him, and he reads a contract with X-ray eyes. There's the story of him perusing the financial pages while on a British tour and seeing that the dollar had weakened against the pound. Before his guitar came out of its case he had negotiated an adjusted fee – adjusted by pennies, but that wasn't the point. As his one-time bass player and current studio engineer Dave Torretta put it: 'He loves the deal more than anything in the world. With the studio, the promoter, Shabba Ranks, whoever. He's a difficult businessman. He has his own way of doing things. He's always suspicious.' Shabba Ranks, a Jamaican rapper, is the unlikely star of what remains at present Berry's last new performance on disc, 1994's 'Go Shabba Go'.

Berry's meanness has been excused by the fact that, like every other black artist in the 1950s, he was ripped off. But the fact is that, being Berry, he wasn't ripped off for very long. He took control of his own career in 1957, paid his band as little as he could get away with, travelled light, and starting tucking away the dollars. By 1959 he was unveiling his grandiose plans for a huge leisure complex, Berry Park, at 691 Buckner Road, Wentzville, a hick town west of St Louis.

Meanwhile Johnnie Johnson, the unsung composer of the music to so many of those hits, descended into a fog of alcoholism and poverty, living in a men's hostel until his third wife, the formidable Frances, rescued him and straightened him out. You do not argue with Frances, and if she decided that Johnnie was going to pull himself together, he really had no choice. Chuck Berry, meanwhile, has always had a keen awareness of his own worth. As Frances puts it: 'That – pardon my French – *motherfucker*. Johnnie needs a certain amount of protection. To have Chuck Berry so friendly when he's ripping J.J. off is distasteful.'

There were no teenage kicks in the blues that preceded 'Maybellene' because there were no teenagers. They hadn't been invented. The blues was for grown-ups. Racism, trouble with 'the man', unemployment, poverty, sex or lack of it. The fuzzy escapism of the search for a Saturday night. Kids had no place in this, and adolescents were invisible, little adults waiting to emerge, just hidden, spotty chrysalids.

The young Fats Domino sang from the barrelhouse bar to posturing, boasting men and noisy, laughing, dancing women. His style of music was just one rollicking jump from the New Orleans whorehouses, from the music of Cousin Joe Pleasants and Champion Jack Dupree, playing in the lobby while customers trooped up and down the stairs. Little Richard celebrated sexual adventurousness, sometimes in camp code, but always in the visionary voice of the church, as a testifying adult sinfully feasting on someone's long, tall sally. Then there was Chuck Berry, inventing rock 'n' roll, dropping the coin right into the slot, singing of lonely schooldays. Playing for kids, newly liberated, with a weekly allowance and the key to the car. Elvis had already identified these kids but he could barely write his own name, let alone compose 'School Day'. Rock 'n' roll had to wait for its Laureate.

For the teenager to emerge as a commercial force, someone worthy of Berry's song-writing efforts, the economic conditions in the United States had to be right. Otherwise he'd happily have skipped rock 'n' roll and concentrated on his real love, property dealing, which was a natural development from his inherited carpentry and electrician's skills. And suddenly, in 1955, those conditions were perfect. Net income received by the nation's businesses was one third up on the previous year. Postal workers received an 8 per cent pay rise, and federal workers almost as much. President Eisenhower signed a bill raising the minimum wage to $1 an hour, to take effect from the following March. The American Federation of Labor and the Congress of Industrial Organizations merged to form one vast trade union.

There was a new confidence apparent in the nation. This gave rise to an unprecedented boom in new buildings, transforming the appearance of the cities. Sales of new cars, bigger and more showy than ever before, increased greatly, as did the passion for household gadgetry and the newly developed colour televisions. Consumerism was on the march, egged on by what writer Vance Packard identified in his best-selling 1957 book as *The Hidden Persuaders*, the advertising agencies.

On the world stage, after the horrors of the McCarthy–Nixon witch-hunts, fears of the 'red menace' eased significantly when Eisenhower proposed that the US and Russia should exchange military information and allow for aerial inspection of each other's installations, the first sign of a thaw in the cold war. Plans were unveiled for the first satellites to circle the earth. There was also the announcement that a vaccine had been developed to prevent the common cold, but they couldn't be expected to get everything right.

The first active steps were taken to dismantle racial segregation. In May 1955 it was banned in all public schools, and in November the Interstate Commerce Commission outlawed segregation on all its trains and buses. In December a Montgomery, Alabama, woman called Rosa Parks took the struggle into the cities when she sat down in a seat at the front of a downtown bus and refused to move, resulting in her arrest. The pastor of the Dexter Avenue Baptist Church in Montgomery, the Reverend Martin Luther King, led a boycott of the city's buses in protest at the treatment of Ms Parks.

However slowly, the times were changing America was flexing its economic muscles, and teenagers were out on the street with money to spend. And with the boom in commercial radio, it was harder than ever to prevent white kids from hearing 'jungle music' through the democratic freedom of the airwaves, and discovering that it was somewhat more interesting than Rosemary Clooney. The year of 'Maybellene', 1955, was also the year of Disneyland and the Ford Thunderbird, of the rebellious-teenager movie *Blackboard Jungle*, with

Bill Haley's 'Rock Around the Clock' behind the credits. And Elvis Presley was touring as bottom-of-the-bill on a country-music package with Marty Robbins.

Soon Berry's discs reached Britain, on continental airwaves, on merchant ships and in record shops with good taste. Imagine a wet Sunday afternoon in the house of a pinch-mouthed maiden aunt, one with all the *joie de vivre* of the Taliban. That was what the early 1950s in the UK could be like, if one ventured beyond the home-made entertainment of solo whist and piano lessons. War was too recent, too painful, too expensive. Life could be as grey as the gutter.

The state gave us orange juice and cod-liver oil to stave off rickets, and grandmothers knitted sensible, scratchy pullovers (not sweaters – they were what Jayne Mansfield wore, and we hadn't heard of her yet). Clothes were black or grey, or that strange muddy green colour still to be found in the windows of provincial gents' outfitters. Lovat or hate it. Sunday shirts were white, with stiff collars and seams that hurt, to remind us of Jesus's suffering. We had yet to see pictures of Marlon Brando astride a motorbike. And, anyway, motorbikes were ridden by sensible, middle-aged men in tarpaulin suits, as a windswept commuting alternative to the more expensive car. But then we heard the first stirrings of rock 'n' roll. Chuck, Fats, Richard, the trinity, in 1956.

Scroll on seven years. For most of 1962 and into the October of 1963 Chuck Berry was in jail. The great rock 'n' roll era was over, as was the period of Berry's fame as the most successful black practitioner of the music, and indeed black music's biggest star before Michael Jackson, who wasn't black for long. To be out of public view for the best part of two years, especially for a man now thirty-seven years of age, would surely be the kiss of death in the faddish world of pop music, where nothing stands still for a moment, and trends spin around and fall as fast as a hula hoop.

While detained at Springfield, Missouri, Berry not only shrewdly studied business practice, preparatory to setting up his own music publishing company and progressively retrieving his copyrights, he also continued to write songs. They were not tired songs, mere retreads harking back to the 1950s – not even 'No Particular Place To Go', which does deliberately revisit the tune of 'School Day' but somehow emerges freshly minted, with a totally different theme. They were not the bitter songs of a man with a huge chip on his shoulder, a man who would surely not have been in jail in the first place had he been white, a man who turned an even more suspicious, steely face to the world when he was released than he had shown before. And they were not, certainly not, third-rate or minor songs.

He emerged, incredibly, with 'Nadine', 'You Never Can Tell', 'No Particular Place To Go', 'Promised Land' and 'Tulane'. Each is a cameo masterpiece, a concise, witty, invigorating demonstration of his genius. Many writers of hit songs would happily swap their entire catalogue for just this quintet of compositions. Far from fading away as the harsh lessons of the rock 'n' roll business would lead one to expect, Berry revived his career with these extraordinary fruits of early middle age, and as the R & B revival gathered pace in Britain and was re-exported to the States, Berry was securely in place as its hero and natural figurehead. As soon as he could, he boarded a plane for the UK, and arrived in 1964 as the King of Rock 'n' Roll.

Now a further move forward, this time two decades, twenty more years of pop-music turbulence, of short-term memories, of brief fame followed by lifetimes of obscurity. On 5 December 1985 *Rolling Stone* announced:

Chuck Berry, James Brown, Little Richard and Elvis Presley are among the ten rock 'n' roll legends who have been elected to the newly established Rock 'n' Roll Hall of Fame. The initial inductees – who also include Ray Charles, Sam Cooke, Fats Domino, The Everly Brothers, Buddy Holly and Jerry Lee Lewis – were among forty-one artistes nominated by the Rock 'n' Roll Hall of Fame Foundation, a group of top music-industry figures formed in 1983 . . .

'This is meant to give recognition to rock 'n' roll's early influences,' said Ahmet Ertegun, the head of Atlantic Records and chairman of the Hall of Fame Foundation. 'It's important to keep their names engraved somewhere for future generations.' The Foundation also plans to honor non-performers such as songwriters and producers, as well as 'forefathers' of rock 'n' roll. Nominees in the latter category include bluesmen Big Bill Broonzy and Blind Lemon Jefferson, and country singer Jimmie Rodgers.

A permanent Hall of Fame display will be installed in a Rock 'n' Roll Hall of Fame museum to be established by the foundation. Locations under discussion include Cleveland, Memphis and New Orleans . . .

In the end, of course, Cleveland, Ohio, provided the chosen site, a stunning waterfront location for architect I.M. Pei's glass pyramids, where Berry is duly honoured. What is most noticeable about the news item in *Rolling Stone* is that in 1985 Berry's name was chosen to lead a field that included Elvis, Holly and seven other worthies, some of whom might have been expected to be more fixed in the contemporary consciousness. Elvis, after all, was still having hits eight years after his death, and Holly was surely the first 'complete' pop musician, one whose influence still informed the pop charts of the mid-1980s.

In 1986 Jerry Lee Lewis found himself in generous mood when nominating the King of Rock 'n' Roll. 'I think Chuck Berry is top of the list. I started out with Chuck. We've had some fights and arguments and everything else, but we're best of buddies. My Mama said: "He's the king of rock 'n' roll." I said: "What about me, Mama?" She said: "What I'm saying is you're great, you sing country and rock 'n' roll. But Chuck is the king."'

Since Lewis once set fire to his piano with a bottle of gasoline and his cigarette lighter, miffed at the fact that Berry was topping the bill, and reputedly said, 'Follow that, nigger,' as he stalked off, it is praise indeed that he endorsed his mother's opinion. 'Burned it to the ground,' he confirmed to biographer Robert Palmer. 'They forced me to do it, tellin' me I had to go on before Chuck Berry.'

By the time of Lewis's more considered tribute the fresh Chuck Berry classics had long ceased to flow, and he had not released a new album for seven years. Live rock 'n' roll was largely relegated to elderly revival packages or the enthusiastic retro of those bored with the limitations of punk. But Berry was still the King, and he remains so into a new millennium. He and Johnnie Johnson wrote the rock 'n' roll constitution, and although those fingers are beginning to assume mere mortal dexterity, that constitution cannot be revised. In 1956, in 1963, in the mid-1980s and in 2002, Chuck Berry reigns.

Berry's pioneering music pre-dated 'rock criticism' by a decade, and once it became respectable to treat popular song as a fit subject for study it still took a while for his true place to be recognized. He was black, but he didn't sit in a field wearing dungarees and singing through someone else's teeth. Nor did he perform in dives on the wrong side of the tracks, charting 'the Negro experience' to the delight of polo-necked university academics. He even figured in the hit parade, not as a novelty act, but as a bona fide pop star.

One of the first serious studies of the black music of the electrically amplified era was Charles Keil's 1966 book *Urban Blues*. 'Serious' is the word. 'It is recognized that singers like Chuck Berry, Fats Domino and Bo Diddley can be called blues singers but are really showmen first and bluesmen second,' says Keil. 'Their appeal rests primarily on novelty songs, catchy lyrics, and visual appeal.'

This surely applies to T-Bone Walker, of whom Keil approves, and who is clearly first and last a bluesman. While Keil does indeed go on to use the labels 'rhythm and blues' and 'rock 'n' roll' in connection with the Berry brigade, to distinguish them from his main concern with purist bluesmen, it seems that as far as academia was concerned, Berry's dense imagery was still regarded as a 'novelty' in the mid-1960s, and that such straight blues pieces as 'Wee Wee Hours', from his first Chess recording session, had perhaps been overlooked. Berry and Johnnie Johnson had taken the blues into previously uncharted areas, revolutionary explorers turning it into rock 'n' roll, but at the time they were still bluesmen at heart.

Three years later, Carl Belz published his pioneering *The Story of Rock*. Although his admiration for Berry is clear, Belz, like Keil, is unable to take him 'seriously'. He calls Berry a 'folk artist of the rock idiom' whose music stubbornly failed to develop because there was no pressing need for it to do so. 'From the beginning it unconsciously expressed the responses of the artist and his audience to the ordinary realities of their world . . .' Belz refers to Berry's 'ingenuous vitality', saying he 'created art unconsciously'.

With the benefit of hindsight, surely this is a patronizing attitude. Belz sees Berry as a naïf, unaware of what he was up to, simply doing what came naturally. This accorded with the view of Richard Goldstein, whose *The Poetry of Rock* was also published in 1969. He refers to Berry's 'accidental art'. Both writers like Berry's music, but cannot bring themselves to credit him with intellect. In the late 1960s, as far as mainstream rock America was concerned, it seemed as if blues artists were still white – and in the case of Johnny Winter, very white indeed. They, presumably, knew what they were doing, just as Bob Dylan knew what he was doing. But apparently Berry didn't.

Nowadays we can see that the writer of 'Nadine', to take just one random example, knew *exactly* what he was doing. He worked and worried at his craft just as George Gershwin and Cole Porter did. Those 'ordinary realities of their world', the world supposedly shared by Berry and his fans, were not the fit subject for popular music until Berry deliberately and perceptively made them so. And as a black man in his thirties, he actually had little in common with the audience he was writing for. As an artist, he knowingly, self-consciously thought himself into their skins, so that he could write about their 'Lonely School Days'. There was surely nothing accidental about it, however casually the Berry of later years might seem to treat his talent.

It took Lillian Roxon, in her *Rock Encyclopedia* published in the same year as Belz's and Goldstein's books, to put Berry in his true place. This is perhaps surprising, because to browse through Roxon's wonderfully idiosyncratic but trailblazing book more than three decades on is to be confronted with hoards of half-remembered west-coast hippies who have perhaps not weathered as well as Berry. And the word 'encyclopedia' is a misnomer – this is a purely subjective work, where no 'fact' should be taken at face value. But the long-haired, tie-dyed, free-wheeling mood of the time did not close her ears to Berry's importance.

He 'may be the single most important name in the history of rock,' she says, not even limiting him to the 'rock 'n' roll' ghetto. The assumption in 1969 that The Beatles were unique meant it took remarkable perception to clamber over them, Bob Dylan, Buddy Holly and Elvis Presley to get to Berry. Roxon also spotted the country-and-western undertone to Berry's music, and made the now obvious, then original, comparison with Presley – one was the hillbilly who sounded black, the other was the black hillbilly, and both therefore had the vital commercial access to white *and* black radio stations, whether or not the disc jockey or programming manager was aware of their skin colour.

In 1971 came another seminal study, Charlie Gillett's *The Sound of the City*. Gillett is an English writer, although the idea for the book arose when he was studying for a master's degree in New York. This was the first book to use record labels, and hence regionality, as the spine around which to hang the flesh of rock 'n' roll, which was indeed a defiantly regional art. Says Gillett: 'If importance in popular music were [*sic*] measured in terms of imaginativeness, creativeness, wit, the ability to translate a variety of experiences and feelings into musical form, and long-term influence and reputation, Chuck Berry would be described as the major figure of rock 'n' roll.' To Gillett, then, Berry is far from a naïf – he does indeed know what he's up to. And the assessment by Roxon and Gillett of his significance, and of the *consciousness* of his art, is surely the true one. Since they first articulated the opinion, it has never been seriously challenged.

A year after Gillett's book was published, Berry had his biggest hit and only no. 1 with the dire ditty 'My Ding-a-Ling'.

# St Louis
# blues

S T LOUIS IS the largest city in Missouri, sprawling on the west bank of the Mississippi just south of its junction with the Missouri. It was first established as a centre of the fur trade in 1764, and as the leading city in the Midwest it grew to be the fourth largest in the country. Nowadays, the flight from the city centre means that its population is less than half of what it was forty years ago, although the suburbs are flourishing. The boundary drawn in 1876 limits the size of the city itself to 61 square miles, but it is the hub of a region fifty times that size which also stretches across the river to the east.

This spread has maintained the importance of the St Louis region in the industrial and cultural life of the country. In 1965, as an expression of civic pride – and perhaps in an attempt to give a tourism boost to a rather drab city – the country's tallest monument was erected beside the river. Designed by Eero Saarinen, the elegant stainless steel Gateway Arch is 630ft high.

Cultural life thrives in the city. An impressive art museum is housed in one of the neoclassical buildings erected for the 1903 World's Fair, in the huge Forest Park, which also has a zoo and a history museum, while a further museum of natural history is in nearby Clayton. Forest Park also offers the strange sight of golfers teeing off down city-centre fairways. The St Louis Symphony Orchestra, founded in 1880, is the second oldest in the country, and the Conservatory and School for the Arts has a national reputation.

Blacks still tend to live in the north-west of the city, above Interstate 44, which is where Chuck Berry comes from, and whites to the south. There are also distinct Italian, German and Eastern European enclaves.

Since the decline of the bohemian Gaslight Square area there is less city-centre nightlife than there used to be, but clubs thrive in various satellite districts. They have one of the strongest traditions for jazz, blues and rock in the country to maintain, a tradition that embraced Chuck Berry as he was growing up, and proved more enticing than the religious music of his parents. In St Louis in 1892 the nineteen-year-old W.C. Handy heard 'shabby guitarists' on the street playing a simple eight-bar blues called 'East St Louis'. He wasn't hugely impressed at the time. 'It had numerous one-line verses and they would sing it all night,' he noted somewhat wearily.

Even when he saw how popular the blues was, when he witnessed a southern trio being well rewarded by an appreciative crowd, Handy still dismissed it superciliously as being repetitive and musically formless. In 1903, waiting for a train in Mississippi, he heard a hobo singing a railroad blues, fretting the guitar strings with a knife to produce a keening, lonesome sound. If this was Handy's road to Damascus it still did not strike him at the time, though he was later to refer to it as his musical awakening.

Music was more a business to Handy than a vocation, an attitude he had in common with Chuck Berry, and before long he could no longer ignore the appeal of the blues. Indeed, he must surely have begun to see it as now being far more relevant to black experience than the neo-classical and European influences of his own minstrel music, though at least his Mahama Minstrels were black musicians, not burnt-cork blacked-up whites mammying away in white gloves.

Handy identified the characteristic 'blue notes', the flattened thirds and sevenths of the scale, and began to write songs in the blues style. 'Memphis Blues' was his first hit, in 1912, and two years later came 'St Louis Blues', with one of the most familiar first lines in the entire genre. 'I hate to see de evenin' sun go down . . .' This song, belatedly harking back to those scruffy St Louis itinerants witnessed by Handy in 1892, has been described by the distinguished Harlem poet Langston Hughes as 'one of America's best-known popular songs all over the world'.

Meanwhile, the Texan pianist Scott Joplin and others were developing another turn-of-the-century black music that was to become sensationally successful, threatening the domination of minstrelsy. The defining characteristic of their so-called ragtime was the musical tension set up between a springy, syncopated melody and an insistent bass line reminiscent of the German–Texan 'oompah' bands. At the World's Fair of 1893, which was held in Chicago, ragtime entertainers including Joplin were strongly in evidence. And ten years later the Fair came to another musical town, St Louis. 'We've been living off it ever since,' says local broadcaster and musician Roy St John wryly, 'waiting for something else to happen.'

With 'Maple Leaf Rag', published towards the turn of the century, Joplin created the genre's biggest hit. His publisher, John Stark, set up business in St Louis on the strength of it, moving to the city from the small town of Sedalia, due west towards Kansas City. While ragtime became adopted as a fast-paced party novelty, Handy persevered in trying to give it greater dignity as an indigenous form of classical music. He wrote extended pieces, compositions intended for musicals, and even a ragtime opera. St Louis at that time was the centre of the ragtime craze, a piano town that nurtured such barrelhouse musicians as Speckled Red and Roosevelt Sykes.

The blues had become the music of the St Louis streets by the turn of the century. That celebrated story of betrayal and murder, 'Frankie and Johnny', was said to have been inspired by a real-life incident in the city, involving a woman named Frankie Baker, and certainly it was being sung there in the red-light-district bars of the 1890s. While minstrelsy reflected the cultural aspirations of the black middle class, or those who yearned for such status in spite of the economic and social obstacles erected by racism, the blues used the language of the streets to express the experiences and emotions of the vast majority of blacks. And in the growing city of St Louis there was room for them all – the black-tie entertainers, the ragtime bands and the busking bluesmen.

'The first music I heard was the blues,' jazzman Harry Dial told *Jazz Journal* in 1958, recalling his memories of childhood early in the century. '[It was] being whistled, sung and shouted from every street corner and alleyway in St Louis. The blues was so much part of our lives that we never gave it a thought as being a special music.'

The St Louis blues sound, unsurprisingly for such a 'crossroads' town, showed much diversity. Although it was rooted in the country blues of the south, it could also take on the more sophisticated colours of jazz. Many of the musicians played both piano and guitar, and this showed itself in the rhythmic emphasis on the left hand, the boogie hand. And so when in the 1950s Johnnie Johnson's left-hand playing became the largely unacknowledged root of the Chuck Berry sound, driving the songs along, forcing the lyrics into rock 'n' roll shape, he was simply developing a St Louis tradition. Since St Louis bands so often included both guitar and piano, guitarists in the city could concentrate on single-note runs and place an emphasis on melody, freed of the necessity to stress the rhythm.

There were many reasons for the gathering drift from the rural south that picked up such pace in the 1920s. The coming Depression bit first at the poorest, the development of mechanical cotton-picking caused mass unemployment and broke the fundamental tie of many black families to the land, and the growth of alternative industries in the factories, car plants, steel mills and meat-packing warehouses of the north acted like a magnet. St Louis, like Chicago and Detroit, was on the transport highways, an obvious destination for southern rural blacks in search of work.

In 1917 the steady influx of blacks prompted a racist backlash that developed into a riot. Nearly fifty people, mainly black, died in the mayhem, many burned alive. A strike of white, unionized workers had been broken by the importation of black labourers from the south, no doubt totally innocent that they were intended to be pawns in a game that set East St Louis on fire, with the police and National Guard siding with the white malcontents.

From New Orleans through the Mississippi Delta to St Louis the journey was an obvious one, whether by the Illinois Central Railroad, Highway 55 or the big river. Sometimes St Louis was the destination itself, sometimes a lengthy staging post en route to Chicago, and the musicians came in their hundreds. So much so that Jimmy Oden, writer of 'Goin' Down Slow', once said: 'There were so many fine piano players in St Louis that I went to Chicago to find a niche.' Before the move, however, he often worked as St Louis Jimmy. Chicago, largely due to the success of Chuck Berry's record company Chess, may be better known these days as a centre of the blues, but in many ways it was St Louis that provided the impetus. Also, for east–west migration towards the fruit groves of California, St Louis was similarly strategically placed.

Wherever the migrant workers went, the entertainers would follow. Often, of course, the bluesmen were also manual labourers – including the hugely popular Lonnie Johnson, who even when selling records by the truckload never quite believed that music was a proper job. This caution served him well during the Depression years.

In the 1920s the elegant Booker T. Washington theatre in St Louis was a prime venue for the classic blues singers, Mamie Smith, Ma Rainey and Bessie Smith among them. Josephine Baker, who found fame in the theatres and cabarets of Paris, was discovered here. Alas, this landmark to the blues and to black entertainment was a victim of the Depression, closed down by the end of the decade and soon demolished.

There was also work for musicians, including the legendary Jelly Roll Morton, on the riverboats carrying gamblers, romantics, businessmen, refugees and migrants up the Mississippi–Missouri to the city where these great rivers meet. And then there were the spit-and-sawdust clubs and bars on the granite-reinforced river banks and in the red-light district around Morgan Street. One musician who worked both the clubs and the boats was pianist Henry Brown, born in St Louis in 1906, whose 'Deep Morgan Blues' took its name from the area. He had a precise, spare style evocatively described by Paul Oliver as 'simple and uncluttered as Shaker furniture'.

Lonnie Johnson was born in New Orleans in 1889, and as a teenager he played the guitar and violin in Storyville barrooms. After a spell in Europe during World War I he returned to America and hit the road north, living first in St Louis before eventually continuing to Chicago. His first job in St Louis, in the early 1920s, was as a member of Charlie Creath's Jazz-O-Maniacs, who played on the riverboat SS *St Paul*. He was the most influential of all the between-the-wars St Louis musicians, both on guitar and piano, and often worked with his brother Steady Roll and his wife Mary.

Recording for Okeh Records in the years before the Depression decimated the record industry, Johnson became one of the bestselling blues artists of the day, and at one time Okeh was issuing a new Johnson disc every six weeks for two years to capitalise on the demand. On the guitar, his favoured instrument, he was a sophisticated and versatile performer – so much so that as an accompanist hired by Okeh he could on the one hand lend a little class and shape to the crude-but-forceful field hollers of Texas Alexander, and on the other adorn a Louis Armstrong record with a nimble, decisive solo. He was skilled in using the blues to comment on topical events, as in his 1927 song 'St Louis Cyclone Blues': 'I was sitting in my kitchen . . . I seen that mean old twister coming just like a cannonball.'

The Depression bit deep into the St Louis economy. The writer Orick Johns, in his 1973 book *Times of Our Lives*, said of the city: 'With a magnificent river site the city has left its crumbling old warehouses, primitive granite-block levees and grimy streets exactly as they were fifty years ago . . . I have never seen such destitution as on the river front of south St Louis.' Having ridden out the storm, Johnson was one of the first to adopt the newly developed electrically-amplified guitar, becoming a formative influence on the first generation of pioneering, purely electric bluesmen led by T-Bone Walker and Lowell Fulson, and hence at one remove on Chuck Berry.

Another bluesman intimately associated with St Louis, one who blazed brightly but more briefly, was Peetie Wheatstraw, born William Bunch in 1902 down in Tennessee. A distinctive pianist and guitarist with a husky, drawling voice, he moved to rough, run-down East St Louis and burnished a bad-boy image by referring to himself as 'the Devil's Son-in-Law' (in 'Peetie Wheatstraw's Stomp No. 2') and 'the High Sheriff from Hell'. In local bluesman Henry Townsend's opinion, 'Peetie's personality was very similar to the one on the records.'

Booker 'Bukka' White arrived in town in the early 1920s, although he frequently travelled in search of work, including stints as a booth boxer and professional baseball player. With a catalogue that included such classics as 'Shake 'Em On Down', 'Parchman Farm Blues' (he served time there for assault in the 1930s) and 'Fixin' To Die Blues',

White was one of the veterans rediscovered during the 1960s blues revival, as was another St Louis stalwart J.D. Short. Big Joe Williams from Mississippi was a long-time resident of St Louis from 1930 onwards, but one who remained an itinerant musician at heart. When he recorded with pianist Victoria Spivey in 1962, for an album eventually released two years later on Spivey's own label, they were joined on two tracks by a fan of both veterans, billed as 'Big Joe's Buddy' — Bob Dylan.

One musician who knew them all was the guitarist and pianist Henry Townsend, born in Mississippi in 1909, raised in Illinois and moving to St Louis just before Williams, in 1929. Others may have come and gone, but Townsend has provided a living link for all generations of St Louis musicians from the years of the Depression to the present day. In 1976 he described the appeal of the blues: 'It's a relief for pressure . . . We all have had something in mind and we didn't want to talk about it to anybody, but the burden was real heavy until you could make some kinda sound about it, you could express yourself to somebody . . .'

Peter 'Doctor' Clayton, an eccentric star of the 1930s, grew up in St Louis and became established there before moving on to Chicago, where he died of tuberculosis in 1947. A year later the pianist James Crutchfield arrived in St Louis from the south and remained there for the rest of his career. Boogie piano player James 'Stump' Johnson, who also spent most of his life in St Louis and whose first hit was 1929's delicate ditty 'The Duck's Yas Yas', evoked the rumbustious riverside atmosphere in 1960 in Paul Oliver's *Conversation with the Blues*: 'All the riverboats would come in there and dock and all the 'ristocratic people would come down there for slummin' and enjoyment. They were very, very tough places though, and they were shootin' dice and drinkin' whiskey and enjoyin' themselves, and it could get kinda rough.' This was the St Louis of the young Chuck Berry, although the red-light district was a different world from his respectable neighbourhood of Elleardsville.

During the war years there was a substantial migration of southern blues singers to St Louis, attracted by the opportunity of work in 'the cartridge factory', a small-arms munitions plant. Muddy Waters and Bukka White were among them. There was clearly a lively blues scene in the city at this time, although the wartime ban on manufacturing records means that it is largely uncharted. After the war, when work at the factory dwindled, many of the workers – notably Muddy Waters – moved on to Chicago.

Others arrived to take their place, however. In Chuck Berry's golden decade, the 1950s, the second Sonny Boy Williamson and multi-instrumentalist Frank Frost were frequent visitors. Williamson, a harmonica virtuoso with a sly, confessional vocal style, became one of the stars of the Chess label with such hits as 'Don't Start Me Talkin'' and 'Help Me', while Frost was a protégé of his who went on to record for the Sun label in the 1960s. Oliver Sain, who came to St Louis from Mississippi in 1959 with Little Milton, began building his reputation, and when he formed his first band in the town in 1960 he hired such locals as Fontella Bass and Bobby McClure, scoring on the Chess subsidiary Checker with 'Don't Mess Up a Good Thing' and 'You'll Miss Me'. Blues guitarist Albert King made his name here, Ann Peebles ('I Can't Stand the Rain') and Jimmy McCracklin ('The Walk') were born here, and it was while playing a gig in St Louis that Ike Turner spotted his future wife, Annie Mae Bullock.

Indeed, talk in St Louis among veteran musicians these days will still refer to the trinity of Chuck Berry, Ike Turner and Albert King. Turner formed his band the Kings of Rhythm in the late 1940s while in his teens, and according to local disc jockey Gabriel he 'just took over the area' when he arrived in St Louis in 1951. Turner's 1951 hit 'Rocket 88', issued under the name of vocalist Jackie Brenston, was prototype rock 'n' roll and it was a boastful song about the singer's car – Berry took note and became the greatest celebrant of four-wheel freedom.

Quite apart from Turner's prodigious talent as a pianist and guitarist, producer and talent scout, he was hugely ambitious and so he could attract the best musicians, eager for a share of his success. He originally billed Annie Mae as 'Little Ann', but following their marriage in 1958 she became Tina Turner, and in the early 1960s they began to record as a double act, with R & B chart hits like 'A Fool in Love' and 'It's Gonna Work Out Fine'. Eventually, says Gabriel, St Louis 'got too small for Ike. He went to California twice and came back again, but the third time he went and never came back.' Phil Spector may have wanted Tina's voice rather than Ike's skills as a musician, but Turner ensured that 'River Deep, Mountain High', on which he played no discernible role, was credited to them both.

Guitarist Albert King was one of the many other migrants from Mississippi, first visiting St Louis in 1949 and making his recording debut in 1953 with 'Bad Luck Blues'. He moved back to St Louis in 1956 and formed a trio, which often included Johnnie Johnson. He worked in the area for ten years until he was signed by the Memphis label Stax in 1966. He was teamed with Booker T and the MGs for a string of hits like 'Born Under a Bad Sign', and crossed over into the pop charts with 'Cold Feet'. Singer–pianist Clayton Love was another of the Mississippi men who made the journey north to St Louis.

By the mid-1960s the St Louis blues scene had been edged sideways by R & B and soul performers like Barbara Carr, and by the end of the decade there was little blues music to be heard in the clubs. According to contemporary performer Leroy Jody Pearson, 'there were still wonderful shows, but always in an academic setting, in the universities'. In the 1970s, however, a newly formed group, the big, fluid Soulard Blues Band, had a similar effect to that of Ike Turner's outfit twenty years earlier. By establishing a new market for local blues they encouraged other artists and the growth of a circuit of clubs.

Blueberry Hill opened in 1972 in the Loop district, the veteran Henry Townsend was the first artist to play the Broadway Oyster Bar in the mid-1970s, and other clubs like BB's and Mike and Min's were established. Existing traditional artists like Townsend, Doc Terry and Tommy Bankhead – who arrived for a six-week visit in 1949 and didn't get around to leaving – found a new audience south of their familiar territory, and local heroes like Berry sidemen Billy Peek and Dave Torretta, who formed the band Fairchild with his wife Connie, had a circuit on which to play alongside veterans like Oliver Sain. By the late 1970s there was a discernible blues revival in St Louis.

So when Chuck Berry joined Johnnie Johnson and began to make his mark in the early 1950s he was just another in a long line of local bluesmen that continues to the present day, and there was a healthy club scene in which to serve his apprenticeship. But Berry was different, and soon began to be referred to as 'the black hillbilly'. The potential for him to bust out of the circumscribed world of the urban bluesman towards greater popularity was always there, once he recognized that while 'Wee Wee Hours' was a good, late-night blues, 'Maybellene' was a revolution. But first, he had to develop a style suitable for the city clubs where he first made his name.

Writing on Charlie Christian in his 1971 book *Combo: USA,* Rudi Blesh pinned down what Christian brought to the technique of playing the newly developed electric guitar. 'Before Charlie Christian, the guitar had barely touched its possibilities of filling both roles: singer and accompanist. Christian created singing single lines of melody in the blues way while giving them a ride on his rhythmic chord riffs.'

His admiration for the saxophonist Lester Young encouraged Christian to adapt Young's virtuoso style to the guitar, which had previously been thought of as an ensemble rhythm instrument, just a mellow banjo. Berry, though never Christian's equal as a technician, was to take it one step further into rock 'n' roll, riffing a rhythm behind the vocal lines and bursting out joyously in the breaks.

Christian's technique developed alongside that of the pioneer electric bluesman T-Bone Walker – literally, since they both took up the newfangled electric guitar at the same time and under the same teacher in Oklahoma City, Chuck Richardson. Walker was to prove an equal influence on Berry.

Walker, born in 1910, was older than Christian by six years. They lived near each other in Dallas, Texas, although Christian's father, a blind musician, relocated to Oklahoma City when Charlie was five. Walker's parents played host to bluesmen when they visited Dallas, and the young T-Bone would guide the itinerant entertainer Blind Lemon Jefferson around town. This encouraged him to take up the guitar himself, and by his mid-teens he was touring with medicine shows. Among those he backed was the blues singer Ida Cox – coincidentally, Christian would record with her in 1939.

In his teens, working the medicine shows, Walker showed all-round talent as a dancer, comedian and compere. As a featured guitarist he developed his flair for showmanship, using a long lead to wander into the audience, playing solos with the guitar behind his head or while slowly doing the splits, the guitar held at 90 degrees to his body, pointing out at the audience. Berry was to pick up on this aspect of Walker's performance, as well as his single-string technique and driving chord work. Walker's first record under his own name was his blues composition 'Mean Old World', still a staple of Berry's stage act, and by the late 1940s Walker was featuring in the R & B lists with such blues classics as 'Stormy Monday Blues' and his signature 'T-Bone Shuffle'.

By this time Christian was dead, succumbing to tuberculosis in 1942 after less than three years as a star instrumentalist in the Benny Goodman band. He was recommended to Goodman in 1939 and was hired immediately, having played a single audition piece called 'Rose Room'. The bandleader featured Christian in both his sextet and his big band. It was a Christian original with the orchestra that is particularly associated with him, and there are constant echoes of this virtuoso piece 'Solo Flight' in Berry's guitar style, with its clear, melodic single notes. Christian played a Gibson ES-150 guitar and this may have inspired Berry's lifelong fidelity to Gibsons.

He made his first record, 'Maybellene', in 1955, with an ES-350TN fitted with P90 pick-ups and pushed through a Fender Twin amp. He switched to the new ES-335 when it came on the market in 1958, and hence to its further development as the 345 and the 355 in 1959. This is the evolutionary line that has served him throughout his career. He uses two humbucking pick-ups (wired in such a way as to eliminate background noise – literally 'bucking the hum').

Berry was only fifteen when Christian died and so did not see him play live when the Goodman band visited St Louis. But he would certainly have seen the big bands in town later in the decade – Goodman's along with those of Tommy Dorsey and Harry James, for example. Jay McShann's band also played in St Louis and Berry was struck by the vocalist Walter Brown, although he would only have heard him on local radio and the jukebox at this stage, and he noted in particular one of his most popular numbers, 'Confessin' the Blues'.

The third crucial element in Berry's music came from Louis Jordan and his Tympany Five (a name the bandleader stuck with, however many musicians he was employing at the time). Jordan himself and one of his featured guitarists, Carl Hogan, were both influential in defining the characteristics from which Berry created something new – Jordan as a showman, writer of tight, witty lyrics and as an exuberant singer, Hogan for his lead guitar lines, some of which Berry adapted wholesale. Another Jordan guitarist of the late 1940s, Bill Jennings, also surely worked his way into Berry's subconscious, and the interplay between his guitar and the piano of Bill Doggett pre-dated the relationship between Berry's guitar and Johnnie Johnson's piano which is at the heart of Berry's records. Berry has referred to Jordan as 'the first rock 'n' roll artist I ever saw', a perceptive confirmation of Jordan's pivotal importance in the growth of a music that, in his heyday, had yet to be given its name.

Just as Christian transformed the role of the guitar in jazz and T-Bone Walker paved the way for it to become the most popular blues instrument, so Louis Jordan pioneered the move from swing to proto-type rhythm-and-blues in his group of the mid-1940s, with such rumbustious boogies as 'Caldonia' in 1945.

Jordan was born in Arkansas in 1908, and in his youth worked both as a professional baseball player and as a touring musician, playing alto sax. In the late 1920s and 30s he appeared with various bands, including that of Louis Armstrong, and played in Chick Webb's outfit from 1936 before signing to Decca Records in 1938. He recorded with his Elks Rendezvous Band, renaming them the Tympany Five in 1939. In the 1940s his popularity was such that he broke out of the black charts and into the national list with such songs as 'Is You Is or Is You Ain't My Baby', 'Choo Choo Ch'Boogie', 'Ain't Nobody Here But Us Chickens' and duets with Bing Crosby ('My Baby Said Yes') and Ella Fitzgerald ('Baby, It's Cold Outside').

Bad judgement led him to increase the personnel in his band in the early 1950s just as fashion and economics dictated the opposite, and as his hit career faded Decca began to score with a more compact group, Bill Haley and his Comets – another confirmation that Jordan is an essential link in the movement from the blues and big-band swing to rock 'n' roll. Revivals in his career continued sporadically until his death in 1975, and his music reached a new audience with the success of Clark Peters' stage revue *Five Guys Named Moe*, which opened mod-estly in the East End of London before transferring to the West End and eventually to Broadway.

At a session on 23 January 1946, during Carl Hogan's time with the Jordan band, they recorded a number called 'Ain't That Just Like a Woman'. Although Hogan's introduction soon resolves itself into a driving chord riff, the single-note run that introduces the song is pure, note-for-note 'Johnny B Goode', something that the twenty-year-old Berry picked up on and perfected. When Berry paid tribute to the song during a 1965 recording session he deliberately avoided aping either the introduction or Jordan's treatment of the number.

Berry has also named Elmore James as another influence on his style, although the musical connection is less clear. What is certain is that, during trips to Chicago in the 1950s, Berry would seek out wherever James was playing, notably at Silvio's Tavern. James, who was only forty-five when he died in 1963, carried the spirit of Robert Johnson into the post-war, electrified blues era, and is noted for his slashing, open-tuned, bottleneck guitar work and impassioned singing. Although Berry sometimes uses a version of James's guitar sound, as in his own song 'Bio' and in 'It Hurts Me Too', a James classic that Berry often features in his stage act and has recorded at least twice, there are few points of contact between James's earthy blues and Berry's rock 'n' roll.

When asked which singers and musicians he admires Berry invariably mentions Nat 'King' Cole. Cole's success as a mellow crooner overshadowed the fact that, with the trio he formed in 1939, he was a quite outstanding jazz pianist. He later neglected this skill to the extent that, on his big 1962 hit 'Let There Be Love', the beautiful, Cole-like piano is in fact played by George Shearing. But it was Cole's voice that Berry particularly admired, and he regularly recorded ballads in respectful, but not particularly effective, imitation of his hero.

The Cole influence has little part to play in the rock 'n' roll sound that makes Berry unique, and the same is true of another singer Berry admired, one who modelled himself on the Cole sound, the mellow Texan blues stylist Charles Brown. There is more of Jordan in Berry's rock 'n' roll voice than anyone else that went before, but in terms of clarity of diction and the light 'whiteness' of his sound Berry created something new from all these influences, just as he took the guitar styles of Walker, Christian and Hogan and hit upon something that came up sounding brand-new – even when he was stealing a lick note for note.

# on Goode
# Avenue

**I**F YOU WERE to consult ten rock encyclopedias regarding Chuck Berry's birthplace you could easily find yourself with a hung jury, five going for San Jose, just south of San Francisco, and five for St Louis. In fact he was born at 6.59 a.m. on 18 October 1926 at his parents' home, the three-roomed 2520 Goode Avenue in St Louis.

Once in the 1950s he claimed to hail from San Jose, trying to impress a young woman who was talking to him after a performance. Since this was Francine Gillium, later to become his secretary and at the time preparing a brief press biography of him, it was soon established as fact. By 1969 he was saying: 'I'm from St Louis, I was born there.' The polite way of interpreting the smokescreen would be to call it mischievous – he would not be the only celebrity to rebel against the repetitive treadmill of publicity interviews by throwing the occasional red herring into the PR pond. And yet Berry has always been devious. Until his candid autobiography appeared in 1987 he was perfectly capable of denying, for example, that he was imprisoned in 1962, even if his interviewer could quote chapter and verse from contemporary press articles.

In 1972, for example, he was telling Patrick William Salvo of *Rolling Stone*: 'That's the misconceptions that people have, that Chuck Berry went to jail. They're just totally wrong, totally wrong. It might have said something in the large papers in the bigger city headlines and things. But, you take a look at any of the local papers and you will see that I was acquitted. I never went to jail.'

The leading local paper is the *St Louis Post-Dispatch*, which reported on 6 March 1960: 'Charles E. (Chuck) Berry, rock 'n' roll singer, was convicted by a jury in United States District Court late Friday 4 March, of transporting a fourteen-year-old Indian girl from El Paso, Texas, to St Louis for immoral purposes.' Although the case dragged on he was eventually imprisoned on 19 February 1962, and was a free man once more on his birthday the following year. He had been in jail before this, and was to serve time again. For decades Berry tried to protect his privacy not just with evasion, but with lies.

To subtract six years from his age, or to allow it to be done on his behalf, was equally confusing but more understandable. He was twenty-eight years old when 'Maybellene' hit the charts, and Chess Records was neither the first nor the last company to give its new star an injection of youth. And so, along with the confusion over his place of birth, any time up to 1932 may be quoted as being the relevant year.

Berry's parents were Henry William, who worked in a flour mill in nearby Baden and was a lay preacher at the Antioch Baptist Church, just down the street, and Martha, who sang in the choir there. Henry was officially the superintendent of the Sunday School. Chuck was christened Charles Edward Anderson Berry, the fourth of six children. The 'Anderson' was in honour of the doctor who delivered him, Anderson Cheatem. His siblings were Thelma, Lucy Ann, and Henry Jr (Hank), later to be joined by Paul and Martha. The Goode Avenue house was in the Elleardsville district, 'The Ville', one of the more respectable black neighbourhoods of the city. This background, which would perhaps be described as 'lower middle class' by sociologists, distinguishes Berry from the humbler origins of the Mississippi blues singers.

During the days of segregation this area, less than a square mile of houses and businesses, was the focus of black life in St Louis. As well as Berry, this was the childhood home of the radical comedian

Dick Gregory, future tennis star Arthur Ashe and Tina Turner. Opera diva Grace Bumbry once sang at Berry's high school Sumner, on Goode Avenue, and another celebrated opera singer, Marian Anderson, performed in the theatre attached to the Poro College, the hairdressing and cosmetology institute that Berry briefly attended as a young man.

Time has not been kind to this part of north St Louis, however. The main thoroughfare running north–south is now called Martin Luther King Drive, formerly Easton, but it is a poor tribute to the great man. It is still a black district, but all those who have been able to escape have fled to the suburbs. There are occasional stores, with perhaps a few second-hand clothes or electrical goods inside, but there is no bustle on the sidewalks, just little knots of unemployed men chewing the fat. While I was there three kids died in a stolen car that went out of control, and locals immediately accused the police of giving the vehicle a 'nudge'. Now, as in Berry's day, the only white people are those driving through, as this is one of the many tarmac arteries that carve through the heart of the city. The positive side to this decline, maybe, is that it was prompted by social integration, with black families moving out into other parts of the city.

Goode Avenue was a little residential street running off the main road, but it is now called Annie Malone Drive – another dubious honour. Otis Woodard, who runs a local food distribution charity and is also a volunteer worker on local radio, explains: 'Annie Malone was one of the first black woman entrepreneurs, in the 1930s. She made her fortune from hairdressing and cosmetic products, and she put money into setting up an orphanage.' It was she who founded the Poro College.

Now only a few houses are left, but the Antioch Baptist Church still stands proudly amid the desolation and vacant, weed-strewn plots. 'A historic church in a historic community,' says the banner. Surprisingly, the church not only survives but is apparently thriving – in autumn 2001 the bulldozers were busily clearing and excavating the adjacent plot of land so that an extension to the church could be built. Clearly it has a catchment area way beyond this silent street – indeed, it is characteristic of St Louis as of so many American cities that prosperity can lie just a block away, and beyond the corner of Annie Malone Drive the houses begin to look sprucer, more confident. Henry Berry would undoubtedly take pride if he could see the land being cleared, to help spread the word he preached for so many years.

So from his earliest days Chuck was surrounded by music, strictly gospel at first, until he mastered the controls on the radio. His mother played the piano, and the church choir would rehearse at his house. Berry's first memories were of his mother's hymn singing as she worked around the house, of the family piano and the old Victrola record machine. Apart from her church duties Martha had a full-time job simply stretching the pennies to keep her family together.

Once, when members of the Antioch choir were sitting around with Martha in her kitchen, the three-year-old Chuck's rubber ball scooted beneath the table. Rather than getting down on all fours to retrieve it, and fearful of an embarrassing reprimand in front of his mother's friends, Chuck discovered that he could also scoot, crouching with his body upright, shuffling forward with his left leg stuck out in front. It got a laugh and saved him from a slap. Years later, performing at the Paramount theatre in New York, he remembered that crouching walk. With his head pecking back and forth, and his guitar slung at his side, he invented what a local journalist tagged the duck walk.

After Sunday morning service the church elders would come back to eat Martha's food, and the children could only sit down at the table once the grown-ups had finished. On one summer night the garden shed next door caught fire, and when the fire engine arrived Chuck saw 'the first white persons I had ever seen up close in my life'. He guessed at the time that fear of tackling the blaze had bleached their faces.

When Chuck was still three the Berrys moved across the road to occupy the upper floor of a two-family house. They were once again crammed into three rooms but had gained an indoor bath. Soon Chuck was allowed to play in nearby Tandy Park, because his mother could now keep an eye on him from the elevated kitchen window. A month short of his fifth birthday he was enrolled at Cottage Avenue, the elementary school around the corner, built in the yard of the local high school Sumner, which was on the same Goode Avenue block as the Berry home.

Tandy Park, with its amusements for children, was to prove an inspiration to Berry. When asked by the *New Musical Express* in 1964 about his own Berry Park, he said: 'It has a swimming pool and all the facilities. We have cabins for groups, tennis, a lake that was dug and an island – we call it Long Island – and we have fishing and the usual games like croquet and handball. It used to be a smooth cornfield that was slightly elevated, but we changed all that. There was a playground on the street where I was born and it was fabulous. It grew up in me to have one of my own.'

Chuck was six when the family moved again, renting a five-roomed one-storey house at 4420 Cottage Avenue. They were still crowded, however, because Henry's cousin Harry and his son soon moved in, following the break-up of Harry's marriage, and mother Martha was pregnant again. Thanks to the family radio Chuck began to discover music beyond the hymns of his parents, and significantly he later recalled the country songs of artists like Kitty Wells as well as the black jazz of Fats Waller and Louis Armstrong.

When brother Paul was born Chuck was seven years old, and soon the family was on the move again to 4319 Labadie Street, a few blocks away. The patriarchal Henry began to work part-time for a company that leased out apartments across the city, doing carpentry, maintenance and repair work, and though as a black man he was paid less than union scale for a long time, he stayed with them until he was seventy in 1964. During the Depression years his work at the mill, which was to give Chuck one of the verses to 'Too Much Monkey Business', fell to three days a week, and so he branched out yet again in a second-hand $30 truck, selling vegetables from door to door. When he was not in school, now Simmons Grade School, Chuck helped with both the carpentry and the vegetable business. This school was the first black institution to be established in The Ville, in 1873, when it was delicately named Elleardsville Colored School No. 8.

Lucy was an enthusiastic pianist, and was particularly drawn to classical pieces. The rebellious young brother Chuck reacted by listening to blues and boogie-woogie on the radio, and so the seed of 'Roll Over Beethoven' was born. From the black radio station beamed across the river from East St Louis he was already hearing the artists whose sound would later amalgamate to create his own.

Soon after Martha Jr was born, completing the family, Thelma got married, and so at the age of two Martha became an aunt. Henry Jr and Chuck were both working for their father now, and in the vacation before going to high school Chuck was kept particularly busy. Henry paid them a nominal wage from his own meagre rate, and Chuck also took an evening job shelf-stacking at a local store.

At Sumner High School in 1941 Chuck appeared in an end-of-term student show called the 'All Men's Review'. Among the standard songs and solemn recitations, he chose to sing the current jukebox hit, Jay McShann's 'Confessin' the Blues', accompanied on guitar by fellow student Tommy Stevens, who was already playing semi-professionally around the locality. It went well, increasing Chuck's standing among the girls in the school, and he was loaned a four-string guitar by classmate Clarence Richmond. Once he had mastered the 'three-chord trick' of the blues by trial and error, Chuck realized that he could accompany dozens of songs that fell into a similar pattern.

He had always had a natural curiosity for photography and, given his developing interest in music, for the radio. When he went to a local radio repair shop and second-hand dealer to buy a radio of his own, the owner recognized his interest and suggested he pay off the cost by working in the evenings. The repairman was also a weekend disc jockey at local dances and so Chuck went along to help him, cueing up the records and noting down requests from the crowd.

As soon as he could afford it he bought his first car, a 1934 V8 Ford, $10 down and $5 a month, though his sister Thelma had to sign for it as he wasn't old enough to enter into a hire-purchase agreement. That V8 Ford was to surface in 'No Money Down'. He traded it in for a Plymouth sedan, a year older but a more impressive, eye-catching vehicle. With the help of the Plymouth, a copy of *Nick Mannaloft's Guitar Book of Chords* and a local musician called Ira Harris, who helped him polish his guitar technique, Chuck could start his career by playing at weekend parties. Simply by adding the four-chord sequence of songs like 'Blue Moon', for example C–Am–F–G, to his three-chord blues he soon built up a repertoire of ninety songs. The Plymouth was replaced by a 1937 Oldsmobile, and 'Maybellene' came ever closer.

Until the age of seventeen Chuck Berry had only indulged in petty adolescent crime, notably an enterprise that involved breaking into a coal yard at night and siphoning off petrol from the parked-up trucks.

He found some moral justification in the fact that the company operated a colour bar, employing only white drivers. But in the summer of 1944 he and his friends Skip and James planned a trip in Chuck's Oldsmobile to California, a trip that would end in jail. They loaded up with provisions and, because the tyres were wearing thin, they took several second-hand spares as well. Chuck also had the barrel of a gun he had found in a parking lot, its handle burned away.

They made a lunch stop at the Southern Air restaurant in Wentzville, just 30 miles west of St Louis. Berry was later to own the restaurant and make his home in Wentzville, and it was at Southern Air that his enthusiasm for home movies of a somewhat specialist nature was to get him into trouble late in life. Perhaps he was spurred to buy the place by the familiar demeaning experience as black customers when they stopped there in 1944, to be served round the back, through a window, on paper plates.

Such was the state of their stock of tyres that they were all used up in making it as far as the first proper stop en route, overnight at Independence, a suburb of Kansas City though still in Missouri. Money was already running out in this ill-planned adventure. Skip disappeared for a short while and when he returned he had a fistful of money, having robbed the till at a bakery store of $62. The next day they continued into Kansas City itself.

The second robbery was at a barber's shop. With James as getaway driver and Chuck waving the defunct weapon, his hand masking the lack of a butt, they took $32. When money ran out again on the fifth day they robbed a clothing store, netting $51 and some shirts, to which they added bedding stolen from the YMCA they had been staying at.

With the car proving troublesome they decided that the adventure was over, and turned east towards home, with yet another tyre stop in Independence. Chuck drove on into the night but at 3.30 a.m. the car finally broke down. At dawn a motorist in a Chevrolet pulled up to offer help and Chuck hijacked his car, once again pointing the gun barrel as if he meant business. The driver ran away, and they then had a daft plan – to use the Chevrolet to push the Oldsmobile, with James steering, all the way back home. After 10 miles two state troopers, alerted on the telephone by the Chevrolet's owner, were waiting for them.

After five days in Boone County Jail in Columbia, they were allowed to phone home. Skip and James were disowned by their parents, but

Henry Berry sent $125 to a Columbia lawyer to defend all three of them. They had been in the prison a month before they met the lawyer, who advised them to plead guilty, and after a twenty-one-minute hearing on the following day they were given the maximum sentence of ten years, armed robbery being the most serious of their crimes. They were committed to the Intermediate Reformatory for Young Men, known as Algoa, near Jefferson City.

The prison stood on a hill 200 feet above the Missouri River. The first thirty days were spent in solitary confinement, although it was possible to talk to those in other cells, and they learned that they were three of only seven prisoners with ten-year sentences, the maximum at Algoa. Even more severe sentences were served at the Missouri State Prison.

Black and white prisoners were strictly segregated, and during the day Chuck's guard was a minister, the Reverend Dave Scott. Scott was illiterate and Chuck managed eventually to gain a favoured position, reading his letters for him and writing out the replies. His official duties were in the laundry. Scott ran Sunday-morning church services in the dormitory, and Chuck had the idea of putting together a vocal quartet to take part in the services. One of the four, known as Po' Sam, was a professional musician from Kansas City, and the group was so well received that they crossed the racial line and sang at the white services as well. Sam and Chuck would also play the blues after hours in the dormitory.

When a white nun, Mother Robinson, took an interest in their welfare the quartet were allowed out of prison, in her care, to be baptized in Jefferson City, and this led to regular trips beyond the walls of Algoa on supervised singing engagements. With the help of sister Thelma, Chuck managed to get them invited to sing in a church in St Louis, and afterwards he was allowed to eat at home with his family. With the success of the quartet, his willingness to volunteer for chores like whitewashing the dormitory walls, and his scrupulous avoidance of winding up the openly racist white guards, Chuck had made prison life as comfortable as it could be. Only the open friendship shown towards him by the wife of the new assistant superintendent threatened his security, but he handled this as discreetly as he could and eventually the couple were moved on to another prison.

Training in the gym and taking up boxing was another passport to brief if painful freedom, and Chuck was entered into a Golden Gloves tournament in St Louis. He and his trainer, a guard named Ellis, stayed at the Berry family home. A couple of walkovers against opponents who didn't show up or withdrew, and a lucky victory in his first proper fight, saw Chuck to the final in his category, heavyweight novice, where he suffered a three-round whipping and was knocked out.

On the advice of an old con Chuck did not apply for parole at the first opportunity, but time was now hanging heavily. The blues jams between him and Sam had led to the setting-up of a fully fledged boogie band as well as the gospel quartet, but when Sam came up for release the band fell apart. Eventually, having served three years, Chuck was given a date for release on parole – 18 October 1947, his twenty-first birthday – and when the day arrived he was given the accumulated earnings from his stay in prison, $69 at five cents a day, and a train ticket from Jefferson City to St Louis, and on the afternoon of his birthday he arrived home.

On his release Chuck was 'free, black, twenty-one, single, and unbelievably horny'. Henry Jr, back from war service in the Philippines, was again working with his father, and Lucy had gone into hairdressing. While in the army Henry Jr had gained the nickname Hank, and it was he who re-christened Charles as Chuck.

Chuck, after paying for his bed and board at home, saved the $4 a day that his father paid him and was soon able to put down $275 as the first payment on a 1941 Buick, his most luxurious car to date and useful as a mobile bedroom in his determined pursuit of girls, so much more discreet than the rent-by-the-hour hotel rooms where customers risked being recognized in the hall. At a May Day festival in Tandy Park he first met Themetta Suggs, whom he nicknamed Toddy. They were soon engaged, and with the permission of Chuck's parole officer Mr Sotorias, who had to approve any official change in his charge's status, the couple started saving towards married life.

The wedding took place on 28 October 1948 at the home of an aunt of Themetta's, who also provided them with their first rented room. In November they moved into spare space at the beauty parlour recently opened by Chuck's sister Thelma, and in January to their first proper home, a room and tiny kitchen in a boarding house owned by Chuck's uncle Ed, at 4352 Delmar.

Ed also pointed Chuck towards the evening shift at the Fisher car assembly factory, where he swept the floor until midnight, before having supper and rising early to work with Henry and Hank, while Toddy worked in a laundry. He then followed Thelma's lead and enrolled at the Poro School of Beauty Culture, to study cosmetology and hairdressing, cutting into his availability to work for his father. And whenever possible, during time off, he was gaining local experience as a guitarist. He continued to juggle these various activities until a full-time career in music became a possibility.

At this stage in his life Chuck decided that savings were only to be invested in property, offering a guaranteed return, a maxim he has followed ever since. And so when the Buick broke down he simply allowed it to be repossessed. He then got a job as a caretaker, which came with a rent-free basement flat, and when the landlord saw how expertly he had renovated his own apartment Chuck was employed to make structural alterations to the rest of the house as well as his menial duties. He could soon afford his next car, a 1933 Plymouth.

The job didn't last long. Chuck took up the invitation of a white woman resident to visit her, with the intended consequences. He was reported by the woman's spurned lover, and underwent an uncomfortable interrogation at the police station, remembering all the time his father's advice that a black man should always know his place in white company. Chuck Berry always has, but not quite as his father intended, and he and Toddy were on the move again. They stayed briefly with sister Lucy before moving into the family home on Labadie, with Chuck now back working for his father.

So he was reduced again to just one poorly paid job, together with his hairdressing apprenticeship, which stimulated him to revive his musical ambitions. Starting as a solo singer–guitarist at friends' parties, he also began to work in bars catering for a white clientele, both on his own and as a sideman. This must have been an intuitive decision, that as a black musician whose musical education depended as much on country-and-western coming out of the family Philco radio as on the blues or his family's gospel, maybe he had something a little different to offer. He also made a more conscious effort to establish himself as a 'personality', using facial expressions and physical movements to complement the words of the songs.

In the summer of 1950 not only was Toddy pregnant but so were sister Lucy and brother Paul's wife Shirley. It was once again time to move, with $450 from their savings as the 10 per cent down payment on the first proper home of their own, a three-room house at 3137 Whittier Street, five blocks away. Chuck once again used his practical skills to turn the basement into an apartment, into which they moved so that they could rent out the main part of the house. On 3 October 1950 Darlin Ingrid Berry was born.

Chuck found a new job as a caretaker at WEW, the second oldest radio station in the United States, still beaming out its eclectic mixture of music and local features from a neat little house at 2740 Hampton Avenue, where it has lived since the mid-1990s. Guitarist Joe Sherman, who had a show on the station, sold Chuck an electric guitar for $30, payable in six instalments. This was a huge stride forward from the archaic four-string acoustic on which Chuck had made his first public appearances, and he found that the slicker fingering opened up new musical possibilities.

The next step towards 'Maybellene' was the purchase of an old reel-to-reel magnetic wire recorder, on which Chuck could try out his own ideas for songs and hone his performance. Many of these ideas were taken from his old mentor Ira Harris, who was still active around St Louis and playing in a style reminiscent of Charlie Christian. Add to this Chuck's interest in Louis Jordan, in particular his guitar player Carl Hogan, plus his worship of T-Bone Walker, and the Berry guitar sound was coming together.

# the
# Cosmopolitan
# Club

**S**INCE GRADUATING FROM high school Chuck had occasionally
bumped into Tommy Stevens, the guitarist who had backed
him on his performance of 'Confessin' the Blues' at the All
Men's Review, but he had never had the opportunity to play with him.
On 13 June 1952 he got a call from Stevens, however, offering him a
job singing and playing with the Stevens trio, two guitars and saxophone, on Saturday nights at a club called Huff's Garden.

The pay was $6 a night, and Chuck stayed with Stevens for the rest
of the year. He heard of the birth of his second daughter, Melody, on
1 November 1952 when he got home from a gig. The material they
played was mainly blues, drawing on artists like Elmore James and
Muddy Waters, but Chuck also began to introduce a hillbilly element,
with songs such as 'She'll Be Coming Round the Mountain' and
'Mountain Dew'. The shows drew a crowd, and the club owner soon
booked them for Friday nights as well, and raised their pay by $2 a
man.

Meanwhile, Johnnie Johnson and his trio were playing at the
Cosmopolitan Club on 17th and Bond Street over in East St Louis in
Illinois, a big venue that had previously been a grocery store. The band

name Sir John's Trio persists in many accounts, and was used by Johnnie's wife Frances in conversation with me, though Johnnie recalls that they were usually billed as the Johnnie Johnson Trio. 'We were playing standard tunes – they were very popular back in those days. A few blues here and there, but mainly things like "Stardust", "Sunny Side of the Street". We'd play clubs, lounges, and sometimes we'd be in a hall playing for a dance or a private party.'

On the day before New Year's Eve 1952, Johnson made one of the most significant telephone calls in rock 'n' roll history. 'Yes, I called up Chuck. I had a saxophone player, Albin Bennett, and he couldn't make the gig. I wasn't specifically looking for a guitar player, but this was a New Year's Eve job. If you're a musician and you're any good you'll usually be working that night, so I was desperate. But I'd seen Chuck before and I had his number, so I called him and found out he wasn't working. So I asked him if he'd go in that night. That one night lasted over thirty years.

'He was playing with Tommy Stevens up the street from one of our jobs. I'd just come to St Louis. And I finished earlier, so when my job was over we'd go to the next club. Change of scenery. That's how I'd met Chuck, because he was on later than us.'

Chuck fitted in well, and the owner of the Cosmopolitan Club, Joe Lewis, suggested to Johnnie that he play there regularly. The trio was completed by drummer Ebby Hardy, though sometimes Lewis would book in a bass player as well. As with Stevens' band, Chuck was keen to introduce his gimmick of playing white hillbilly music to a black audience, and it got the band noticed. One effect was that white customers began to patronize the Cosmopolitan, and so – most unusually for the time – Chuck would see both 'salt and pepper' in the crowd for their shows. Although most of their material still drew on such artists as Nat 'King' Cole and Muddy Waters, his parallel liking for country music inevitably had an influence on his diction and style of singing, which has always been more clearly enunciated than any other black artist, and this would be vital in allowing him to convey his complex, witty lyrics later in his career.

On one occasion Berry missed a Cosmopolitan gig in order to play with his old friend Tommy Stevens, back on the Missouri side of the river at the Crank Club, at 2742 Vanderventer. Since Berry's singing was now a popular part of the Johnson band, and his replacement that night didn't sing, the club owner insisted that Berry signed a contract to guarantee his appearances at the Cosmo.

He was also branching out, and one Crank Club poster of the period advertises 'Chuck Berryn' with a combo made up of saxophonist Richard Culph, pianist Erskine Rodgers and drummer Bill Erskine. Berry explains the distortion of his surname as being an attempt to conceal his involvement in the sinful world of secular music from his father, though since the poster also carried his photograph this seems unlikely. Equally mysteriously, the poster promises that Mr Berryn would be performing every Monday, Wednesday, Friday and Saturday, which would clearly be in conflict with his obligation to the Cosmo Club.

He also played at Club Imperial, owned by George Edick – whose son Greg, bass-playing leader of St Louis band The Joint Jumpers, later backed Berry on record and on tour. 'My dad opened the Club Imperial in 1952,' Greg recalled in 1994. 'He had all the big acts. Louis Prima, Stan Kenton, Jimmy "Night Train" Forrest. My dad gave Chuck Berry some of his first local gigs.' And with father and son later sharing the management chores the club survived. 'Every once in a while Chuck Berry or his daughter Ingrid will join us on stage,' said Greg. 'That's always a nice surprise.' Before joining Johnson, Berry would also occasionally sit in with a touring outfit called the Ray Band Orchestra.

According to Berry, it was when he was required to sign a contract that he suggested that the name of the Johnson band be changed to the Chuck Berry Trio, an arrangement that suited Johnson, who had no taste for the business side of music. Johnnie remembers it differently, and that the change of name didn't occur until after the success of 'Maybellene' in 1955. 'An agent got hold of him and hired him after that,' he says. 'So he asked me and Ebby to play with him. We still had the same people playing, we just changed names.' This accords with his recollections recorded in his biography: 'The band that recorded "Maybellene" and "Wee Wee Hours" was still called the Johnnie Johnson Trio. The record came out under Chuck's name, but we didn't think nothin' of it . . . Me and Ebby didn't care nothin' 'bout no records . . . We did a job, we got paid, we went home.' Chuck, as he says, was the 'go-getter'.

'Whatever he try to do he usually bring it down,' says Johnnie. 'He had his own peculiar ways, even back then. Sometimes he'd talk to you, then he'd walk. He'd hibernate, and you wouldn't see him for a while. But I never tried to understand the way he is. All I was interested in was doing my job on stage. Getting paid, and going my way and he'd go his way.'

It may be that the apparent conflict of loyalties between the Cosmo and the Crank, together with the alleged change of name and what seems to be an alternative band at the second venue, which Johnson says he knew nothing about, was part of a deliberate scheme by Chuck to increase his fees *and* gain control of the Johnson band. Johnnie, of course, is too good-natured to claim that the change of bandleader was anything but a natural progression, *after* 'Maybellene'.

One highlight of the trio's performances was the growing rapport between the increasingly proficient Berry and the self-taught Johnson. They developed a call-and-response style of instrumental break, with Berry trying to out-fox his partner by playing slurred and bent notes, and the pianist producing the perfect response from his unyielding keyboard. This interplay was to form the heart of the records they made together, which would have been the lesser without Johnson's extraordinary flights of fancy. Berry also began ad-libbing extra verses to songs and even improvising new words to existing tunes, the process that led directly to 'Maybellene', in its raw form a barely disguised country song 'Ida Red', which Berry called 'Ida May'.

However, when he signed with Chess Records Berry had already been inside a recording studio. He auditioned for Duke Records in Memphis, possibly as early as 1952, though nothing came of it. In 1954 he also tried his luck with Chess's chief rival in Chicago, Vee-Jay, but was turned down. In that year another St Louis musician, guitarist Oscar Washington, set up a little record label at 4741 Leduc Street, and cut vocal group The Swans on a version of the instrumental 'Night Train', a 1951 hit for Jimmy Forrest to which Washington added lyrics. In 1962 a revival of the tune by James Brown reached no. 5 on the R & B chart and was also a sizeable pop hit, peaking at no. 35. Knowing of Berry's growing reputation around town, and having seen him play a number of times in local clubs, Washington booked him for a session on the afternoon of 13 August, although Berry has always denied being involved in any recordings before 'Maybellene', as well as having failed previous auditions.

Washington and vocalist Joe Alexander had written a couple of songs with a Latin tinge, 'Oh Maria' and 'I Hope These Words Will Find You Well'. On the session Alexander and Washington (under the name Faith Douglas) and 'Charles Berryn' were joined by bongo player Freddy Golden. Berry played lead guitar on the second title. 'We practised in my basement, because the piano was down there,' Washington recalled in 1982. The session was held at Premier Studios and four sides were cut in two hours, although the other two have disappeared from the records.

'Oh Maria' was announced somewhat optimistically in a *Billboard* ad as 'a calypso hit', but sales were poor. In fact, the Ballad label did not last long, although Berry did try to persuade Washington to record him under his own name. Washington turned him down. 'The biggest mistake I ever made,' he later admitted ruefully. Alexander gigged in St Louis for a while after the failure of the record before moving to Chicago and turning to gospel music. Golden also became a singer, with a group called Quartette Très Bien, who later found success in the Paris cabaret clubs, while Washington remained in St Louis as a writer and producer.

In early 1955 Berry was making enough money as daytime carpenter and evening musician to buy his first new car, a Ford Esquire station wagon, and to add a couple of rooms to the back of the bungalow. In May he set off for Chicago in the Ford, taking with him an old school friend who wanted to visit his mother in the Windy City, Ralph Burris. The city's blues scene was at its peak that year, just before Bo Diddley and then Berry rewrote the rules. On their first night in town the two tourists looked in on every blues bar they could find, seeing Howlin' Wolf and Elmore James among others before just catching the end of a Muddy Waters gig at the Palladium on Wabash Avenue.

Once Muddy had wound up with a song that Berry recalls as 'Got My Mojo Working', although this Willie Dixon number wasn't recorded until the December of the following year — Muddy's most recent R & B chart success had been 'I'm Ready', and his biggest hit of the past year was 'Just Make Love to Me' — Berry joined the crush trying to press the flesh with the star, and managed to stammer out a question about where he should go to try and cut a record. Berry recalls the answer in his autobiography as: 'Yeah, see Leonard Chess. Yeah, Chess Records over on 47th and Cottage.' He also denies the embroidered story about him sitting in with Muddy that night – he would never have had the nerve. 'It has always hurt me when a writer replaces the truth with fictitious dramatic statements to increase interest in his story.'

That is not what he had told students on the Berkeley campus back in 1969. 'When I first walked into Chess Records in May of 1955, after a previous night of visiting one of Muddy Waters' dates, which was around the corner, on the south side of Chicago . . . and I played a song with him, it was a great thrill, him having let me do so . . .' It is also possible that Waters, playing in St Louis and with some evenings free, caught Berry playing with the Trio at the Cosmopolitan Club.

Extending the trip beyond the intended weekend, Berry drove to 4720 Cottage Grove Avenue early on Monday morning and followed a man into the Chess Records building. It turned out to be Leonard Chess himself, who listened to his story and asked to hear a demo tape. Berry pretended that he had one ready back at home in St Louis, and that he would be happy to come back with it. He drove home, contacted Johnnie Johnson and Ebby Hardy, and plugged a microphone into his cheap tape recorder. They put down two songs, Berry's 'Ida May' and the languorous blues from the Cosmo Club, 'Wee Wee Hours'. 'That was the tape,' recalls Johnson. 'Those days they were only making 45s, so we just had the two songs.'

In his 1969 Berkeley talk, Berry refers gracelessly to his fellow musicians, as well as exaggerating the number of songs. 'I had a $79 tape recorder, monaural, and I cut six songs on it with some jive musicians on it – I say jive musicians, because I don't even remember their names now . . .' He also airbrushed Johnson and Hardy out of the historic recording session that resulted from the tape. 'Two weeks later I came back and cut a session with some Chicago musicians, and that started the ball rolling.'

On 29 November 1938, in Dallas, Bob Wills and his Texas Playboys recorded a lively number called 'Ida Red', with Tommy Duncan on vocals. The first known recording of the song had been cut fourteen years earlier, by Fiddlin' Powers on Victor Records. No composer credit was given when the Wills version was released on Vocalion, implying that it was assumed to be in the public domain, and it became a staple of the Wills songbook. Some five years later he cut a second version for Armed Service Radio Transcription, and in the meantime he had featured it in the 1941 Glenn Ford movie *Go West Young Lady*.

In the mid-1940s Wills returned again to the song when recording a huge selection of his repertoire for Tiffany Music, Inc., who sold the discs to radio stations across the country as thirty-minute ready-made sponsored shows. By the time Wills revisited the song yet again in 1960 he had claimed half the composer credit, along with someone called Moore – possibly his former electric mandolin player Tiny Moore.

There were plenty of opportunities, then, for the young country-music fan Chuck Berry to acquaint himself with the Wills tune via the family radio. 'Ida Red, Ida Red, I'm a fool about Ida Red.' A song for sticking your thumbs behind your braces, waggling your elbows and hammering your heels into the hardwood floor. But Fred Rothwell, author of *Long Distance Information: Chuck Berry's Recorded Legacy*, has identified further possible sources of the inspiration for what was to become 'Maybellene'. In 1951 Bumble Bee Slim recorded 'Ida Red Blues', and in the same year there were several hit versions of a country boogie called 'Hot Rod Racer', a car chase with the automobiles 'rollin' side by side'.

The likeliest answer is that all three songs worked their way into Berry's subconscious and emerged as his own hillbilly novelty 'Ida May'. He himself makes no reference to possible influences, but when Berry returned to Chicago with what he regarded as a self-penned song on the home-made demo tape, both Leonard Chess and Willie Dixon counselled a change of name – similarity of melody, theme *and* title to 'Ida Red' could cause trouble. 'If it went over,' said Dixon, 'whoever was involved with "Ida Red" would come running.'

In 1972, talking to *Melody Maker*, Berry denied that his song was a straight rewrite. 'It was always "Maybellene" after it became a hit record, but I was doing "Ida Red" in the same tune. Actually, they're two different songs. "Ida Red" is traditional country and western and it wasn't my tune.' Well, we know that, but there is no mention here of his halfway stage, 'Ida May', which clearly had a close relationship with its near-namesake, as well as establishing the 'Maybellene' theme of a high-speed car chase after a girl.

Dixon had no such qualms about the appeal of the song, however. 'The minute I heard it, I knew it had that certain quality and feeling.'

This came as a surprise to Johnnie Johnson: 'I'd always figured people liked the hillbilly stuff at the Cosmo 'cause it was a novelty. But Chess was a serious blues label.' What became the flip side, 'Wee Wee Hours', was the stronger contender as far as Johnson was concerned, and more what he felt the band to be about, particularly as it was his tune. Muddy Waters, whose old-style Chicago blues was to be over-shadowed by his protégé's reworking of it, was also struck by the novel appeal of 'Maybellene'. 'You'd better record that,' he told Leonard Chess. 'That's something new here.'

Leonard and his brother Phil were Jewish refugees from Poland who moved from drinks wholesaling into nightclubs and then bought themselves into a record label, Aristocrat, set up in 1947. Two years later they took over the label, renamed it Chess, and began to record local talent. It soon became clear that their blues recordings were the label's particular strength, notably those of Muddy Waters. In the course of the 1950s every major blues star either resident in or passing through Chicago was represented on the label – with the exception of Jimmy Reed, who was rejected by Leonard Chess and went down the street to rivals Vee-Jay. In 1955, with the signing of Chuck Berry and Bo Diddley, Chess also found itself in on the birth of rock 'n' roll.

When Chess demanded a new title for 'Ida May', Berry claims that he immediately thought of 'Maybellene'. He may have been remem-bering the name of a cow, Maybelle, in a children's cartoon book. He confirmed that version in the 1972 *Melody Maker* interview. Johnnie Johnson credits Leonard Chess himself, spotting a bottle of Maybelline mascara and changing one letter, again to avoid accusations of plagia-rism, although with Berry's training at the cosmetics college, the inspiration could indeed have been his. And which of the rugged Chess bluesmen was using mascara, anyway? Little Richard never entered the building, and was on the west coast, after all.

Berry expounded his theories on the close relationship between the blues and hillbilly.

There really is no difference from the white man singing the blues as opposed to the black man. Blues comes primarily from poor background, and not from cultural differences and not from ethnic differences. If you was a black person living on the street in the ghettos and a white person living on the street in the ghettos they would still sympathize with each other because they are both poor.

And a hillbilly who lives there in the mountains and he has bad times and he sings those country hillbilly songs about, you know, down and out living – his tears are the same . . . With 'Maybellene' now, it's a physical thing. It all has to do with timing, the 2/4 time and the musical reference. Actually, it all started back when I was listening to station KMOX in St Louis, which is theoretically an Okie station and I got turned on by the sounds . . .

Also significant was the fact that in 1954 another local radio station, KATZ, began broadcasting live gigs from clubs in the town. Since both whites and blacks had access to the airwaves, the next obvious step was that attendance at these live performances would become racially mixed.

By 1979, in an interview with *Goldmine*, Berry had changed his story about the origin of the name 'Maybellene'. '[The title] had nothing to do with the cosmetic thing. I was through with hairdressing by that time, and the cow's name [in the cartoon book] was Maybelle. I just got to playing with the song, trying different names, and Maybellene popped up. Anyway, Maybelle wouldn't fit.'

The words were also worked on, and the arrangement was developed along more original lines. When Berry, Johnson and Hardy returned to Chicago, heading for Universal Studios at 111 East Ontario Street, for the recording session on 21 May 1955, the song continued to move further and further away from 'Ida Red'. They were augmented by Dixon on slap bass and a maracas shaker, possibly Jerome Green from Bo Diddley's band, though they were on the road continually at the time, so maybe it was Leonard Chess himself.

Looking back now, after decades of hearing 'Maybellene' simply as one of the cornerstones of rock 'n' roll, its hillbilly origins do seem muted, lying somewhere in its skipping lightness of touch compared to the foursquare solidity of a typical Chess blues. Hardy's urgent drumming and Dixon's vibrant slap bass complete the picture. However, a respectful live version by the young Elvis Presley, who picked up on the song immediately and sung it on the *Louisiana Hayride* show, does indeed transform it into pure rockabilly, while at the same time following the original closely, and it must be this hillbilly quality that Presley heard in the original. Years later, Presley admitted: 'I just wish I could express my feelings the way Chuck Berry does.'

Berry's precise, clear way of talking, and therefore of singing, was another reason for the crossover tone of the record, but it is something he claims to be unaware of. 'It doesn't register to me that someone would judge you by your enunciation,' he told *Melody Maker*. 'It doesn't make any sense . . . You're trying to say, is Chuck Berry black or white? Well, I'll tell you, Chuck Berry is black and he's beautiful!'

In a 1970s *Rolling Stone* essay Robert Christgau developed the theme of Berry's crossover appeal. 'Berry was the first blues-based performer to successfully reclaim guitar tricks that country and western innovators had appropriated from black people and adapted to their own uses twenty-five or fifty years before. By adding blues tone to some fast country runs, and yoking them to a rhythm and blues beat and some unembarrassed electrification, he created an instrumental style with biracial appeal.'

Christgau also notes the distinctive quality of Berry's voice: '. . . an insouciant tenor that, while recognizably Afro-American in accent, stayed clear of the melisma and blurred overtones of blues singing, both of which enter only at premeditated moments'. The blues singer Jimmy Witherspoon once observed: 'Chuck Berry is a country singer . . . If [he] was white . . . he would be the top country star in the world.'

As Berry recalls it, the session also produced the two sides of his second single, 'Thirty Days' and 'Together (We Will Always Be)'. This conflicts with Johnson's memory, and indeed seems unlikely. 'Maybellene', for all its energy, humour and freshness, took thirty-six takes to record, partly no doubt due to Berry's lack of studio experience. For 'Wee Wee Hours', however, it was simply a question of fitting a few stanzas to a mellow, slow blues they had routined at the Cosmopolitan Club, with Johnson's playing to the fore and Berry singing in his finest Charles Brown voice. This tune is perhaps the most convincing evidence of Johnnie Johnson's uncredited but vital musical input into the Berry catalogue. As Johnson's wife Frances puts it: 'That "Wee Wee Hours" was in the Sir John Trio repertoire before Chuck joined.'

'I was just foolin' around with a regular old blues in G,' Johnson told his biographer Travis Fitzpatrick. 'Later on, when Chess asked for another song, Chuck had me play that blues again and he started puttin' words to it. Wasn't but fifteen minutes later we had "Wee Wee Hours", which was the first song we did, Chuck and I, that was all our own . . .'

To complete the confused recollections of this trailblazing session, Willie Dixon would have you believe that Johnson wasn't present at all, and that the piano part is played by Chess studio musician Lafayette Leake. But the beautiful piano figures on 'Wee Wee Hours' are quintessential Johnson, and the tune is surely his from the days of the Trio. Leake did play on some later Berry sessions when Johnson wasn't available, and it may be that as a good friend of Dixon, who filed the recording details, his name was sometimes slipped on to the sessions sheets even if he wasn't there.

Phil Chess set up the session while his elder brother took care of business elsewhere in the Universal studio building, although Berry recalls that Leonard did operate the tape machine when they got down to work. In Dixon's recollection, however, the older brother was out of town. Once again it would seem that his memory let him down, since Berry also describes reading the relevant recording and publishing contracts while Leonard watched him for any reactions, and he would surely remember that incident vividly. Dixon went on to claim that he, Leake, Harold Ashby and Al Duncan 'were the first road band Chuck Berry had', when it is clear that Johnson and Hardy fulfilled the role.

Dixon, secure in his recognized position as the pivotal figure of Chicago blues, had no reason to lie, no need to move himself even more centre-stage than he already was, so it seems most likely that in old age his memory let him down at times. Phil Chess confirms this. 'I don't know what Willie was thinking. The only reason Leake would come in is if Johnnie couldn't make it or if we had to redo the recording for some reason.' This version is backed up by Johnson's recollections.

On and on, take after take – though most were swiftly aborted, and many were surely spent simply getting that startling introductory guitar figure right – they worked on 'Maybellene' into the evening. Once again Phil Chess confirms the story. 'We didn't have anything to compare it to,' he told Fitzpatrick. 'This was an entirely new kind of music. Maybe some of them were fine as they were, but we just kept playing with it.'

Tape was a reusable commodity to the penny-wise Chess brothers, but how musical history could do with the evidence of those thirty-five aborted attempts. They would surely show rock 'n' roll being born, inch by inch, in the time it took a black bluesman to take what he wanted from hillbilly and put it to revolutionary use.

Unfortunately, the confusion over Dixon's recollections also means discarding one of his most entertaining anecdotes – about how Leonard Chess was actually out of town during the time it took to cut, press and distribute 'Maybellene' to disc jockeys, and how he came back to Chicago and burst into the office saying, 'Man, somebody's got a record on the air that's burning it up,' without knowing it was one of his. He would surely have recognized Ida Red's daughter Maybellene, even if he met her unexpectedly while on a business trip.

'Playing with it', in Phil Chess's words, included employing the Chess Records patent method of getting a little echo on the voice, by moving the singer into the bathroom and pumping the fractionally delayed vocals back to the studio through a long length of plumbing pipework. Once Take 36 was approved Berry and Johnson concocted their B-side, which was quickly and satisfactorily laid down, and Berry was handed two contracts to sign, for recording and publishing.

He read them carefully but in confusion, trying to kid Leonard Chess that he understood every word, and signed excitedly. He was soon to overcome this innocence and become one of the most tediously argumentative analysts of a contract, but for now he was happy, and once they'd loaded up the car they set off for home. Leonard Chess immediately sent acetates of the two sides to Alan Freed in New York to be played on his syndicated radio show, and Freed reported enthusiastic response to 'Maybellene', for which service he was soon to be rewarded. The record was rush-released, and one local radio station disc jockey was so impressed that he played it over and over without a break.

Berry was then to get a stern lesson in the ways of the music business. As far as he was concerned he was the sole composer of 'Maybellene'. At the time Johnson wouldn't have disagreed with him – in spite of his undoubted contributions to Berry's songs, which started simply as verses written down on paper until Johnson began to make musical suggestions to go behind them – the piano player never thought of himself as the writer of the music. 'I can't read music, and I never wrote it down,' he says, and until comparatively recently in his mind this meant that he didn't *write* the music. 'I just made it up, you know?'

Ironically, while Johnson's very real claim to a credit was ignored, Berry found that he did apparently have two co-writers. When 'Maybellene' was copyrighted on 5 July his was the only name on it, but within a month the names of Russ Fratto and Alan Freed had been added to the certificate of registration. And when the sheet music was published, misspelling the title as 'Mabellene', Fratto and Freed were on the cover.

In the case of Freed, the most influential radio disc jockey promoting this type of music, this was quite simply a form of payola. His name appeared as co-author of many songs, including The Moonglows' 1954 smash 'Sincerely'. This was, Leonard Chess explained to Berry, the way that things worked. Although Freed was to be the main victim of the 'payola' scandal of the early 1960s, which led quickly to alcoholism and early death, he was not the only disc jockey on the take. The arrangement was usually strictly cash, and the writer credit was just a variation on the theme, a convenience for a small company only known for its blues 'hits' that sold far fewer than successful pop records. As a result, Freed played 'Maybellene' to death, and helped to ease it up the chart.

It is less clear what hold Russ Fratto had over the Chess brothers. He supplied their stationery, letterheads, record labels and the like. In Phil Chess's recollection he actually paid Berry an agreed sum in return for a share of the publishing, but Berry denies this, and it would indeed seem a very strange way to behave. More likely, it was simply an alternative way of the Chess brothers settling their printing bills, one that it would appear they used several times. Berry states that he first knew of this arrangement when he received his first royalty statement, and that even then he was too naive to realize that they shared the revenue as well as the credit. Since his first cheque came to around $10,000, it didn't occur to him that he could have been owed even more. Berry finally gained sole ownership of 'Maybellene' in 1986, once the original copyright had expired. It had previously been held by Arc Music, Chess's publishing arm, jointly owned by the Chess brothers and Harry and Gene Goodman, bandleader Benny Goodman's brothers.

*Billboard* magazine greeted the record with enthusiasm, in its unique journalistic style: 'Berry socks across an amusing novelty with ace showmanship and expressive good humor. The tune has a catchy rhythm and a solid, driving beat. Fine jockey and juke wax.' This may be the first time, but it was certainly not the last, when rock 'n' roll was seen as a novelty, although every other word is spot on.

With the record breaking out locally in various parts of the country as well as shooting up the national R & B list, Berry was signed in August 1955 to the Gale Booking Agency on a three-year deal. Already it was apparent from the sales pattern of the record that something unprecedented in the experience of the record company was happening, because the disc was being bought in places, as Nadine Cohodas has noted in her book *Spinning Blues Into Gold*, that the traditional Chess fare had failed to penetrate, for example Boston, New York and Philadelphia.

Phil Chess was by this time on a family holiday in an out-of-the-way place in Wisconsin, no doubt anticipating a drowsy summer lull in the sales graph, but when he found he was hearing 'Maybellene' every time he switched on the radio he knew it was time to cut the holiday short and head back for Chicago to assist in the promotional effort. The entire Chess Records staff, including the brothers, worked overtime boxing up the records and sending them out to keep up with demand.

The 'Hot Hundred' chart published weekly by *Billboard* was not inaugurated until November 1955, but prior to that they published a weekly list of bestselling singles nationwide. 'Maybellene' soon reached no. 4, an unprecedented achievement for a record by a black artist. It was also listed in the charts reflecting jukebox and radio plays, and climbed all three R & B lists, record sales, jukebox plays and disc jockey selections. Regionally, it was the top record in cities right across America. Collation of these statistics may have occasionally been somewhat haphazard, and the Chess brothers were not in the habit of publishing their sales figures, just in case one of their bluesmen could read, but there can be no doubt that for the work of an unknown, black artist 'Maybellene' was a commercial as well as a cultural phenomenon.

The Gale contract guaranteed Berry at least $40,000-worth of work a year, something he neglected to mention to Johnson and Hardy when he invited them to join him on the road for a more modest wage. It is at this point, according to Johnson, that his Trio became Chuck Berry's. 'I figured we'd keep on gettin' gigs with Chuck in charge,' he told Travis Fitzpatrick, 'and that maybe I'd be able to work full time as a musician if I stayed on his payroll and did what he said.'

One wonders if, just sometimes, Berry the businessman, Berry the dollar-hoarder, ever realizes the extent of his extraordinary luck that it was such a naive, trusting, unambitious, *good* man, a musical genius as a bonus, who once phoned him up with the offer of a one-off New Year's Eve gig. With the success of 'Maybellene' and a contract in his pocket, Berry sold the hairdressing booth he had kept on since leaving the Poro College, and was a fully fledged professional musician.

The first fruit of the agency deal was a three-night booking for $500 at the Peacock Lounge in Atlanta, Georgia, playing thirty-minute sets, no problem to the group seasoned by long nights at the Cosmo Club. The neon sign outside announced The Four Fellows, Miss Wiggles and Chuck Berry – his name in lights for the first time, a moment alluded to in 'Johnny B Goode'. They returned to the Cosmo (at their usual fee of $21) to wind up their long residency before driving to Cleveland, Ohio, for a week-long engagement at Gleason's Bar. As the record sold more and more the agency would wire them to stay on the road, adding dates as they went along.

Without knowing it or agreeing to it, Berry acquired a manager, Teddy Reig, assigned to him by an agency contact, Jack Hook. Berry's deal was 60 per cent of the gross with a guaranteed $150 minimum, and he soon began to notice that, no matter how big the crowd, it was never quite big *enough* according to Reig's accounting to trigger more than the minimum fee. Against his better judgement, though, and for the only time in his career, Berry formalized the relationship with Reig by appointing him as his manager. He regretted it immediately, when a packed house at a large venue produced just $100 more than the guarantee.

Berry noted that once Reig had the security of a contract he didn't bother to put in an appearance at gigs so often, but he still managed to control the take. The relationship didn't last long. According to Berry, Reig soon asked for an extra percentage, even though he seemed to be doing less work – and, Berry now assumed, was also skimming off the difference between the guaranteed minimum and the actual fee at most of the gigs. Berry claims that Reig cashed a cheque illegally, and that this gave him the opportunity to sever the contract. Since then, he has been his own man and his own manager.

The next milestone in Berry's career on the road was a week-long engagement at the Paramount in Brooklyn, New York, on a bill that included Tony Bennett, Nappy Brown and the Red Prysock Orchestra. In celebration he bought the trio brown suede shoes and matching but cheap stage suits, and it was here that he first unveiled the duck walk. 'Alan Freed had a house full,' he told *Rolling Stone* in 1969 '. . . and I had to outfit my trio . . . and I always remember the suits cost me $66, $22 apiece. We had to buy shoes and everything, so anyway, when we got to New York, the suits, they were rayon, but looked like seersucker by the time we got there . . . so we had one suit, we didn't know we were supposed to *change*. So we wanted to do something different, so I actually did that duck walk to hide the wrinkles in the suit – I got an ovation, so I figured I'd pleased the audience, so I did it again, and again, and I'll probably do it again tonight.'

The format of the show was typical of that offered by the big-city theatres of the day – in this case a live performance five times a day beginning at 1.00 p.m. and continuing into the small hours, separated by screenings of a current movie. The Berry trio were first on, and at 7000 capacity this was by far the biggest gig Berry had ever witnessed, let alone played. They performed the two sides of their single and retreated to the dressing room for a couple of hours.

Before the week was over the agency confirmed that they were to move on for a further week-long booking at the famed Apollo in Harlem, this time a ninety-minute live show interspersed with a half-hour of cartoons, trailers and advertisements. Whereas the Paramount crowd had been white, Berry, Johnson and Hardy were now playing at the Mecca of black musical entertainment. It was a raunchy place, where hookers were always on hand to offer the performers, in Berry's neat words, 'anything you could want from matzo balls to matrimony'.

There was no colour bar here, though. Rock 'n' roll existed in an anarchic cocoon, a meritocracy based on talent, popularity and sales figures. Within this cocoon, for example, Buddy Holly and Little Richard could become good friends. Outside it, a rural Texan redneck and a black, city gay were rarely to be seen enjoying a joke together. White performers who appealed to a black audience were booked on that basis, and everyone mingled backstage.

There's a scene in *The Buddy Holly Story*, effective and amusing in its context, where The Crickets find themselves booked into the Apollo on the assumption that they are a black act, and when the curtain goes back the audience are stunned into silence – though of course Buddy and the boys soon have them jitterbugging in the aisles. It's a nice piece of fiction. 'That'll Be the Day' doesn't sound black, it sounds Texan. But black New Yorkers bought it, so they got the gig. They were, however, unusual Texans in that they had seen Bo Diddley perform and were buying Chuck Berry records.

The crossover attractions of 'Maybellene' were confirmed when country singers immediately picked up on the song. Apart from the Elvis version already mentioned, featured on the TV show *Louisiana Hayride*, Marty Robbins had a regional C & W hit with it and it was also covered by disc jockey–singer Jim Lowe, of 'Green Door' fame. These were just the first of over a hundred covers of the song, by artists as diverse as duetting country giants George Jones and Johnny Paycheck, British groups The Searchers and Gerry and the Pacemakers, rockabilly Mac Curtis, Berry's rival Jerry Lee Lewis, and further performers in Denmark, Latvia, Finland, Belgium, Australia, Canada, Norway, Holland, Sweden, France, Switzerland and Mexico! On its release it also prompted two answer songs, both called 'Come Back Maybellene', by John Greer and Mercy Dee.

Rarely, if ever, can a debut disc have had such wide-ranging and lasting appeal, unconscious recognition that maybe this was indeed the song that kick-started rock 'n' roll. When Elvis Presley, at this time still a local sensation in Memphis but yet to become famous across the continent, reversed the process – a white man singing black – the revolution had arrived.

# on the road

FOLLOWING THE APOLLO engagement the band had been instructed by the agency to join up with the Alan Freed *Rock 'n' Roll Jubilee* tour, the second annual package show organized and emceed by the disc jockey. Indeed, the bus was waiting for them outside the Apollo and they hit the road at 3.30 a.m., en route to the Nu Elms Ballroom in Youngstown, Ohio. These caravans had a steadily changing cast, prompted by illness or exhaustion in some cases, or when an act hot on the charts replaced one whose record was on the way down. An artist with a regional break-out might join the tour just for the period when it swept through the area where the record was hot.

'One hundred and one one-nighters,' says Johnnie. 'In 101 days!' And yet he recalls the uncomfortable marathon of these 1950s tours with affection, because of the resulting camaraderie. 'On the tour you all became friends because you were together for three months. I got to know everybody. One of my close friends was Della Reese. Faye Adams. Illinois Jacquet, who was one of the band. We was all one big happy family. I still think about it sometimes. Not too often, though. Now I'm too busy thinking about what my future is . . .' Johnson's 'future' only really began with the release of Berry's sixtieth birthday tribute film *Hail! Hail! Rock 'n' Roll* in 1987, after which he emerged as a solo star and national treasure, and eventually kicked his debilitating drink habit.

Life on the 1950s tour bus, not the executive coach of today with its plump seats, video screens, attendant and miniature 'rest room', but a rocking and rolling, lino-floored boneshaker with no heating and no escape, with cola bottles rattling from one side to another at every bend, was a revelation. Berry was particularly struck by the gambling that seemed to reflect the live-for-the-moment 'other world' of rock 'n' roll, a reminder that his rival as the biggest-selling black artist of the year was Johnny Ace, but in Ace's case the honour was posthumous, since on the previous Christmas Day he had killed himself in a backstage game of Russian roulette.

'I saw my first live gambling,' Berry recalls in *The Autobiography*, 'a bold and blazing crap game in the aisle of the bus that carried on until dawn. When I woke up at the announcement of a breakfast stop, only three were left in the game and maybe twenty thousand dollars had changed hands in the aisle.' Berry was soon to lose his gambling virginity, since on a similar tour in 1957 there he was at the back of the bus, rolling dice with Buddy Holly. This was a rare indulgence, though. Gambling risked losing money, and money was what Berry held most dear.

Getting on together in this way, across the racial divide, was essential if life was to remain tolerable. Not only was there the juddering claustrophobia of the bus, but the backstage areas of the theatres had not been designed to accommodate a huge rock 'n' roll revue in either privacy or comfort.

On that first major tour, limited to playing their hit and, if they were lucky, the B-side as well, there was plenty of time for Johnnie and Ebby to indulge in their favourite hobby, drinking. Johnnie would also seek out the nearest club at each stopover, always ready to sit in. The teetotal Berry, however, kept himself to himself, often writing lyrics in his hotel room. His disapproval of drinking brought to his mind the chiding phrase 'Johnnie, be good', which was steadily transformed into one of rock 'n' roll's greatest anthems. Although it was initially inspired by Johnnie, the spelling of Goode in memory of Berry's first home, and the fact that the hero was a guitarist, turned the song towards autobiography. He was no 'little country boy', of course, but the adjective was a replacement for the original description 'little colored boy'. When the tour reached New Orleans and Berry could see his name displayed in a musical city that until then he could only dream of, the song really took shape.

Before that there was the urgent problem of a follow-up to 'Maybellene', the sales of which could peak at any time although it was still one of the top sellers in the country. In September Berry and the band were hauled off the road briefly and taken back to Universal for an emergency recording session. Berry had another song, 'Thirty Days', which was in a similar vein to his first hit. So thirty-six takes were not necessary this time round, and in Johnson's recollection they were in and out of the studio in an hour.

'Maybellene' was still selling well when the follow-up was released, and this may explain why 'Thirty Days' sold comparatively poorly. Although it reached no. 8 on the *Billboard* R & B chart in mid-October, it failed to come anywhere near matching the across-the-board appeal of its predecessor. Had it found a later place in Berry's chronology 'Thirty Days' could have done better, as it has a strong, witty lyric about the singer's determination to do anything necessary to get his errant girl, 'Maybellene' in spirit, back home. It also drives along beautifully, with Hardy and Dixon slapping out an infectious rhythm and Johnson's improvisations providing the perfect framework, with an outstanding interplay on the guitar solo between Berry and Hardy. The B-side, 'Together (We Will Always Be)', is a disappointment after its sensual, reverb guitar intro, with Berry doing a rather listless impersonation of his hero Nat 'King' Cole.

The release of 'Thirty Days' as the second single suggests that Berry's memory is faulty when he says, as he has done at various times, that his earliest demo tape also included 'Rock 'n' Roll Music' and 'Too Much Monkey Business'. He has also said that 'You Can't Catch Me' was cut at the first session. Johnson is sure that they only had the two songs ready to begin with, and had these slightly later masterpieces been available Leonard Chess must surely have gone for one of them as the second A-side.

Four years later, in June 1959, 'Thirty Days' did indeed make the Hot Hundred, peaking at no. 45, but it was in a curious disguise. The

Canadian rocker Ronnie Hawkins, whose backing group at that time, the Hawks, became superstars ten years later as The Band, was one of the finest and most successful white interpreters of both Berry and his stablemate Bo Diddley – his manic reworking of Bo's surreal epic of despair 'Who Do You Love' is especially masterly. But his debut hit not only mysteriously gave the girl a generous 'Forty Days' to get back home, it donated the writer credit to Hawkins himself. Memories at Chess's publishing arm Arc Music were not that short, and Hawkins' record company Roulette was soon forced to attribute the song correctly. Incidentally, on the French cover version by heart-throb Johnny Hallyday the time limit issued to the girl was just *'huit jours'*.

Before Berry, Johnson and Hardy were summoned back to Chicago, however, the tour swung south from Ohio to Charleston, West Virginia; Raleigh, North Carolina; Columbia, South Carolina; and Jacksonville, Florida. When they hit the Carolinas Berry had his first taste of southern racial attitudes, with segregated accommodation and food counters for the company. At the Florida gig, in spite of the fact that the Duval Armory was packed, a roped-off empty corridor down the middle of the hall kept black and white apart, though in defiance of the authorities fans of both colours climbed on stage at the end of the show, to mingle with the performers. Berry noted, however, that his nod to hillbilly music, 'Maybellene', was better received on the white side of the hall, and 'Wee Wee Hours' by the brothers.

Apart from Berry's combo the only other musicians on the tour were the Buddy Johnson Orchestra, who filled a second bus and provided backing for all the vocal acts, solo and groups, doo-wop, rhythm-and-blues and ballads. The caravan moved on into Texas and when they reached Waco only the first bus pulled up in front of the theatre. The local police were combing through the orchestra bus in search of drugs. With the crowd getting restless the promoter asked Berry, Johnson and Hardy to get out on stage and fill in, as they were the only musicians available. Their Cosmo Club experience proved invaluable and they worked through their varied repertoire for forty minutes, while the delayed musicians arrived and set up their gear behind them.

When the tour wound up it was again urgently necessary to get some more songs in the can, particularly as 'Thirty Days' had come and gone quickly. It spent just eight weeks on the R & B chart, half the longevity of 'Maybellene'. Following a phone call from Leonard Chess the group reported back to Universal on 20 December 1955 for their third session. At least this is the recollection of Johnnie Johnson, who says he was there (and indeed sounds to be, on the evidence of the tracks) and of Berry himself, who noted disapprovingly that Johnson and Hardy brought beer into the studio. Some accounts, though, credit the piano to Otis Spann, then in the Muddy Waters band, whose most recent session had been in October. As always, exactly whose hands are shaking the maracas is something of a mystery. The Bo Diddley band were hot at this time, touring on the strength of their own first two hits 'Bo Diddley' and 'Diddley Daddy', and it is unlikely that Jerome Green was always conveniently on hand in Chicago.

'You Can't Catch Me', the first cut of the session, is the ultimate Chuck Berry road-racing fantasy, when he outdrives not only the 'flat tops' who have the nerve to overtake him but also the cops who then pursue him. Musically it is wonderfully achieved, with the narrative verses building up staccato tension and the triumphant chorus exploding into extra boogie energy, to be brought down again by the stretching of the word 'cool' in the final chorus line 'goin' like a cool breeze'. The piano, let's assume it's Johnson's, then rocks in until the story picks up pace once more. The fertile furrow that Berry first cut with 'Maybellene', tapping so perceptively into the teenage cocktail of the open road, the fast car, the chicken-run competitiveness and the sexual chase, is now stripped back to a heady celebration of illegal speed.

For Berry, the car was the ultimate expression of the freedom he was either celebrating or yearning for in his songs. It had had a comparatively short history as the ultimate consumer durable, certainly among poor and lower middle-class black communities, and so it was still not to be taken for granted. Berry's car songs drool over the brand names and the details, 'the extras', as status symbols. This is the total opposite of a millionaire like Frank Sinatra or Bing Crosby singing 'Who Wants to be a Millionaire?' Berry isn't, and he wants it more than anything else. And he is singing to his peers and to younger whites struck by the same aspirations.

To the car's potency as symbol of freedom and of economic aspirations must be added a third quality, that of sex appeal and machismo. As Ian Hoare noted in his 1973 *Let It Rock* piece 'Cruisin' and Playin' the

Radio': 'Chuck Berry's words are loaded with self-advertisement, he's always celebrating the fact that he's the slickest and the fastest. And the car is blatantly used as a virility badge as much as anything else. The attributes of a car are seen as representative of a guy's personal attributes by virtue of ownership.' In the rock 'n' roll world that Berry was inventing, the car was the perfect vehicle – aspirational, assertive and sexy.

Two instrumentals which Berry claims were simply warm-ups or unconstructed jam sessions were given the names 'Rolli Polli' and 'Berry Pickin'' and were used by Chess later as album fillers, appearing on 1957's *After School Session*. The mysterious 'Down Bound Train' was cut next. Berry's country side peeps through again here, as there are distinct echoes of 'Ghost Riders in the Sky' in this anti-drink morality tale. 'Riders' was recorded by The Sons of the Pioneers, the group formed by future cowboy film star Roy Rogers, and Berry could not have avoided their work on the radio. But the song also has links with moralizing gospel music, and Berry's discographer Fred Rothwell has identified a 1926 recording, 'Death's Black Train Is Coming' by Reverend J.M. Gates, as another influence. The urgent, strummed rhythm and the echoing voice atmospherically evoke the hellish journey of the train. It is unlike anything else Berry has recorded, but I was reminded of it when listening to a demo version of a new Berry song, 'Dutchman', in autumn 2001. This is a recitation in the style of 'My Dream' from *San Francisco Dues*, a barroom narrative again giving a dreadful warning about the evils of drink.

'Down Bound Train' was chosen as the B-side to the next song cut at the session, another motorvatin' masterpiece, 'No Money Down'. The 'stop' rhythm is familiar from earlier Chess hits, notably Muddy Waters' 'Hoochie Coochie Man' and Bo Diddley's 'I'm a Man', which Muddy immediately adapted as 'Manish Boy'. The verses are spoken in a jive tone, as the customer lists for the car salesman all the extras he wants on his car. As with 'You Can't Catch Me' Berry has tapped into another car-oriented teenage fantasy, of having sufficient funds and confidence to be able to talk down to the salesman and drive away in a Cadillac with every imaginable additional feature.

Shortly after it was released a record called 'Clothesline' by Boogaloo (real name Kent Harris) came out, in which the narrator adopts a similar approach in a clothes store, and 'No Money Down' may well have been the inspiration. Although nothing happened to 'Clothesline', Jerry Leiber and Mike Stoller took the idea and turned it into one of their comic cameo masterpieces for The Coasters, 'Shoppin' for Clothes'. But whereas Berry drove away in his Cadillac, Coaster Carl Gardner is superciliously informed by the salesman that 'your credit didn't go through', and he rubs salt in the wound by adding 'that's a suit you'll never own'. The record fades on the great pay-off line, 'I got a good job, sweepin' up every day', showing that Leiber and Stoller could cram both comedy and social observation into just a few words.

The December 1955 session was completed with a ballad, 'I've Changed', in which Berry employs his intimate crooning voice to greater effect than on 'Together (We Will Always Be)'. Although it is a well constructed and effective love song, this is not what we want Berry for – if we're in the mood for a song like this we can do what he would do in the same situation and play Nat 'King' Cole.

Thanks largely to Berry and 'Maybellene' – and also to the eponymous 'Bo Diddley' – 1955 was confirmed as Chess Records' most successful trading year to date, and in the annual polls conducted by both *Billboard* and *Cash Box* Berry was the winner in the Most Promising New Artist category. Berry and Bo were beginning to edge out the old-style Chicago blues spearheaded by Muddy Waters, and were appealing to the mass market rather than just the black audience.

In spite of this, even though the Hot Hundred was now up and running 'No Money Down' failed to score on the pop charts when it was released in January, and only enjoyed a five-week run on the R & B list, peaking at no. 11. Although Berry could not be dismissed as a one-hit wonder there was some concern at Chess Records as to whether he could ever recapture the magic of 'Maybellene'. The triumphant answer was to come in April.

Meanwhile the band was back on the road – Washington, Baltimore, a return to the Apollo, and a date in Chicago. It was at this point that Berry seized the opportunity to fire his manager, and the first booking following this decision was back east, in Buffalo, New York, playing in a nightclub rather than the usual theatres.

Berry's next career move was to augment the band, the first change in the trio since he had responded to Johnson's New Year's Eve invitation just over three years earlier. Back in St Louis he hired tenor saxophonist Leroy Davis and bass player Albert Moseby for a gig at a whites-only ballroom, the Casa Loma, and as a five-piece they set off for a string of dates in California, where Berry paid $800 for a band bus. 'Leroy was the perfect sax player for the kind of music we was doin',' was Johnson's reaction. As a regular road band, however, this arrangement didn't last long. Although he gave away as little as he could, Berry soon tired of parting with four wages from his appearance fees.

While Chess Records usually used Universal Studios for their sessions until they moved to plusher offices and a purpose-built studio at 2120 South Michigan Avenue, late in 1956, there was also a rudimentary studio set-up available at the old address, 4750 South Cottage Grove Avenue, and it was here that the next Berry session was set for 16 April 1956. Johnson and Davis were present, and as ever Willie Dixon was the in-house bass player, but Hardy was replaced by Chicago stalwart Fred Below.

This was the beginning of the end for the Chuck Berry Combo. While Below became the most regular drummer on sessions, Berry was now musing on the advantages of playing live gigs as a solo performer. He'd had enough of touring with two drunks, and he could see a way of making more money if he travelled light, charging the promoter with the responsibility of providing a house band. This in spite of the fact that he was already taking three-quarters of what the trio were paid for gigs, leaving Johnson and Hardy to scrape along on one-eighth each. It would also mean that he could fly wherever the money was, rather than having to work within driving distance of the previous booking. It took him a while to put this plan into action, however, and in the meantime he had reached make-or-break time in his career.

Fats Domino had been lording it in the R & B chart since 1950, when his debut single 'The Fat Man' reached no. 6, and now, in early 1956, he began to 'cross over' into the Hot Hundred, selling to a predominantly white audience. Although 'Bo Weevil' only reached no. 35 in February, two months later he was in the top ten with 'I'm In Love Again'. From then until 1964 Domino was a permanent presence in the pop charts, becoming one of the biggest-selling artists of all time.

Little Richard had beaten both other members of this pioneering triumvirate when 'Tutti Frutti' reached no. 21 in the Hot Hundred just after Christmas 1955, a month after climbing to no. 2 in the R & B list.

Had this chart been inaugurated in the summer, 'Maybellene' would undoubtedly have featured in it, maybe right at the top, but by early 1956 Berry now had stiff competition as a black artist appealing to a wider audience from the other two pioneers.

Not only that, but from their country-and-western background the first wave of white artists were producing what was undeniably their own version of rock 'n' roll. In February 1956 Elvis Presley was at no. 1 with 'Heartbreak Hotel', with Carl Perkins's 'Blue Suede Shoes' just three rungs behind him. The revolution was clearly under way – Presley replaced 'The Poor People of Paris' by the Les Baxter Orchestra at the top. And the success of Presley and Perkins prompted Capitol Records to sign their own rockabilly, the crippled ex-sailor Gene Vincent, whose 'Be-Bop-a-Lula' hit the top ten in June. Having failed to match the success of 'Maybellene' with his two subsequent releases, when Berry went into the studio for his fourth Chess session he could hear the competition snapping at his heels.

# roll over
# Beethoven

THE FIRST SONG tackled at the eight-hour session on 16 April
1956, 'Drifting Heart', once again shows Berry's fixation with
Nat 'King' Cole, one that was never going to be commercial.
The song has a vaguely Spanish feel, although Johnson's piano owes
more to chop suey than paella, Davis noodles away in the background,
and the results are rather soporific.

What a contrast was provided next: 'Brown Eyed Handsome Man'
is a stunning piece of work, a surreal cameo shot through with memorable imagery: 'Flyin' 'cross the desert in a TWA I saw a woman
walkin' 'cross the sand.' The interplay of instruments sets up an irresistible rhythmic texture, and there's no doubt that Berry cast himself
in the title role, with 'brown eyed' being his code for 'black skinned'.
Significantly, though, the woman in the song is clearly white.

The song jumps from courtroom to desert to baseball stadium with
little pretence of logic, just a cascade of imagery from deep within what
Berry modestly described as his 'sometimes unbelievably imaginative
mind'. His starting point, he says, was a plane flight that began in
frozen, snowbound St Louis and ended in baking California sunshine.
The song stimulated Buddy Holly, either in his west Texas garage in

Lubbock or in nearby Venture Studio late in the year, to tape one of his finest nods towards current black music. When released in the UK in 1963, in a version expertly overdubbed by The Fireballs and producer Norman Petty after Holly's death, it reached no. 3 in the charts. From Holly and a clutch of Berry's other contemporaries, including Carl Perkins and Jerry Lee Lewis, to Paul McCartney in 1999, the song has attracted heavyweight cover versions in spite of its idiosyncratic imagery.

After laying down his first rock 'n' roll masterpiece since 'Maybellene' Berry simply went on to surpass it. 'Roll Over Beethoven', as anthemic an instruction as Carl's 'Don't you step on my blue suede shoes', sprang from memories of sibling rivalry back in Goode Avenue and Labadier. Berry's early love of music was more frustrated than encouraged by elder sister Lucy's monopoly of the family piano, particularly because of her penchant for classical pieces.

A quarter of a century later, Berry took brotherly revenge. Lucy 'delayed rock 'n' roll music twenty years,' complains Berry, tongue-in-cheek no doubt, but of course she also inspired one of its finest moments. 'This side has humor, a driving beat and, most of all, Berry's own distinctive and wailingly primitive style,' was *Billboard*'s opinion. This was the record that at last broke him into the Hot Hundred, where it peaked at no. 29 in June. On the R & B list it made the seventh slot. The song has been covered countless times – immediately, in the case of one Helene Dixon, and most famously and brilliantly by The Beatles.

Although the structure of the song includes dramatic pauses and changes of rhythm, at its heart is the 'chunka chunka' groove that is reckoned to be quintessential Berry, and which is therefore the very soundtrack of rock 'n' roll. Here it is heard in particularly treble-heavy, fluid form, with Berry's rhythm guitar comparatively high in the mix and Johnson pushed right back. No would-be guitarist of the late 1950s or early 1960s could even dare to emerge from the bedroom without some mastery of this sound. And so it is particularly instructive to listen to what the modest Johnnie Johnson has to say about it.

I mentioned to him that, although they tended to pick up on what his right hand was doing in the Chess studios, those ridiculous flights in and out of the keys that decorate, provoke and respond to Berry's guitar, surely it was his left hand, the boogie hand, that was actually driving the sound, even when it is barely discernible in the mix. He calls it a 'chopping bass' technique.

'You could play it slow like a lazy blues, or as fast rock 'n' roll. It went with whatever Chuck was doing on the guitar. He could fit in with it, play over it or stop playing, but that chopping bass would carry on. And that's how we wrote those songs. Like "Beethoven". I'd come up with the rhythm that seemed right for the words he wrote. My right hand responds to what he's doing, and the left hand drives the song.'

And in 'Roll Over Beethoven' what it's driving is rock 'n' roll's declaration of independence, of teenage defiance towards the old order. Berry's beef may have been in particular with Lucy's choice of piano pieces (and one suspects that less rhythmically useful names like Bach were also on his hit list) but it's not just a question of 'down with the classics'. And anyway, many of us have eventually learned to appreciate them, as long as they are part of a balanced rock 'n' roll diet. What we will never come round to, though, is the sort of musical soup that 'Roll Over Beethoven' was threatening to replace – the drab orchestral confections of Lawrence Welk or the UK's Mantovani, the tyranny of A & R man Mitch Miller at Columbia, determinedly trying to steer everything into the middle of the road, the anodyne balladry of Patti Page or crooning colleen Ruby Murray.

'Yes, I wrote that at home,' Berry told Charlie Gillett in 1973. 'My sister did a lot of classics, Strauss, all those names. And when I was hanging around I tried to read the sheet music she left on the piano, which was far in advance of my one-finger chromatic scale technique. So I wrote a song about moving all that stuff out of the way.'

Even after this triumphant capping of 'Brown Eyed Handsome Man', the session wasn't over. 'Too Much Monkey Business' was the day's third miracle. Just as Berry had coined the word 'motorvatin'' in his pursuit of Maybellene, he was now writing about 'botheration', the frustrations and annoyances of everyday, blue-collar life. Although most of the verses deal with school, military service and the workplace, perhaps the finest observation is: 'Blonde hair, good looking, tryin' to get me hooked, wants me to marry, settle down, get a home, write a book.' Rhythmically it is as dense as it could be, the perfect example of how, at the heart of Berry's music, is an airtight weld between lyric and rhythm. And the 'write a book' pay-off opens up a wonderful world of suburban dreams. He's 'working at the filling station' and fretting about the mortgage, doing his best, and all the time she's nagging him to better himself. Predictably, she's blonde – Berry's favourite colour.

Eventually, of course, Berry himself wrote a book, his autobiography. The wit and precision of his lyrics – written, as it were, to order for a specific market – deserts him when he can indulge in such a personal piece of writing. The pedantic carefulness of his speaking voice comes to the fore, and the writing is often archaic, convoluted, deliberately complex. Although Berry came from a background of greater comfort than the dirt farms that were the usual childhood homes of his blues heroes, his education was nevertheless fairly basic. It is as if, in his speaking and prose style, Berry is trying to sound more sophisticated and educated than he actually is, but the results simply seem stilted. There is an echo of him, then, in that blue-collar worker being urged to write a book in 'Monkey Business'. Berry's literary genius, partly under the influence of Louis Jordan's writing style, was in distillation, not expansion.

Fred Rothwell correctly hears an echo of 'Monkey Business', both rhythmically and in its expression of being put upon, in such Jagger–Richard lines as 'Go on try it, go on buy it, you can pay me next week' in 'Satisfaction', but an earlier influence was undoubtedly that on Bob Dylan. 'Johnny's in the basement mixing up the medicine, I'm on the pavement thinkin' 'bout the government' – the echoes of Berry, and of 'Too Much Monkey Business' in particular, leap out of the lines. When Dylan chose to illustrate this song, 'Subterranean Homesick Blues', in D.A. Pennebaker's documentary *Don't Look Back*, it was by standing in a London alley peeling off sheets of cardboard, containing successive phrases from the song. Once again this stressed the nervy, dense, jump-cut approach to imagery that he had learned from Berry. Even on songs that go beyond surreal alliteration and are more conventional in purpose, like 1974's beautiful 'Tangled Up in Blue', the spirit of Berry lies behind the way in which Dylan's words, melody and rhythm act as one.

Remarkably, having made the breakthrough into the Hot Hundred with 'Beethoven', Berry couldn't repeat the trick when a powerful coupling of 'Too Much Monkey Business' and 'Brown Eyed Handsome Man' was chosen as the follow-up in autumn 1956. On the R & B list, though, it matched its predecessor, peaking at no. 7. This is a reminder of how enthralled white artists like Holly were with black music, picking up on a B-side that had had no crossover success. But he still heard it somehow, bought it and pored over it, deciphering the images.

After this remarkable session Berry returned to the road with the *1956 Show of Stars*, headlined by Fats Domino. In June, while playing at the Rock and Roll Club in Pittsburgh, Pennsylvania, he began talking to a young white woman who had been in the audience. This was Francine Gillium, who later became his secretary. When she offered to prepare a publicity biography for him he could not resist embroidering the truth, and for some reason he decided that San Jose was a more glamorous birthplace than St Louis. From Francine to Chess Records, from there to his official publicity release, and on into history, the confusion about his birthplace was born.

At around this time in early summer – the precise date is unrecorded – Berry cut at least two live tracks for Alan Freed's radio show on WINS in New York, *The Camel Rock 'n' Roll Dance Party*. Remarkably, the Freed house band backing Berry on 'Roll Over Beethoven' and a truncated version of 'Maybellene' is the Count Basie Orchestra, moonlighting between more accustomed bookings. Although the audience is enthusiastic and the supporting musicianship proficient, Basie and his boys are no rock 'n' rollers, and Berry's guitar work is sometimes lazy. It should not be too big a step from Basie's orchestrated swing to the looser-limbed requirements of rock 'n' roll, driving the rhythm from just behind the beat, but the Basie band cannot quite bridge it.

One is reminded of Yehudi Menuhin, at the time the most celebrated classical violinist in the world, sounding so wooden and metronomic when forming a 'dream team' with jazz virtuoso Stéphane Grappelli. Or, closer to rock 'n' roll, how Eric Clapton's guitar work seemed stiff and out of place when gigging with Carl Perkins on a 1980s TV special, even though he could comfortably hold his own with the greatest of black blues players. The Berry and Basie recordings, designed to sell Camel cigarettes, were unearthed in the archive of the Armed Forces Radio and Television Service, who made such material available to radio stations broadcasting to homesick GIs abroad.

Ebby Hardy drifted away from Berry in the autumn of 1956, which pleased his wife at first, but without the regular discipline and pay from the trio he was soon scuffling. A time playing with Albert King in 1958 didn't work out, again because of his drinking, and after that he was limited to playing local gigs whenever he could get them. He died in poverty in the 1980s. Johnson, however, stayed with Berry into 1957, and the trio was now completed by drummer Jaspar Thomas. Very often, though, Berry would now travel with Johnson alone – Thomas was another one who liked a drink, and so to the disciplinarian Berry he was no improvement on Hardy. 'Jaspar was real good, better than Ebby,' recalls Johnson in his biography, 'but Ebby held his liquor. You never knew what was gonna happen with Jaspar on the road.'

Berry told *Melody Maker* in 1972: 'I don't indulge in alcohol, period . . . I don't have anything against any guy who can hold his liquor or whatever . . . but when it inhibits your performance, that's another thing . . . I can swallow half a cup of wine or a hi-ball and I can also smoke a joint . . . My system must be freaky or something because I've never had an unsober moment and that's why I don't understand it.'

When Berry toured with Johnson alone, using a pick-up band hired by the promoter, it was Johnson's unpaid duty to talk them through the set, something that Berry had no interest in. And when Berry was out there travelling on his own, they weren't even talked through it. Often Berry didn't even bother to meet the band before the gig. Without his faithful sidekick, Berry would turn in more and more lacklustre performances, through a combination of meanness, arrogance and a stubborn insistence on pushing himself to the limit of potential catastrophe.

Alan Freed extended his empire – first radio and then package tours – still further with the feature-film quickie *Rock, Rock, Rock*, starring Tuesday Weld (though when she opened her mouth to sing, Connie Francis came out). Berry was booked along with such current acts as The Moonglows, The Flamingos, Frankie Lymon and the Teenagers, LaVern Baker and, importantly since this is their only celluloid appearance, The Johnny Burnette Rock 'n' Roll Trio, one of the most dynamic of rockabilly groups. History has been less kind to another featured act, The Three Chuckles.

The plot, if such it can be called, involves the heroine trying to raise the money to buy a dress to attend the high-school hop, but of course the interest is in the (mimed) performances, including Berry with 'You Can't Catch Me'. The poster screamed 'The Greatest Rock 'n' Roll Music Played By The Biggest Rock 'n' Roll Groups This Side Of Heaven', and coupling it with a Randolph Scott horse opera *7 Men from Now,* the distributors announced 'The Greatest Double Programme Of The Year'.

Berry later told of his inexperience in the film business. 'I was told that I had a picture to make in – it wasn't Hollywood – Culver City,' he told *Rolling Stone.*

> They gave me a ticket, sent me to Culver City with my guitar; they threw a script in front of me and we started shooting the next day. The next day I came and I think I had read the script, but after I'd read it, you know it's like a book, it doesn't say anything. You're not interested in it and I didn't remember any of it. They bring this big camera right up before me and say, 'Speak louder, Mr Berry.' And I'd say my line, you know a picture's made in parts, about three minutes at a time, which was beautiful, or I'd never have made it. And there was about twenty minutes in between each three minutes, so that's how I got my script together . . .

The movie prompted the Chess brothers to put together their first ever album release, sentimentally given the catalogue number Chess LP 1425 in memory of their first ever home in America at 1425 South Karlov, built by their father. Given the same title as the movie although containing numbers not in the film, it was released in November 1956 and Berry is featured with 'Maybellene', 'Thirty Days' and 'Roll Over Beethoven' as well as 'You Can't Catch Me'. 'This looks like one of the strongest rock 'n' roll packages extant,' said *Billboard.*

On 15 December 1956 Berry returned to the in-house studio at Chess Records with Johnson, Dixon and Below to cut a demo of a new composition, one that sought to capitalize on the sentiments of 'Roll Over Beethoven'. He has always unashamedly admitted that his motivation as a writer and performer is money, and late in 1956 he was beginning to appreciate the market that he had opened up – rock 'n' roll for white teenagers, R & B for kids. Caucasian was the predominant race in the USA, and their youngsters had the most disposable cash. No more third-rate Nat Cole impersonations then – although he would continue to ring the musical changes on occasion, briefly test-marketing the demand for Spanish, calypso or mellow blues. He now knew where his core audience was to be found.

And we know what we want from him. When he steps up to the microphone he pleads: 'Just let me hear some of that rock 'n' roll music.' It is the most enticing promise of an evening's entertainment ever written – whether or not the man goes on to deliver the goods – and it contrasts significantly with the instruction in 'Roll Over Beethoven' to 'dig these rhythm and blues'. From black to white (or 'salt and pepper' at least) in one twist of a phrase. And for the three seconds that he takes to deliver the instruction he *is* his own audience, defining their wishes, watching, clapping and dancing to their rock 'n' roll star.

In December his next anthem 'Rock 'n' Roll Music' was still unfinished, and the demo is further proof of Johnnie Johnson's creative input, hitting his grooves in response to Berry's unfinished lyrics, searching to put illustrative musical shape to Berry's words on paper. And the groove is a relaxed one, less frantic than the finished article, but enticing nonetheless. Confirmation that this was strictly a 'work in progress' session comes with the other cut, an unnamed instrumental that was to emerge a year later in polished form as 'Rock at the Philharmonic'. In the meantime a newly perfected slice of teenage life was ready to roll, and it would prove to be one of his most successful records, triumphantly putting him back on top.

# ring! ring!
# goes the
# bell

THE SESSION ON 21 January 1957 was Berry's first at the studio built in the new Chess Records building on South Michigan Avenue, and it seems that 'Rock 'n' Roll Music' was not yet ready to rock. He was joined once again by Johnson, Dixon and Below, and the guitarist who put so many chilling licks behind the demonic voice of Howlin' Wolf, the great Hubert Sumlin, also looked in at one point. 'I helped him out on "Deep Feeling" and "School Day",' Sumlin told *Living Blues* in 1989. 'I played second guitar behind him.'

Berry relaxed his fingers with a melancholy blues instrumental that clearly met with Johnson's approval, since it inspired him to a beautifully judged accompaniment and a crisp solo, hammered out in the top register. It also inspired the Chess Brothers to an outrageous con trick – having titled the cut 'Blue Feeling' they produced an additional half-speed version christened 'Low Feeling' – and even had the nerve to use both a year later as fillers on Berry's third album *One Dozen Berrys*. Chess fans will recall that they had used this trick in reverse five years earlier, when John Lee Hooker's 'Walking the Boogie' had a manic, double-speed guitar part dubbed over it, along with foot stamping that sounds like a clog-dancing mouse.

'Lajaunda' (or 'La Jaunda' – it has received both titles at times as well as the wrongly spelt 'La Juanda') is one of Berry's Spanish practices, a forgettable story-in-song about a *femme fatale*. Of far greater interest is the instrumental 'Deep Feeling', with Sumlin chugging along anonymously in the background. Berry puts down his Gibson guitar for the first time in favour of the same manufacturer's Electraharp pedal steel, an instrument more familiar in country music. Since he had only bought it two weeks earlier, his proficiency is commendable.

This atmospheric, shimmering piece inspired by 1939's 'Floyd's Guitar Blues', recorded by Andy Kirk and his Clouds of Joy and featuring Floyd Smith, proved inspirational in its turn. The difficulty of copyrighting a wordless blues, however striking in instrumentation and treatment, is shown by the fact that the sharp-eared Berry and the Arc Music lawyers failed to slap a writ on 'Albatross', Fleetwood Mac's 1968 mega-hit (or, for that matter, on Jeff Beck's frankly titled 'Stealing'). However, since the Floyd Smith tune was still only twenty-nine years old when Peter Green offered his 'homage' to it, maybe Arc decided that it was best not to stir up any mud.

And so to the session's masterpiece, the song that finally established Berry not just as an R & B artist, not just as a rock 'n' roller, but as a bona fide pop star. 'School Day (Ring! Ring! Goes the Bell)' – the awkward subtitle avoided the prospect of having royalties sent to the composers of several similarly titled numbers – was the finest demonstration yet of Berry's ability to write for an audience half his age, the real rock 'n' roll generation.

'I had no idea what was going on in the classes during the time I composed it,' he admitted, yet his blow-by-blow description of the boredom and frustration of the school routine, building up to the long-awaited escape to hear 'something that's really hot' on the jukebox, struck a chord with teenagers on both sides of the Atlantic. For the rest of his career Berry could rely on effortlessly persuading his audience to join in with the crucial couplet: 'Hail! Hail! rock 'n' roll, deliver me from the days of old.' In fact, he usually leaves them to it these days. Beethoven had not just rolled over by now, he was spinning in his grave, and for good measure Berry was pronouncing a death sentence on dusty old Tin Pan Alley.

It was, according to *Billboard*, 'another sensational jumpin' story novelty', and the magazine predicted that it would again break him out of the R & B ghetto into the pop charts. They were right. On the three R & B charts then in operation, those reflecting radio play, disc sales and jukebox activity, 'School Day' was Berry's first number-one hat trick since 'Maybellene', and on *Billboard*'s pop chart it easily surpassed 'Roll Over Beethoven' to reach no. 5, remaining in the Top Hundred for half the year; it went two places higher on the rival *Cash Box* list; and it marked Berry's UK chart debut, just nipping into the Top 20.

Nowadays, with the pop market fragmented by the variety of formats, the far greater significance of album sales and the proliferation of wall-to-wall TV channels running pop videos, gossip and performances, these mathematical details may seem overstated, but back in the 1950s the tables were pored over, and the rises and falls carefully charted, just as carefully as a stockbroker checked the markets. And if the kids were analysing the charts, the industry certainly was. 'School Day' was as big a breakthrough for Berry as 'Maybellene' had been, in that it inaugurated a period when *every* single by him made the charts, an achievement that would carry him into the next decade.

Johnson, as so often, was the unacknowledged partner in the creation of 'School Day'. 'We decided right away to put a shuffle behind it. I guess it was becoming our sound . . . The only problem was how to start it out . . . Chuck had that Carl Hogan intro he liked to use, but it didn't seem to fit . . . Finally I said . . . we could use the intro from "Johnnie's Boogie", which I got from [Meade Lux Lewis's] "Honky Tonk Train" . . . When Chuck played it on his guitar, we thought it sounded like a school bell ringin' . . .'

In February 1957 Berry joined *The Biggest Show of Stars*, a Freed-style package assembled by rival New York promoter Irving Feld, of the General Artists Corporation, and opening at the Apollo. Fats Domino, Clyde McPhatter – former lead singer with The Dominoes and The Drifters, but now a big solo star – and Chess stablemates The Moonglows were among the acts crammed into two buses for a seventy-two-date tour. Unlike Berry's first experience of these caravans, travelling and playing every day and night, this tour took a total of three months, allowing for a slightly less rigorous schedule. From New York it headed up through New England into Canada, and then criss-crossed the national border as it moved west, before running down through California and into the south, where the racial attitudes were no more enlightened than they had been two years earlier.

From St Louis onwards Berry abandoned the bus and travelled in his own Cadillac, which he says was bought when a substantial royalty cheque caught up with him. According to Johnson he got the idea from the teenaged Paul Anka, who was already using his own car. The tour finished in May and Berry was hurried back into the studio with Dixon and Below. Although Johnson says that he was at the session, he recalls the tracks that were cut on that day incorrectly, and it seems likely that his memory is faulty. He was, after all, a problem drinker at the time, and presumably his employers at the American Steel Foundry were rather anxious to see him back after yet another leave of absence for the *Show of Stars*.

Discographers Les Fancourt and Fred Rothwell both credit the piano on all the remaining 1957 sessions to Ellis 'Lafayette' Leake, who frequently worked with Willie Dixon and would have been a logical choice if Johnson was indeed unavailable. No doubt Johnson had been involved to some extent in the creation of the songs as usual, and would have played them countless times since on the road, and so in his mind his involvement has become seamless.

Berry brought along a melancholy blues ballad, 'How You've Changed'. The subdued backing and Leake's solo are pleasant indeed, but no matter how hard he tried (and he seemed reluctant to give up the attempt), Berry was *never* going to be Nat 'King' Cole. His voice is flat and exposes the somewhat mundane lyrics. What a contrast there was, moving from there to one of the most stirring openings of all his classic anthems, that insistent demand: 'Just let me hear some of that rock 'n' roll music.' The theme of 'Roll Over Beethoven' is continued into 'Rock 'n' Roll Music', and Berry's guitar has an almost acoustic sound, playing a supporting role to Leake's driving piano. This is the most straightforward of Berry's greatest songs, a simple demand for rock 'n' roll above all alternatives, and he slips in a newly minted reference to Elvis Presley's current chart-topper 'All Shook Up'. A second version, with the vocal double-tracked, stayed on the shelf until it surfaced on Berry's 1986 compilation album *Rock 'n' Roll Rarities*.

Surprisingly, it was the day's next offering that Chess chose for the first single from this session. 'Oh Baby Doll' takes Berry back to school, worried about losing his girl during the long vacation, and at the very least it is at the top of the second division among his catalogue. The simple little story works well, he moves it along with his most insistent scratching rhythm, and the guitar solo leaps joyously out of the mix. It was released in July and was something of a disappointment commercially, failing to climb beyond no. 57 in *Billboard* and faring little better in *Cash Box*. As the current single, however, it was chosen as the featured song for Berry's second Alan Freed film quickie, *Mister Rock and Roll*.

As soon as 'Oh Baby Doll' began to slip down the charts Leonard Chess produced his next trump card and rush-released 'Rock 'n' Roll Music' in September. Of course it did the trick, reaching no. 6 in the R & B chart, no. 8 in *Billboard*, and no. 14 in *Cash Box*. This was timely, giving Berry not just a fresh hit but a classic one at that to tout around the country on the second *Biggest Show of Stars* of the year, picking up sales as he motored on.

The session also included a coy little song in cha-cha style about the 'Thirteen Question Method' for courting a girl, an unissued warm-up instrumental (although in 1963 it did receive a title, 'Cranberries', suggesting that it was intended as an album filler or B-side) and a curiosity, Berry's cover version of 'How High the Moon'. Beginning as a show song in 1940 this melodic number was soon picked up by jazz artists like Count Basie, but above all by the electric guitar pioneer Les Paul and his wife Mary Ford, whose breakneck, multi-tracked version topped the charts in 1950. The Berry version is similarly brisk and energetic, kicked into life by a crunching Leake solo and driven along as if Fred Below had a train to catch. Berry and Dixon then take turns soloing before Berry has another go, throwing in every jazz lick he can think of. It ain't rock 'n' roll, but it's great fun.

Berry played an Alan Freed *Summer Festival* before joining Feld's second *Biggest Show of Stars*. The bill was a stunning one, with Berry, Domino, McPhatter and LaVern Baker retained from the earlier caravan. Domino was riding high with 'Valley of Tears', McPhatter had followed up 'Just To Hold My Hand' with the equally successful 'Long Lonely Nights' and LaVern Baker, whose sequence of Atlantic hits had begun early in 1955 with 'Tweedlee Dee', was in the charts with 'Jim Dandy Got Married'. To these were added Frankie Lymon and the Teenagers, The Drifters, The Everly Brothers, Paul Anka, Jimmy Bowen, Buddy Holly and the Crickets and Eddie Cochran. Naturally no act was on stage for long – a maximum of four numbers – but what an evening! Holly had already cut his own version of the Domino hit – the session date is unrecorded, but was certainly before July 1957.

The package began in Pittsburgh on 6 September and swept through the country for two and a half months. Again they hit segregation in the south but, as Niki Sullivan of The Crickets recalls, when they all found themselves booked into a whites-only hotel by mistake, the white artists voted to stay with their travelling companions in black hotels from there on. According to John Goldrosen and John Beecher's biography *Remembering Buddy*, when Buddy Holly's mother asked how he got on with Negroes, his reply was: 'Oh, we're all Negroes now.' Once again, the much-maligned rock 'n' rollers were in the vanguard of a better, more equitable society (the reason, of course, that they *were* much maligned in the land of the lynch mobs).

It was on this tour that Berry and Holly would pass the time shooting dice, and Berry also recalls that he was putting the finishing touches to 'You Can't Catch Me' – a song that he had in fact recorded two years earlier. It seems likely that it was 'Sweet Little Sixteen' occupying his mind.

Berry was now rich enough to treat himself to far more than a Cadillac. He had already begun to dabble in property in St Louis, and ever since he had helped his father with repair jobs at the whites-only Glencrest Country Club he had dreamed of creating something similar but less exclusive, a recreation and amusement park with no colour bar. In April 1957, just before the 'School Day' session, the dream began to take shape with the purchase of 30 acres of farmland just outside Wentzville, a small farming town 40 miles west of the city. It was a dream, of course, that was firmly married to Berry's conviction that investment in real estate was the passport to real money, secure money, and he laid down $8000 for the land.

The idea was not to build capital-consuming white-knuckle rides – and looking at this peaceful agricultural scene forty years on it is doubtful if the town elders would have been overwhelmed at the idea anyway. He wanted instead to augment the natural conditions, shape them, to provide fishing, hunting, bathing and musical entertainment for both day-trippers and families to be accommodated in self-catering lodges. In the early days the tour bus he had bought in California came in handy, converted into a simple mobile home.

Berry drew up plans for the development of the site and began to spend every spare moment there, particularly in the summer break between the Irving Feld tours. A one-acre lake was excavated on the road side of the property, and a guitar-shaped swimming pool was constructed. Whenever possible Berry watched over the contractors, suspicious of being palmed off with weak cement or substandard timber. Next came the nightclub and bar, with a stage, and two office buildings.

He had kept in touch with Francine Gillium, the self-assured twenty-year-old who had offered to write his publicity biography, and she now persuaded him that he should form a corporation to bring his professional activities under one umbrella. Francine seemed to be the ideal candidate for company secretary, and so she moved from New York to St Louis and began working for him in November 1957.

The cautious Berry, a one-man operator since splitting from Teddy Reig (punningly called 'Roag' in Berry's autobiography), soon realized that Francine could be a great help at 'percentage' gigs, those where his fee only climbed above the agreed minimum if sufficient punters had paid to come in. And so one of her earliest duties was as door-watcher, to see if her estimate of the crowd tallied with that claimed by the promoter. And she also had to represent Berry in dealings with the building contractors back at the park when he was off on his own, in the meantime dealing with a growing amount of fan mail.

She was not best pleased when Berry proudly announced the address of the park on Dick Clark's television show *American Bandstand*, since it seemed to formalize the foundation of a fan club for which she would inevitably be responsible. At the time, December 1957, she was busy setting up Chuck Berry Music Inc. and a company to look after his property investments, Thee Investment Inc. Berry, the sharp and suspicious businessman, had luckily bumped into the ideal assistant, industrious, loyal and skilled way beyond her typing speed and telephone manner. It is, of course, a loyalty that has been reciprocated by Berry over the years, and the impression is that he is always on his best behaviour in his dealings with Francine.

Their next enterprise was the opening of Club Bandstand in March 1958, at 813 North Grand Boulevard. While they applied for a liquor licence to open a bar in the club they held their fan club meetings there, but these had to move into another Berry property on Easton when the licence was granted, as teenagers were barred from licensed premises. Club Bandstand, named after *American Bandstand,* which was proving so important to Berry's career at this time, promoted bands every night and cabaret shows at the weekends. Fran was now effectively Berry's secretary, business manager and barmaid, supervising the development of Berry Park, running business and the fan club from the office and working at nights in the club. It would be 1960 before she could move into Berry Park and centralize all her various activities there.

During a package show at the Ottawa Coliseum Berry saw a little German girl, seven or eight years old, pursuing the singers for autographs to add to her 'wallet full of pictures', seemingly more interested in the trophy signatures than in the music being performed on stage. The idea for one of his most successful songs was born, although the girl who provided the inspiration was a little too young even for his taste, and so she became 'Sweet Little Sixteen'.

Early in December 1957 Berry, Leake, Dixon and Below laid down a demo of the song. The number is clearly complete by this stage, and until Berry stumbles over his lines with a laugh this is a good enough version to master. Below biffs a muscular turnaround into each chorus, Berry's guitar lays down a solid chugging rhythm and Leake's solo is ready to roll.

On 29 December the band reassembled for a long and productive session. Again, Johnson insists that it was he, not Leake, who was present, and recalls that 'Reelin' and Rockin'' 'was . . . the first song where Leonard Chess asked me to rip the keys. What rippin' the keys meant was you dragged your hand up the keys . . . like Jerry Lee Lewis does.' And he also refers to ripping the keys on 'Sweet Little Sixteen' – 'I 'bout tore my thumbnail off.' To add to the confusion he dates the session as 6 January, and says that Jaspar Thomas was the drummer.

Two complete takes of 'Sweet Little Sixteen' are known to have survived. The alternate version, which first surfaced on the 1980 bootleg *America's Hottest Wax*, is taken at a quicker tempo. Strangely, having chosen the slower take to master for single release, Leonard Chess then speeded up the tape! The song perfectly captures the excitement of its teenage heroine, and is another striking demonstration of Berry's ability to think himself into the mind of someone half his age.

The song starts with the line: 'They're really rocking on *Bandstand*, Pittsburgh, PA.' This product placement had the desired effect, and Berry was booked by Dick Clark to perform the song on *American Bandstand*. In his ghosted memoir *Rock, Roll and Remember*, Clark says: 'Sometimes we heard a hit first time we played a record – Chuck Berry's "Sweet Little Sixteen" was like that.'

An incident just before Berry was due to appear on the show is demonstration that he was already fine-tuning his stubbornness, lack of cooperation with those who are meant to be working with him, and his perverse delight in deliberately throwing a spanner into any works he can find. When he was greeted by Clark, about twenty minutes before he was due to perform on live television, Berry began by making the gnomic statement: 'Ain't going to do any dancing.' It was down to the show's producer Tony Mammarella to unravel its meaning – Berry had decided that he would not perform his trademark duck walk and furthermore he refused to lip-synch to the record. 'Chuck Berry ain't gonna open his mouth and have nothing come out.'

As for what he is alleged to have said, Berry states rather primly: 'It's hardly likely anyone whose mother taught school would be trained to speak in such a fashion.' And he claims that he was simply ignorant that the economics of the show demanded cheap miming over expensive live performance. Clark phoned Leonard Chess in Chicago, and Chess gave Berry a dressing-down. Clark guessed that what Chess was saying was something like: 'Get your ass out there and do that thing, motherfucker.' Berry, shocked as a church-going spinster at Clark's turn of phrase, says that 'the negroid dialect and profanity . . . never transpired'. But the miming did.

'He's never gotten any easier to get along with, he's still an ornery son of a bitch, but I love him dearly,' sighs Clark. 'I doubt that he loves me,' responds Berry with a metaphorical toss of the head, but as one of the hottest attractions in rock 'n' roll he was booked back onto *American Bandstand* time and time again.

When released in February 'Sweet Little Sixteen' proved Berry's biggest hit to date (and remained so until 'My Ding-a-Ling' clouded the horizon in 1972) by climbing to no. 2 in both *Billboard* and *Cash Box*, denied the top spot first by The Silhouettes and 'Get a Job', then by Elvis's 'Don't'. It did, however, reach the top in the R & B chart, while in the UK it gave him his second hit, peaking at no. 16. 'A very ordinary rock number,' wrote Keith Fordyce in *New Musical Express*, 'with nothing especially exciting or catchy about it.'

Back to the session. 'Rock at the Philharmonic' is far more than a warm-up instrumental, it's a structured piece that showcases Berry's guitar in a jazzier setting than usual, and as already mentioned it had been demo'd in embryonic form at the same time as 'Rock 'n' Roll Music'. Perhaps the allusion to the celebrated concert series *Jazz at the Philharmonic* is a little pretentious, but as a conscious tribute to Berry's hero Charlie Christian it is excusable. Fred Rothwell has spotted an ancestor of the tune in the 1949 recording 'Big Three Stomp' by the Big Three Trio – featuring, as does 'Rock at the Philharmonic', Willie Dixon on bass, although the writer credit naturally goes to Berry. Did Dixon not make the connection?

'Guitar Boogie' is a pleasant warm-up number, a finger-stretching 12-bar that the magpie Jeff Beck once again borrowed, this time calling it 'Jeff's Boogie', and 'Night Beat' is another throwaway, though it succeeds in conveying a smoky, introspective mood; Berry also doodled around with another improvisation that was later given the name 'Chuckwalk'. 'Time Was' is a curious choice, a cover version of a wistful Mexican ballad given English lyrics in the 1940s, which Berry would have known from a hit version by the Jimmy Dorsey orchestra.

Among all these disposables lurked the next Berry classic. 'Reelin' and Rockin'' gets under way as if Berry at last means business. It has the distinction of being Berry's last hit to date, when released in 1972 in a live version as a follow-up to 'My Ding-a-Ling', and it has always been a mainstay of his stage act, a customary closer. It takes its idea of rocking around the clock not from Bill Haley, but from a 1945 Wynonie Harris record, 'Around the Clock Blues', although Berry was also aware of a slightly later version by Big Joe Turner.

Both these are explicit in describing what went on around the clock, as has Berry been in more recent years (including the 1972 Lanchester Festival that gave rise to the later hit version), but in 1958 the song was apparently strictly about dancing. So prolific was Berry at this time (or so profligate was Chess) that the company could afford to issue this as the B-side of 'Sweet Little Sixteen', leaving the disc jockeys to decide if they wanted to play it as a double-sided potential hit or concentrate on 'Sixteen'.

# go, Johnny, go

**O**N THE NEXT day (or perhaps on the *same* day if the possible January date once referred to by Johnson is in fact the correct one for this remarkable session) Berry produced his 'Blue Suede Shoes', his 'Be-Bop-a-Lula', his 'Summertime Blues', his 'Long Tall Sally', his 'Bo Diddley' – all rolled into one song, one of the most celebrated ever written. 'Johnny B Goode' is, after all, out there in space on a Voyager rocket with a movement from a Beethoven string quartet, the twin ambassadors for earthling music. No Mozart, no Duke Ellington, no Beatles, just Ludwig and a 'little colored boy', blasted off from Cape Canaveral on 20 August 1977.

It seems unlikely that 'Johnny B Goode' *was* recorded alongside 'Sweet Little Sixteen', partly because surely not even Berry at the height of his creativity could have maintained the energy level for a very long session including so many classics, but also because, significantly, Johnson makes no claim to have been on the track. 'He never did tell me who he recorded "Johnny B Goode" with, but I'd say it was probably that Leake fella,' is his opinion.

Significantly, the archetype Chuck Berry guitar intro and instrumental break are an amalgam stolen from his heroes. The song starts with a rocked-up but note-for-note version of Carl Hogan's lead in to Louis Jordan's 'Ain't That Just Like a Woman', and continues by chicken-pecking across adjacent B and top E strings in perfect homage to T-Bone Walker. But the total effect is like nothing they could have dreamed of — the most famous musical notes in rock 'n' roll history.

From his initial idea of an admonishment to Johnnie Johnson for his drinking, Berry developed an 'American Dream' movie synopsis in three minutes, of the poor boy made good thanks to his guitar playing, of the journey from the 'little cabin made of earth and wood' to the neon lights proclaiming 'Johnny B Goode Tonite'. The song's early reference to New Orleans is not accidental, as Berry explains: 'The gateway from freedom . . . was somewhere "close to New Orleans" where most Africans were sorted through and sold.' And it was in this area that Berry's great-grandfather did indeed live 'way back up in the woods among the evergreens'. The saga is strengthened by the reference to Berry's own 'Goode' birthplace.

Three takes of the song have surfaced from the session, the rejected ones being included on the 1986 *Rock 'n' Roll Rarities* collection. But before the single could be released Berry needed a B-side, which he cut at his next session on 28 February. Apart from the engineer, probably Malcolm Chisholm, he was on his own this time, and he warmed up by laying down the backdrop for a blues shuffle that briskly appeared the following month on the *One Dozen Berrys* album, variously titled 'Ingo' and 'In-Go' ('Indigo' as in the colour of the blues? 'Ingrid' after his daughter Darlin Ingrid?). When he dubbed on the lead guitar part he ran through his repertoire of T-Bone Walker licks to pleasant effect, adding a further chord-heavy lead guitar and a piano solo.

The session's main work, and the B-side to 'Johnny B Goode', was to prove a mainstay of the British beat boom — perhaps because so many diehards sought out 'Johnny B Goode' as a single, having heard it on Radio Luxembourg. 'Around and Around' develops the theme of rocking all night long from 'Reelin' and Rockin'' and all those earlier R & B and jump blues numbers on the same topic. A second attempt at the song varies only in that, having laid down all the other parts, Berry tried a slightly different guitar solo. The song 'sprouted from a jam session during a rehearsal before a concert,' he recalls. A rare concert indeed, with Berry actually warming up with the band beforehand. For two hours, he claims.

The most notable cover version, of course, was the 1964 track by The Rolling Stones, cut in the same studio as the original at 2120 South Michigan Avenue and one of their most passionate and inventive nods to Berry's influence. Indeed, the song had always been in the band's repertoire from the days when Mick Jagger sat in with Alexis Korner's group in 1961, and it featured on the demo tape that wound up at Decca Records and led to their being signed in 1963.

During 1957 Berry's live concerts were often attended by a rich white female fan who 'popped up in the most weird places', even optimistically inviting him to her downtown hotel in segregated Jackson, Mississippi, and turning up at *his* hotel when he pointed out the difficulty. She was the inspiration for 'It Don't Take But a Few Minutes', an amiable story with a chicken-wing strut to the rhythm that, like 'Ingo', was rushed onto *One Dozen Berrys*. The session also included a work-out on Berry's Electraharp to be called 'Blues for Hawaiians' and, allegedly, a demo version of 'Do You Love Me', which he returned to a year later during the 'Back in the USA' session. This last number, though, has never surfaced.

Leonard Chess had no hesitation in picking 'Johnny B Goode' as the next single, released in April. In *Billboard* it gave Berry his third top-tenner in a row, reaching no. 8; it climbed to no. 11 in *Cash Box* and just failed to make the top spot on the R & B chart. It also peeped into the UK chart for a week at no. 17. While this was a very respectable performance, and as far as the USA was concerned it was his biggest hit until 'My Ding-a-Ling' in 1972, it does not quite reflect its subsequent status as a cornerstone of the rock 'n' roll era. This may be due to Chess's over-anxiousness to release it, within weeks of 'Sweet Little Sixteen', which was still selling strongly – after all, it was 'Sixteen' that caused the miming row in May on the Dick Clark show, not Berry's more recent record. Clearly Chess felt that they were on a roll with Berry, one that could best be maintained by hurling product into the marketplace – two singles and an album in two months!

I cannot be objective about the result of the next session, on 20 April 1958. Although I was already familiar with Berry's singles through the boom and fade of night-time Radio Luxembourg, 'Beautiful Delilah' was the first of his records, released in the UK on the London label, for which I laid down hard cash. Sixpence precisely, paid to a school friend who had bought the record in town before making the extraordinary decision that he wasn't a Chuck Berry fan after all.

Where others have heard crudeness in the execution of the song I hear raw inspiration, and what Fred Rothwell regards as a flawed, even out of tune, recording I insist on hearing as improvisational genius. Berry flicks his plectrum up into the strings, creating a tense, unexpected rhythmic pulse, interspersed with stomach-rumbling wah-wah punctuations, like a punkish version of 'You Can't Catch Me'. It is indeed somewhat crude – unpolished, in its best sense – but it finally convinced me (although clearly not my classmate) that Berry was a mighty man.

The session personnel is confused. Either Leake or Johnson plays the piano, either the outgoing Hardy (surely he had left some time before, however) or the incoming but untrustworthy Thomas was on drums, and there may be a mysterious G. Smith slapping Dixon's bull fiddle. The song is about a teenage temptress, 'swinging like a pendulum, walking down the aisle', who has all the boys in thrall. The boys included the Davies brothers, who cut a 'garage' version with The Kinks, released as a single before Ray Davies found his own unique voice with 'You Really Got Me' in 1964.

Remarkably, a Chess trade ad at the time announced the July release of Berry's next single as 'Vacation Time' b/w 'Beautiful Delilah'. The supposed A-side, the other result of the session, is one of Berry's regular excursions into Croonsville, 'just me and my honey bun', and he was clearly unsure about it. Having smooched his way through the version on the single he tried to rock it up (labelled by Chess as '21', with a fluffed 'Maybellene' intro) and then to fit it with slightly more success into a chunka-chunka blues arrangement ('21 Blues'). Both these rejected approaches simply take Chuck Berry guitar figures off the shelf and try to fit them into an unsuitable context. All this song tells us, as with so many of these persistent attempts by Berry to be someone else, is to question if he really knew where his genius lay. Once again we are reminded that the main reason he pioneered rock 'n' roll was because he saw it as a business opportunity.

It is another indication of Chess's energetic milking of their hottest act at the time that, far from leaving this forgettable love ditty on the shelf, they bunged it straight out – even, according to that *Billboard* ad, briefly deeming it to be the follow-up to 'Johnny B Goode'! When the wonderful 'Delilah' became the plug side it was still a summertime failure, creeping to no. 81 in *Billboard*, nowhere in *Cash Box* (who were at this time only listing their Top 75) and missing out on the R & B chart as well. *Billboard* had tipped better things for the 'primitive-type folk tune about a beautiful chick,' and praised Berry's 'vigorous, winning style'.

Meanwhile, following the 'Delilah' session Berry joined Buddy Holly as headliners on Alan Freed's *Big Beat Show*. When the package reached Boston, where racially mixed shows had had trouble in previous years, there was a riot. The venue was the Boston Arena in a rundown quarter of the town where, according to Freed's business partner Jack Hooke, quoted in Ellis Amburn's *Buddy Holly: a Biography*, 'the dregs of society lived'. Before the show a gang moved through the crowd, and several girls were raped. Rioting spread through the streets as the police attempted to restore order.

As Amburn states: 'Inside the arena, a riot was about to erupt. The bigoted Boston audience resented black R & B stars and had been spoiling for an opportunity to disrupt an integrated show.' Irish immigration to Boston had begun in the 1830s, the years of the potato famine, and the steady increase in the black population had always caused friction among what journalist Cy Egan called 'flannel-mouthed Irishmen with great skills at talking but no brains and filled with prejudices and resentments'.

The ignition point for chaos was when a white girl in the crowd leapt onto the stage and grabbed the crotch of a black singer. Freed appealed for calm but was informed by a policeman: 'We don't like your kind of music here.' It was left to Berry to try and end the show, a hopeless task. Missiles began to rain down on the stage and Berry ran for it, before security men waded in and eventually drove the crowd out into the streets. *Time* magazine called it a 'Rock 'n' Roll Riot', as if integrated music was to blame. And for Berry this frightening experience was merely the prelude to a process that was to end in his second jail sentence.

On 2 June 1958 a warrant was issued against him. Reported the *St Louis Post-Dispatch* on the following day: 'Charles (Chuck) Berry, St Louis rock 'n' roll guitarist and singer, was at liberty today on a $1000 bond on a warrant charging the carrying of a concealed weapon.' He and a white woman, Joan Mathis, had been travelling in his pink Cadillac from a gig in Topeka, Kansas when he had to pull in to the side of the road, on the outskirts of St Charles, Missouri, to change a flat tyre. He says he had first met Ms Mathis on the previous Christmas Eve, at a gig in St Louis, and claimed to have given her a lift to visit friends in Kansas.

A Highway Patrol officer, Don Medley, also pulled up, and found a .25-calibre automatic pistol containing ten cartridges under the driver's seat, together with a stash of money. Berry said he had bought the gun in Texas, as security when carrying large amounts of cash earned at gigs – he had already developed his preference for the folding stuff over traceable cheques. Both Berry and Ms Mathis were handcuffed, and taken to the county jail.

Berry paid the bail bond, together with another of $250 for his companion. He was also fined $30 because his driver's licence had expired and for an irregularity in the registration of the car. Because of Berry's previous conviction for armed robbery he was debarred from possessing a firearm, and this was confiscated. Later, he says, Ms Mathis told him that the police had tried to suggest that she had been abducted or molested, which would have enabled them to charge Berry under the Mann Act.

This was the federal law that Berry would eventually fall foul of following another incident – clearly the authorities remained persistent. It prohibits the transportation of minors across state lines for the purpose of sex, including prostitution, even if they are above the age of consent in the state concerned. Ms Mathis refused to cooperate with the police in their attempts to nail Berry for something more serious than possession of the gun.

The main question arising from this incident, surely, is quite why a patrol officer, when he sees a stranded motorist changing a tyre, should find it necessary to search the car. In 1958 the answer, presumably, was that it was prudent when the driver is black, his female companion is white, and the car is an exotic one.

On 11 July Berry was arrested again, once again with a young woman in the passenger seat, when police officers allegedly saw him weaving dangerously in the traffic. He was charged with careless driving, and they again threw in the other charge of having improper licence plates – Berry was a St Louis resident, giving his address as 3137

Whittier Street, but the Cadillac had New York plates. Bail this time was $500, and the following week he was fined $15 in his absence. 'Rock 'n' roll singer fined for rock 'n' roll driving,' headlined the *Post-Dispatch*.

However trivial the alleged offence, the police were not going to let Berry relax. He began more and more to fly to gigs, thousands of feet above the Highway Patrol. Eventually, the far more serious matter of the gun was allowed to rest on file, because they had found a better way of harassing him that would eventually lead to jail, thanks to the Mann Act.

In between these two encounters with white man's law Berry was back in the studio on 12 June, with the same disputed personnel (except that the aural evidence surely confirms Johnson's presence), to cut his next single, and his purple patch of creativity was yet to slow down – 'Carol' is a marvellous noise. If it is indeed Jaspar Thomas and the mysterious G. Smith driving it along on drums and slap bass then they do not merit their obscurity, giving each line of the stop-start song a chunky rhythmic texture that makes it stand out from other first-grade Berry material of the period.

The session also included an enjoyable minor work, 'Oh Yeah', an up-tempo rocker in which Berry celebrates his career to date by listing twenty-one of his song titles; a forgettable pseudo-Spanish song called 'Hey Pedro'; a second attempt at 'Time Was', which he first cut six months earlier; and another cover, 'House of Blue Lights'. This boogie was co-written by pianist Freddie Slack, who cut the first version in 1946 with vocals by Ella Mae Morse, and Don Raye, who also wrote another Berry cover, 'Down the Road Apiece'. 'Blue Lights' is less successful than the 1960 cut of the latter song, with Berry's initial guitar part blithely out of tune.

'Carol' was greeted by *Billboard* as 'a hard-hitting gal-titled rocker' and it fared better than 'Beautiful Delilah' when released in August, reaching no. 18 in the *Billboard* Hot Hundred and no. 31 in *Cash Box*. Once more The Rolling Stones leapt on the song and included it on their first album.

On 5 July Berry became the first rock 'n' roll artist to appear at the annual Newport Jazz Festival, and he was one too many in the opinion of some serious goatee beards in the audience. The event was filmed for the celebratory film *Jazz on a Summer's Day*, in which he performs 'Sweet Little Sixteen'. This song, together with 'School Day', 'No Money Down' and 'Johnny B Goode', together with other festival performances, surfaced in 1992 on the Swedish CD *Blues in the Night*.

Also in July, Berry laid down two multitracked songs alone in his office at 4221 West Easton Avenue, using a cheap reel-to-reel tape recorder. 'Jo Jo Gunne' is a jungle tale about a mischievous monkey, probably inspired by the bawdy folk song 'The Signifying Monkey' but in Berry's hands Disney-clean. A second-division piece, perhaps, but the intricate lyric is to be admired, there are amusing little guitar references to other songs in the instrumental fills, including the theme to a then-current television advertisement for Gillette Razors, and it gave its name to at least one subsequent band, the Los Angeles outfit Jo Jo Gunne, formed in 1971 by ex-members of Spirit, whose 'Run Run Run' reached no. 6 in the UK charts a year later. Jo Jo also made a brief appearance in The Beatles' 'Get Back'. It was released late in the year as the flip to 'Sweet Little Rock 'n' Roller'.

The other result of Berry's home taping is one of his greatest songs, and is a distinct departure from his anthemic rockers. This was not apparent to Chess at the time, since they sat on 'Memphis Tennessee' for a year before releasing it as the B-side to 'Back in the USA'. The song is if anything strengthened by its budget production values, which lend it a mournful, booming sound in sympathy with its wistful story-line. And it is indeed a story – the singer is desperately trying to get in touch with 'my Marie' by long-distance telephone, and in the last verse she is revealed not to be his wife or girlfriend but as his six-year-old daughter. 'We were pulled apart because her Mom did not agree / Tore apart our happy home in Memphis, Tennessee.'

The tumbling, pulsing melody has attracted many cover versions, including one by the Count Basie Orchestra, and in 1963 as 'Memphis' it made no. 5 in the Hot Hundred in a stunning instrumental version by guitarist Lonnie Mack, which reworks it totally in virtuoso style. In the same year Sheffield singer Dave Berry, who took his stage name from his hero, reached no. 19 in the UK with a respectful cover version. This prompted Pye Records, who by now had acquired the UK rights to the Chess catalogue, to release the original as a double-header with 'Let It Rock'. Chuck chased Dave up the charts and soon overtook him, peaking at no. 6.

Back in 1958 Berry featured the song in his third Alan Freed quickie movie *Go, Johnny, Go*, directed by Paul Landres, which is notable for a poignant appearance by Ritchie Valens singing 'Ooh, My Head'. By the time the film reached the cinemas Valens was dead at the age of seventeen.

# sweet little rock 'n' roller

**W**HILE 'CAROL' WAS restoring Berry to the Top 20, he and Johnnie Johnson went back on the road in late summer 1958, completing an east-coast run with a ten-day engagement at the Fox theatre in New York. They returned to the studio on 28 September, now reunited with Willie Dixon and Fred Below, and cut the weakest song to be accorded A-side status (given that the cloying 'Vacation Time' had soon given way to 'Beautiful Delilah' as the disc jockey preference). 'Anthony Boy' is a childish sing-along set to a bumpity-bump rhythm, seemingly aimed at the Italian market at the request of Phil Chess. It may be another neat example of Berry's ability to write to order, but it advances our appreciation of popular music not a jot.

The session's other piece, however, was a vast improvement. 'Sweet Little Rock 'n' Roller' has an irresistible drive to it, and even if it is 'Sweet Little Sixteen' revisited in some ways, although the heroine is only nine years old this time, its enthusiasm carries the day. It also highlights Berry's unexpected turn of phrase, as in the well-sketched line: 'She's the daughter of a well-respected man, who taught her how to judge and understand.' She was 'dressed up like a downtown

Christmas tree' because Berry was trying to write a seasonal rock 'n' roll song at the time, something he soon achieved with 'Run Rudolph Run'.

Fred Rothwell and collector Morten Reff have identified thirty-seven cover versions of 'Sweet Little Rock 'n' Roller' worldwide, notably the swaggering Rod Stewart version with Ron Wood on guitar. It was picked as Berry's autumn release, backed with 'Jo Jo Gunne', and disc jockeys again expressed differing preferences, making it a modest double-sided hit. The songs reached no. 47 and no. 83 respectively in *Billboard*, 52 and 74 in *Cash Box*. With its customarily reserved approach to the English language, *Billboard* greeted 'Sweet Little Rock 'n' Roller' as 'another good jumper right up the teeners' alley'.

On 19 November the same musicians were back at Chess's South Michigan Avenue studio for Berry's first Christmas record. For the smoky blues 'Merry Christmas Baby' he turned to one of his heroes, the Texan-born balladeer Charles Brown. As singer and pianist with the Los Angeles group Johnny Moore's Three Blazers, Brown cut the original hit version in 1947. With its cool, understated backing and Johnson's appealing piano improvisations, this is one of Berry's most successful attempts to step out of his rock 'n' roll shoes.

But he cranks up the tempo again for the wonderful song that brought him another double-sided hit just in time for Christmas. On 'Run Rudolph Run' (though the exhortation in the lyric is actually 'Run Run Rudolph') co-writer credit goes to Marvin Brodie, composer of 'Rudolph the Red-Nosed Reindeer', but this is surely pure Berry, with the little boy in the song asking Santa for 'a rock 'n' roll electric guitar' and the girl hoping for a doll that 'can cry, sleep, drink and wet'. Maybe at Chuck Berry Music Inc. they were just being cautious, ascribing to Brodie the rights to all Christmas reindeers called Rudolph, since the cross-reference to his seasonal chestnut is quite clear and intentional.

*Billboard* could hardly distinguish the relative popularity of the two contrasting songs, which it reviewed as 'a hep rockin' novelty' and a 'pretty Christmas romancer', and it showed 'Rudolph' reaching no. 69 and the blues peaking two rungs below. When re-released Slade-style a year later the disc wasn't a hit, though in the UK it was revived for Christmas 1963 and reached no. 36. The song became a seasonal mainstay in the repertoire of Brinsley Schwarz, kings of the London pub and club circuit in the 1970s and the springboard for Nick Lowe's later fame, and Keith Richards put his version out as a solo single in 1979.

Berry's creativity for the day hadn't been exhausted, however. 'Little Queenie' is a further classic, similar to 'Rudolph' in its relentless rhythmic groove and melody but in its subject matter owing more to Delilah than any reindeer. The singer is eyeing up a girl who is 'standing over by the record machine, looking like a model on the cover of a magazine', wondering how best to approach her. It tellingly evokes the world of teenage dances, something that Berry hadn't experienced for at least thirteen years, and the beat is carved from solid rock. Since the 'go, go, go, little Queenie' injunctions are presumably only in the singer's mind, we are left not knowing if he overcomes his shyness or not. I have a feeling that he left the dancehall on his own. 'I leaned toward a story for the teen market which had gone so well for me,' is how Berry puts it with his usual commercial awareness, and in his typically stilted version of the English language. What is identified as Take 8 of the number also survives, but lacks the dynamism of the best-known version.

The song was rushed into the movie *Go, Johnny, Go* but Chess were seemingly less sure. In January they released the feeble 'Anthony Boy' (or 'cute Italian flavored bouncer' if you believe *Billboard*) with the productive Christmas session's last cut on the flip, the 1931 oldie 'That's My Desire'. This intimate smooch song about a romantic rendezvous proved irresistible to rockers for some reason – they included Buddy Holly and Eddie Cochran at his most breathily seductive – but Berry turns it into a curious and mildly enjoyable cha-cha with no seductive qualities. 'Anthony' clearly had some appeal, after all – he reached no. 60 in *Billboard* and 76 in *Cash Box*. Meanwhile 'Little Queenie' sat on the shelf for a few months.

On Christmas Day 1958 Berry flew from St Louis to New York City to join yet another Alan Freed package, *Christmas Jubilee*, although this time the cast were spared the discomfort of the road in favour of an eleven-day run at Loew's theatre. And what a cast – in Berry's recollection they included Jackie Wilson, Bo Diddley, The Everly Brothers, Frankie Avalon, Jo Ann Campbell, Eddie Cochran, King Curtis, The

Flamingos, The Crests, The Cadillacs, Dion and the Belmonts, Johnnie Ray 'and others'.

Immediately afterwards Berry joined up in Los Angeles with the co-stars for his first Australian tour, stopping over in Hawaii – Bobby Darin ('Queen of the Hop' was his current hit), Jo Ann Campbell again (a country star in the making, best known for her 1962 answer record '(I'm the Girl) on Wolverton Mountain') and George Hamilton IV (the most recent of his country hits to edge into the pop charts was a revival of Hank Williams's 'Your Cheating Heart'). Buddy Holly and the Crickets had opened up Australia to rock 'n' roll in the previous year, and the package was well received – though Berry's 'Back in the USA', written at this time, suggests that he would always be happier with American asphalt under his wheels.

Then, on 3 February 1959, 'the music died'. So many rock stars have since perished in planes and cars that it is easy to underestimate the impact of rock 'n' roll's first major tragedy. The innocence was over almost before it started. Eddie Cochran was to follow Buddy Holly, Ritchie Valens and The Big Bopper a year later when his taxi skidded into a Wiltshire lamppost, Little Richard returned to the church, Jerry Lee Lewis was seen as a paedophile pariah, Elvis Presley was being sanitized in the army, and Chuck Berry was still being pursued by those persistent law-enforcement officers.

The four-seater Beechcraft Bonanza should of course not have taken off on that frozen, snowblind night, but when the *Winter Dance Party* limped into Clear Lake, Iowa, on the previous evening it was already in terrible trouble. Holly's tour drummer Carl Bunch was in hospital with frostbite, the 'clear lake' had been frozen over all winter, the promoters had failed to come up with any of the things they had promised to improve the conditions, and there was now the prospect of another freezing, bumpy, marathon 500-mile trip in an unheated, lurching bus to the next night's concert in Moorhead, Minnesota. Holly had had enough, and arranged to charter the plane to fly from Mason City, just outside Clear Lake, to Moorhead's nearest airport at Fargo, North Dakota.

The only pilot that the charter company could raise was Roger Peterson, twenty-one years old and worn out, having been on duty in these dreadful conditions for maybe seventeen hours previously, and now facing a further seven-hour round trip before he could go to bed. Berry's old dice-shooting partner died instantly of massive brain injury.

One characteristic of Holly's brief career had been his musical curiosity. By the end of his life he was adding the distinctive saxophone of King Curtis to 'Reminiscing', and banks of pizzicato strings to 'It Doesn't Matter Anymore'. Berry, by contrast, has tended to stick to what he knows best. But his first studio session after Holly's death, on 17 February 1959, not only featured his regular band, but also Chess's top vocal group The Moonglows. Their leader Harvey Fuqua also brought along his girlfriend, Etta James, who was to be one of the biggest Chess stars of the 1960s. Johnson approved of the innovation. 'We had been usin' the same music so long that I was getting' tired of it. At least when they came in, we had something new.' When he went on to admit to heresy – 'I was gettin' tired of rock 'n' roll' – it was another sign that sometime soon Berry would lose his faithful but exploited sidekick. After all, Holly's death had done nothing to ease Johnson's lifelong fear of flying, and Berry was becoming increasingly dependent on airline schedules.

The Moonglows were signed to Chess in 1954, when they reached second slot on the R & B chart with their doo-wop classic 'Sincerely', while their most fruitful run in the pop list was with 1958's 'Ten Commandments of Love'. After that Fuqua, who ran the band and owned the name, decided to fire the others and replaced them wholesale with a Washington, DC vocal quintet, The Marquees. These were bass singer Chuck Barksdale, later a mainstay of doo-wop's longest surviving group The Dells, James Nolan, Reese Palmer, Chester Simmons – and the young Marvin Gaye.

The musicians probably limbered up with an instrumental jam later titled 'Blue on Blue', which gives Johnson plenty of elbow room as the only featured soloist, something he takes full advantage of. Then they launch into a Berry blues ballad 'Do You Love Me', an uncharacteristic number where the interplay of lead vocals and backing singers works well. This continues into the bouncy 'Almost Grown', hardly a classic though once again it shows Berry's innate skill in thinking himself into the mind of an adolescent, and the instrumental combination of chanting singers, chugging rhythm guitar and Johnson's tinkling piano keeps it moving engagingly. The next Berry anthem completed the session, with The Moonglows chirping 'A ha ha, a ha ha, oh yeah' to great effect in the background of 'Back in the USA'.

This celebration of Homer Simpson's blue-collar America, where cars zoom along the freeway and 'hamburgers sizzle on an open grill night and day', was in part Berry's reaction to Australia, which had yet to succumb to junk food. Although he had experienced good ol' American racism at first hand at the southern lunch counter, the seg-regated hotel, the gigs divided into 'salt and pepper' and at the hands of the ever-vigilant traffic cops, there seems no trace of irony or satire in this simple love song to his home country. Its patriotism and energy have guaranteed a useful shelf life, with successful covers by Bruce Springsteen, Linda Ronstadt and The MC5, and it also inspired The Beatles' parody 'Back in the USSR'.

'Almost Grown', with 'Little Queenie' thrown away on the flip, was released in March once 'Anthony Boy' had slipped out of the Hot Hundred, and proved a stronger performer – no. 32 in *Billboard*, 31 in *Cash Box*, who were now also listing their top one hundred records each week. 'Back in the USA', with 'Memphis Tennessee' dusted off to complete a killer single, followed in June and also made the 30s. With Chess hurling Berry at the market so frequently, and sales of singles at an all-time high, these were as impressive performances as almost any chart-topper of today.

Meanwhile 'Little Queenie' was really getting up arch-rival Jerry Lee Lewis's nose. His treacherous mother Mamie had come out of the closet as a Chuck Berry fan, and was wearing out her copy of the single by filling the house with Berry. On 28 May Lewis insisted on a session at the Sun studio in Memphis, assembling regular guitarist and drum-mer Roland Janes and James Van Eaton together with second guitarist Brad Suggs and bass player Cliff Acred. There was only one song on the agenda, and the 'pumping piano man' ripped into a version designed to obliterate memories of the original. It doesn't for a moment, but Lewis's frustration is certainly translated into pure rock 'n' roll energy. However, it wasn't the hit needed to restore his fortunes after the 'child bride' scandal of a year previously, when it transpired during a UK tour that he had married his thirteen-year-old cousin.

For a mammoth two-day session on 27 and 29 July 1959 the vocal-group experiment continued, this time with an otherwise unknown outfit called The Ecuadors, and with Berry's former road saxophonist Leroy Davis fattening the sound on several of the cuts. From a mixed bag of variable standard, as so often, leaps one masterly addition to Berry's catalogue, this time the intriguing fragment 'Let It Rock' (a command that appears nowhere in the lyric).

First, however, he added to his list of girl songs by serenading 'Betty Jean', with the backing group urging, 'Sing your song, Chucky boy.' This has headlined more than one magazine piece about Berry over the years. Although the song is a standard pop–blues, lines like 'I love the way you walk, looks like you're dancing but you're not,' and the infectious, humorous drive lift it out of the rut.

For 'County Line' Berry sets up a Bo Diddley rhythm and chants one of his most complex lyrics on a familiar theme, that of the car chase. In this case it's a race between a Jaguar and a Thunderbird, pursued by the sheriff across the county line. In the following year he was to tell the same tale, relocating from Pennsylvania to Indiana, calling it 'Jaguar and Thunderbird'. Although there's little to choose between the two songs – if anything, 'County Line' has the edge for its freshness and tongue-twisting complexity – presumably Berry or Chess Records or both preferred the rewrite, because 'County Line' stayed on the shelf until 1974's *Golden Decade Volume 3*.

'Childhood Sweetheart' is a mid-tempo 12-bar that thumps along in routine manner, purloining the odd phrase like 'I broke my mother's rule', with The Ecuadors proving that a shoo-wop backing is somewhat superfluous in the standard blues format. Far more impressive is a show-off reading of Count Basie's 'One O'Clock Jump'. The relish with which Johnnie Johnson attacks his leading role is clear in his joyously sprightly playing. Berry puts together some fine Carl Hogan licks and Davis stresses his jazz background with a driving saxophone solo before Johnson elbows his way back in. After some more Davis, with Berry remaining in the background, they all riff on merrily as if loath to surrender the groove.

The Willie Dixon–Muddy Waters classic 'I Just Want To Make Love To You' (confusingly called 'Just Make Love to Me' in its original version) is given the Berry treatment to no great effect, particularly as for years it was only available in the version released in 1963 on the *Chuck Berry On Stage* album – which is nothing of the sort, of course. Just as Vee-Jay Records apparently once recorded Jimmy Reed 'live at the

Carnegie Hall', so Chicago rivals Chess took a collection of Berry studio cuts, dubbed on fake audience applause and even a master of ceremonies. For the French release he was transported to the Paris Olympia, sounding much the same but in Franglais.

Showing another lapse of judgement Chess decided that the session's next effort, 'Broken Arrow', was to be the follow-up to 'Back in the USA', and it was released to an indifferent public in September. It combines mundane lyrics, the melody of 'Old MacDonald Had a Farm' and a Bo Diddley beat – a bad idea that only Bo himself or the raucous Capitol session band The Piltdown Men could hope to get away with.

But Berry was fooling us all along, because if the matrix numbers are to be believed he then rolled up his sleeves and launched into 'Let It Rock'. This is one of his most enigmatic songs, as haunting in its way as 'Memphis Tennessee' even though it is a straight-ahead rocker. He sets up the story with a deft couplet: 'In the heat of the day down in Mobile, Alabama/Working on the railroad with a steel-driving hammer.' In the absence of the foreman the workers are sheltering from the heat and playing dice in a teepee between the tracks, oblivious to the fact that 'an off-schedule train' is heading straight for them.

Berry gets an extraordinary sound out of his Gibson to imitate the train's warning siren but the railroad gang remains unaware of the danger, and chaos descends when it is recognized too late. In the end Berry sings the chilling line, 'Can't stop the train, gotta let it roll on' – and that's it, barely a minute and a half after he started the story. There are just three short verses, and Berry's slightly uncertain vocal launch into the second and third suggests that the song is a newly minted gem. How on earth could he jump from 'Broken Arrow' to this as if they had equal weight – and how could Chess compound the lack of discrimination by releasing the former? Occasionally, it seems, the seat-of-the-pants businessmen who ran the record companies made strange errors of judgement. At around this time, for example, Carl Perkins cut one of his masterpieces, 'Put Your Cat Clothes On'. Sam Phillips left it in the can, and it was not released until the 1970s, when the small British independent Charly discovered it.

For a fragment destined to be a B-side, 'Let It Rock' has taken on a life of its own. The first ever attempt in the UK to produce an intelligent rock monthly, in the mid-1970s, stole the title, virtually every band of the 'beat era' covered it and The Rolling Stones have been performing and re-recording it for forty years.

The magic couldn't last, though, and Berry then turned his attention to a song co-written by Billy Davis, soon to join Chess as their top A & R man. 'Too Pooped To Pop' is about an ageing man trying to remain 'with it', and as he approached his thirty-third birthday maybe Berry saw an element of autobiography in this forgettable novelty. It would have taken the comic genius of The Coasters to squeeze what humour there is out of the song, and Fred Rothwell has suggested that perhaps Leonard Chess persuaded Berry to cut it as bait to Davis, whose A & R talents did indeed prove central to Chess's survival in the 1960s.

For the rest of this long session Berry played the role of lead guitarist behind The Ecuadors, who shooby-dooby their way through 'Say You'll Be Mine' to a Bo Diddley beat, following it up with the amusing 'Let Me Sleep Woman'. Although there are clear echoes of better-known groups, The Cadets, The Coasters and Frankie Lymon and the Teenagers among them, on this brief evidence The Ecuadors do not deserve their total obscurity, and it is fascinating to hear Berry dutifully and energetically performing as a session guitarist. The tracks were released on Chess's Argo imprint without success, and a third Ecuadors cut from the session, 'Up There', has never been issued.

Whether it was part of the Davis deal or sheer lack of taste, 'Too Pooped to Pop' was preferred to 'Let It Rock' as the plug side of the follow-up to a very broken arrow in January 1960, by which time Berry had other things to worry about. The record performed reasonably well, reaching no. 18 in the R & B list, and it was another double-sider in the pop chart, with 'Too Pooped to Pop' getting to no. 42, 'Let It Rock' (which actually lingered in the Hot Hundred for two weeks longer) to no. 64. It was to be Berry's last American hit until he emerged from prison with 'Nadine' under his belt.

# bye bye
# Johnny

**O**N 12 FEBRUARY 1960 Berry was back in the Chess studio for a long session of higher than usual consistency, though once again a real gem – in this case 'Bye Bye Johnny' – was buried in the middle. Johnnie Johnson got further leave of absence from the steel works, Leroy Davis was on call and Willie Dixon slapped the bass. Discographies are undecided on the identity of a second sax player (who could, in any case, be a double-tracked Davis) and whether the drummer is Fred Below, Jaspar Thomas or even the prodigal Ebby Hardy.

There are also backing vocals on a couple of tracks (The Ecuadors?), but what is undisputed is the identity of the second guitar player, largely confined to a rhythm role and often picking out single-string bass riffs that add a new chunkiness to the Berry sound. Matt 'Guitar' Murphy, Mississippi born but growing up in Memphis, was the guitarist with Sun Records' early 1950s stars Junior Parker and the Blue Flames, before he moved to Chicago with Memphis Slim and later worked with the second Sonny Boy Williamson. He achieved wider fame later in life as Aretha Franklin's husband in the 1980 film *The Blues Brothers*, and along with such other giants as Steve Cropper and Donald 'Duck' Dunn he toured in The Blues Brothers Band.

Maybe Murphy's presence prompted Berry to dig some old blues favourites out of the bag. 'Drifting Blues', like 'Merry Christmas Baby', comes from the Charles Brown–Johnny Moore catalogue, and is given a respectful, walking-tempo treatment. Far superior is a rollicking reading of Little Walter's 'I Got to Find My Baby', with a little Berry rewriting, booted along by Davis's sax solo and Murphy's solid riffing. Next up was Tampa Red's 'Don't You Lie To Me', recorded in 1940 and revived by Fats Domino in 1951. Although the Domino version failed to make the R & B chart ('Rocking Chair', from the same session, was his only success of the year) Berry must have been aware of the New Orleans record. Although he avoids the Domino treatment, the insistent pulse provided by Davis's saxophone has a distinct Crescent City feel. Murphy takes the guitar solo, remembering at one point to throw in a few Berry-like phrases.

The most straightforward 12-bar of this little blues set is also the most successful – one of those moments when Berry, as later with 'Down the Road Apiece' and 'Route 66', takes someone else's song and makes it sound like an original. 'Worried Life Blues' was first recorded by Big Maceo, a pianist who spent most of his working life in Chicago (and often played with Tampa Red). A tad slower and the tempo could have plodded, but Berry sets up an attractive chugging rhythm for Murphy to decorate, and the vocals have greater conviction than many of Berry's excursions into straight blues.

Back in 1957 The Everly Brothers had woken up little Susie, and in 'Our Little Rendezvous' Berry asks to take her home in a song that starts off as a rewrite of the first Sonny Boy Williamson's 'Good Morning Little Schoolgirl' and then takes Susie out into space. 'I'll build a spaceship with a heavy payload' is perhaps not the most seductive line that Berry ever wrote, and the song has a throwaway feel to it.

On the session's highlight, 'Bye Bye Johnny', Berry and Murphy mesh their guitars together to give the sequel to the 'Johnny B Goode' story an irresistible chunka-chunka drive. The story is everything – they dispense with a guitar solo and just keep motoring on. The song takes Johnny away from Louisiana to 'the golden west', where just like Elvis he is going to be a film star. In spite of its constant references back to 'Johnny B Goode', the song stands alone, and was yet another Berry piece that the young Rolling Stones immediately picked up on. In the days when the extended-play record was an ideal compromise if the record-buying budget wouldn't stretch to an LP, they included it on their first EP in 1964 along with masterly covers of 'Money', 'You'd Better Move On' and 'Poison Ivy'.

With 'Worried Life Blues' on the flip it was released as the next Berry single in May but surprisingly failed to score in *Billboard*, either in the pop or the R & B list, though in *Cash Box* it climbed to no. 64. The latter paper had greeted it enthusiastically. 'Looks like Chuck Berry's gonna get back in the big hit groove with his newest rock delighter,' it opined. 'It's a pile-driving sequel to "Johnny B Goode" (who on this deck heads out to Hollywood . . .). The kids'll love it.'

After 'Bye Bye Johnny' most numbers would sound mundane, particularly a plodding 12-bar like 'Run Around', with Berry on his Electraharp doing Elmore James impersonations. Even Johnnie Johnson in his element cannot lift it above the routine. The evening's final master was Berry's rewrite of his own 'County Line', 'Jaguar and Thunderbird', with Berry chanting the story interspersed with the chorus 'Slow down little Jaguar/Keep cool little Thunderbird Ford'. It adds nothing to the earlier attempt, although the intention was presumably to simplify 'County Line' into a clearer car chase narrative, and the chorus is irritating. When released as the next single but one it once again missed out in *Billboard* and died at no. 93 in *Cash Box*.

The reason for Berry's slump in popularity, even though numbers like 'Let It Rock' and 'Bye Bye Johnny' proved that the creativity was yet to dwindle, may be that, like Jerry Lee Lewis, he was beginning to feature in the headlines for the wrong reasons. The problems that began with a flat tyre in 1958 were coming to a head. So much so that in February 1960, the month of the 'Bye Bye Johnny' session, he was only booked for three gigs, one of those a benefit, and none in the following month.

On the previous 1 December Berry had a booking in El Paso. Killing time during the day, he and his musicians – Johnson, Thomas and Davis were all on this trip – crossed over the Rio Grande and into the Mexican town of Ciudad Juárez, where by his own admission they amused themselves for several hours by visiting strip clubs. In the late afternoon they were in a cantina chatting up two young women, Beatrice and Janice, who agreed to come back to the gig with the band.

To travel happily across a national border with a rock 'n' roll band they had only just met does suggest that they were not of unimpeachable virtue, and clearly the band's intentions were no more honourable.

Janice Escalante was an Apache, and though she wouldn't tell Berry her age, Beatrice claimed that Janice was twenty-one. Although Beatrice was flirting with Thomas, a man who turned out to be her husband arrived during the performance and put an end to her evening, leaving Janice alone backstage. She then told Berry that she was indeed alone, and claimed to have only recently arrived from her home town of Yuma, Arizona.

Berry offered Janice a job 'as a hostess' or a hat-check girl at Club Bandstand, with the idea of dressing her up as an Apache, and she accepted. And so she became part of the entourage, moving on with the band to Sante Fe and then Denver. She shared hotel rooms with Berry, and the fact that she would walk around the room naked certainly allows for a certain amount of reading between the lines of his autobiography.

With Christmas approaching Janice began work at Club Bandstand as a waitress, but within a couple of weeks Berry was back on the road. A few days later Francine phoned to say that Janice had not turned up for work since he had left St Louis. She called again to say that the police had been asking to speak to Berry regarding a teenage employee he had brought with him from El Paso.

He was back in St Louis on 21 December when two policemen arrived at the club and took him to the station, where he was questioned about Janice and then put in a cell until his bail was approved. The sergeant mentioned the Mann Act, and said he could get ten years. On 25 January he was again indicted under the Mann Act, this time concerning his interstate journey with Joan Mathis in 1958. They were going to get him one way or the other.

There can be no doubt that the eighty-one-year-old Judge George H. Moore was a racist, referring to Berry dismissively as 'this Negro', and seemingly determined to put a racial slant on everything. And although no birth certificate for Janice could be tracked down, it was alleged that she was fourteen, that she had worked as a prostitute in El Paso and was now supplementing her Club Bandstand income in the same way. Berry referred dismissively to the proceedings as 'the Indian trial'.

On 4 March 1960, after a two-week hearing, Berry was convicted 'of transporting a fourteen-year-old Indian girl from El Paso, Texas, to St Louis for immoral purposes'. The *Post-Dispatch* reported:

Judge George H. Moore deferred sentencing until 18 March and declined to allow bond for Berry. The singer faces a maximum of five years in prison and a $5,000 fine for violation of the Mann Act. The girl's home is in Arizona. She told Assistant United States Attorney Frederick H. Mayer that she and Berry left El Paso on 1 December and arrived in St Louis December 10. Berry is a former convict. Mayer said investigation showed his income had been as high as $115,000 a year.

On 12 March, earlier than had been expected, the paper confirmed that Moore had passed the maximum sentence. Berry lodged an appeal.

His trial under the same act regarding his journey with Joan Mathis, however, went his way, helped particularly by her claim to be in love with him. On 1 June, after the jury had deliberated for six hours, he was found not guilty of 'transporting an eighteen-year-old woman from St Louis to Toledo and St Louis to Omaha in 1958'. On 16 August there was further good news. Judge Randolph Weber went against a jury verdict and found him not guilty on the firearms charge, because he felt there had been irregularities in the conduct of the court proceedings.

Berry later ruefully observed that the 'guilty' verdict received ten times more publicity than his acquittal in the Mathis case. He won another victory when, in view of the openly racist conduct of the Escalante proceedings, a retrial was ordered. Under the headline 'Appeals Court Remands Case Over Questions By Judge Moore', the *Post-Dispatch* reported that Moore had constantly interrupted proceedings with repeated questions about race during the trial. The paper quaintly described Berry, by this time the most famous man in St Louis, as 'a Negro orchestra leader and nightclub operator'. The Appeals Court felt that Moore's choice of language 'was intended or calculated to disparage the defendant in the eyes of the jury, and to prevent the jury from exercising an impartial judgement'.

However, the three appeal judges who reviewed the conduct of the trial clearly had little sympathy for Berry, and even bent over backwards to find excuses for the judge's shortcomings. Their statement said:

In fairness to the trial judge it should be said that much occurred to try his patience. The record shows that he had difficulty in hearing witnesses, that he apparently was in physical discomfort much of the time, that the trial dragged, that he was unable to see eye to eye with counsel in their conduct of the trial, that there was convincing evidence that Berry's treatment of the girl named in the indictment, who was a fourteen-year-old Apache Indian who had become a prostitute, was inexcusable, and that his testimony about his intention in transporting her in his automobile from El Paso to St Louis, being to make an honest woman of her, had its irritating aspects.

Of course the idea that Berry's intentions and actions were pure still overstretches the imagination, however badly the case had been handled, but the appeal judges do seem to be excusing Judge Moore for being irascible, hard of hearing, too ill to conduct the trial properly and easily bored, as if these qualities were indeed par for the course among the judiciary, as many have always suspected. It was the racism that they were a little queasy about. 'It seems safe to say that ordinarily a trial judge who in the presence of the jury makes remarks reflecting upon a defendant's race, or from which an implication can be drawn that racial considerations may have some bearing upon the issue of guilt or innocence, has rendered that trial unfair.' And so Berry was free but in limbo, neither guilty nor innocent, awaiting the summons to a new trial.

The police, temporarily thwarted, changed their tactics and started constantly harassing him over Club Bandstand, suddenly citing fire safety measures and noise complaints. Berry decided that being a club owner was proving too much trouble, and he closed it down. He would concentrate his energies into Berry Park instead, still with the dream in his head of creating an interracial leisure park.

While these problems were building up around him Berry returned to the studio just three days after his previous session, on 15 February, unencumbered by the distraction of gigs. There was a deliberate element of stockpiling in this activity, although strangely he didn't record again for nearly a year, so distracted was he by his court battles. Berry confirms this in his autobiography, although confusing the chronology, saying, 'Leonard Chess was anticipating a negative result for the appeal' when in fact he wasn't even tried until the following month. 'He wanted to get as many songs on tape as he could before I should have to go off to prison.' Even allowing for the mix-up over the order of events this was no doubt the case, and Berry confesses that he found it hard to keep his mind on the job.

The same personnel (presumably, since the precise identity of some of them remains unclear) was assembled, together with unidentified female backing singers, and Berry wowed them with one of the sentimental croons that he could never quite bring himself to abandon. 'Diploma for Two' might have worked for Perry Como or Andy Williams – at least we could have ignored it – but as with 'Vacation Time' and its ilk it does nothing to burnish the Berry legend. Brought up as he was absorbing anything that flowed out of the family radio, he still maintained catholic tastes, including one for sentimental mush, long after he had ploughed his own unique rock 'n' roll furrow.

He battled on regardless with the rockaballad 'Little Star', a dire showcase for his female chorus, and 'The Way It Was Before' is equally grim and very similar. 'Away From You' has a slightly greasier feel to it and some bluesy trilling from Johnson, together with a treble-heavy guitar solo (either Berry, or Murphy in fair imitation of him – the sound is not spot-on Berry in either case), but remains utterly forgettable. If Berry really was stocking up for a possible period in jail then this was not the way to set about it, and in the following March these turkeys were slipped onto the album optimistically titled *New Juke Box Hits*. These songs are the nadir of Berry's career to date, indicative of the slapdash approach his state of mind had induced. And only two of them could have made it to a jukebox anyway – 'Little Star' and 'Diploma for Two' were to be issued as B-sides, though in the UK we were fortunately spared the latter.

For the first time at a Berry session – a worrying sign perhaps – it took a cover version to pull the day into shape. Murphy's wonderfully swirling guitar leads into 'Down the Road Apiece' (Berry overdubs the second guitar break and the fade-out lines himself) and the interplay between the two is masterly, topped by Berry's sly vocals about a fantasy roadhouse where the boogie and the fried chicken keep coming at you all night long.

This Don Raye boogie was first recorded in 1940 by The Will Bradley Trio, with the crucial piano role filled by Freddie Slack, and was later covered by Merrill E. Moore and Amos Milburn, among many others. Ironically, Berry's own piano genius Johnnie Johnson is comparatively muted in face of the duelling guitars. It is a further irony that Berry, creator of one of the most distinctive guitar sound, in rock 'n' roll, should have gained so much from the input of another axe man. Briefly, Murphy helped to shape Berry's music as surely as Johnson had always done.

Although never released as a single, 'Down the Road Apiece' featured in July 1960 on the *Rockin' at the Hops* album, a strong selection in contrast to those supposed jukebox hits of the following year, and in the UK it became part of a generation's education when in 1963 Pye put together a 'best of' called simply *Chuck Berry*. The early Stones covered this song, together with 'Confessin' the Blues', 'Come On' and 'Around and Around' from this hugely influential collection, and every competing combo from The Animals on down also plundered it.

Perhaps surprisingly, Berry was five years into his recording career before he reprised the Jay McShann blues, first cut in 1941 with McShann on piano and vocals by Walter Brown, that he and his guitarist friend Tommy Stevens had controversially performed at their high school concert amid more polite offerings. 'Confessin' the Blues' continues the form of 'Down the Road Apiece', again helped by the twin guitar interplay and Berry's buoyant vocals. It made sense to return to it now, however – given the perceived urgency of getting material down on tape, Berry says that 'most of the songs were cover tunes that I had always done at the Cosmopolitan Club'. And some of them were certainly preferable to the new material that he brought along on this particular day.

At the time of this session one of the hottest blues records in the country was B.B. King's version of the meditative 'Sweet Sixteen', just beginning to sink down the R & B charts having risen to the second slot. The 1952 original gave ex-Basie singer Big Joe Turner his second Atlantic hit, and was written by the label's co-owner Ahmet Ertegun. In spite of a skittering guitar lead by Murphy, the Berry effort is laid-back almost to the point of listlessness, little more than a blues that happened to be fresh in his mind which was probably always destined to be an album filler. Yes, it was a 'new jukebox hit' in 1961.

When Berry got back to his own compositions there may have been those in the studio who began to wonder if he had lost the knack for ever, because he returned to a three-year-old song that was always going to be a turkey. 'Thirteen Question Method', with its coy and rather laborious plan for wooing a new girlfriend, is now set to an annoying cod-Spanish rhythm and has been reworked to no effect.

And if the Chess brothers were already worrying a little, they were probably chewing their knuckles when he launched into 'Stop and Listen'. Actually, this slow bluesy piece of nonsense is so weird that I love it, with its doomy atmosphere dripping with echo, its lyrics where each verse starts out seeming to make some sort of sense before descending into gibberish, and a weird female in the background who is either crying or pleasuring herself. It has 'new juke box hit' written all over it, and indeed it was.

Next up is a pleasant but lightweight blues shuffle, 'I Still Got the Blues', one of the tracks that was destined to be smothered in fake 'live' applause until Ace Records in the UK stripped the *On Stage* cuts of their extraneous noise in 1993. A little better, but no way forward in career terms, is an easy-listening cover of Duke Ellington's 'I'm Just a Lucky So and So', which probably didn't chime with Berry's mood at the time. It may have been popular with certain patrons of the Cosmopolitan Club, but that didn't make it appropriate so many years later.

Two Electraharp instrumentals completed a long day. 'Mad Lad', probably named in tribute to local disc jockey E. Rodney Jones, 'The Mad Lad', who later worked for the Chess brothers on their radio station WVON, has a catchy melody and was issued as the B-side to 'I Got to Find My Baby' in August. 'Surfing Steel' is simply a further and rather meaningless variation on the 'Deep Feeling' theme that was washed over with audience reaction for the *On Stage* set before being re-presented on its own as 'Cryin' Steel', with no surfing connotation. At the time of the *On Stage* release in 1963 Jan and Dean had just reached the top of the charts with 'Surf City', while The Beach Boys had followed up their rip-off of 'Sweet Little Sixteen', 'Surfin' USA', with 'Surfer Girl'. Leonard Chess's reaction was to give a Berry tune an arbitrary surfer tag, and to pack Bo Diddley off to the coast for *Bo Diddley's Beach Party*.

Meanwhile Johnnie Johnson was also at a low ebb, personal rather than legal. Separated from his wife Rose and his children, he turned up drunk at their house one September evening simply, he says, to say hello to the children. A furious argument developed, so furious that Rose pulled out a gun and shot twice at Johnson. One bullet hit him in the elbow and remains embedded in his arm to this day. He started running but she chased him into the yard and kept firing, and another bullet entered his lung. An inch either way and he would have been dead.

Suddenly realizing what she had done, Rose called for an ambulance. When he left hospital Johnson had nowhere to stay, so instead of pressing charges against his estranged wife he moved back in with her! It wasn't long before he found safer accommodation, however. In the meantime Berry, though keen to get back into the studio, was constantly distracted by his drawn-out legal wrangles, so promised sessions never materialized and gigs remained few and far between. In November 1960 Johnson, anxious to keep playing, joined the Albert King band, while Berry tried to occupy himself out at Wentzville, creating his country park.

# have mercy
# judge

ELEVEN MONTHS AFTER his most dispiriting recording session to date, Berry was at last back in the studio on 10 January 1961. 'The Indian trial' still hung over him, and this effort to kick life back into his faltering career had an element of 'make or break' about it. Of course at this time no one, not Berry, not the Chess brothers, could have predicted the brief but marvellous songwriting renaissance still to come, epitomized by 'Nadine'; and the idea that a new generation of rock 'n' rollers – from staid old Britain, of all places – would conquer America and crown Berry as their king would have seemed laughable. Berry had enjoyed a good run, gathered a bigger bag of hits than most, and written himself into the pop music history books. Now, as he approached rock 'n' roll middle age, he was presumably going to fade away, first to jail and then, probably, into St Louis property dealing.

But if we ignore a pallid and bafflingly pointless cover – and it is advisable to do so – of Little Richard's 'Rip It Up' then, creatively at least, this session managed to put that decline on hold for a while, because he also brought along the road song 'Route 66' and his own 'I'm Talking About You'. Johnson was there, either Thomas or Hardy was manning the drum kit, and for the first time ever in a Berry session an electric bass player was booked – probably a local contact of Willie Dixon's, Reggie Boyd.

'Route 66' was composed by veteran writer and pianist Bobby Troup, who worked for many years with Tommy Dorsey before providing Nat 'King' Cole with a brace of 1946 hits, this one and 'Baby, Baby All the Time'. His later songs include 'The Girl Can't Help It', sung in the movie by Little Richard. Troup's wife was Julie London, whose sensual reading of 'Cry Me a River' in the same film caused many an adolescent tremor at the time.

It took The Rolling Stones to turn 'Route 66' into a snarling rocker – the Cole version was smoky and laid-back, and Berry simply beefs it up a little and sets it to a vaguely Latin beat. The singing is relaxed and the sound is sparer than usual, because Berry contents himself with just the one guitar part. It's no classic, and Johnson seems a little uncertain as to what he should be up to, but it stopped the rot and put Berry back on course.

The brief session's highlight is undoubtedly 'I'm Talking About You', another of Berry's songs that was eagerly picked up by British groups in the mid-1960s. Boyd's bubbling bass gives it a distinctive pulse, and Berry sets up the theme immediately with the neat introduction, 'Let me tell you 'bout a girl I know, I met her walkin' down an uptown street.' It may be that Berry's worries about 'the Indian trial' mean that there is less attack and commitment in his vocals than there might be, as if part of his mind is elsewhere, but this is still an automatic choice for any 'best of' compilation, with unexpected little touches to the melody and a well-crafted lyric, a relief after the drivel he turned up with eleven long months earlier.

This was a natural choice as the next single, released in February, though it was weakened by the appearance of 'Little Star' on the flip. 'Route 66' would have been more logical, but to this point Berry had only surrendered composer rights twice when it came to singles – 'Too Pooped to Pop', as Leonard Chess's concession to writer Billy Davis, and the classic 'Worried Life Blues'. While Berry was in jail the record was re-released, this time with the sickly 'Diploma for Two' on the back, but it still didn't reach the Hot Hundred. Berry may have been back on form, but he was still out of favour with teenage America.

The retrial took place in March, but as Berry and Chess Records had feared the conviction was upheld. On 14 April Judge Roy W. Harper sentenced Berry to three years in prison – a reduction of two years from the maximum handed out by Judge Moore – and imposed the same $5000 fine. Berry immediately lodged an appeal, and was released on a bond of $10,000. If things went against him, as he expected, he calculated that the family would be financially secure while he was unable to provide for them, although he was later to reckon that the long-drawn-out process siphoned off half his savings.

What was expected to be a final recording session for a while was called for 29 July, and continued five days later in an attempt to put more masters in the bank. The backing personnel was made up of Johnson and Davis, there was a new drummer in occasional Chess session-man Phil Thomas, Reggie Boyd was probably once again on electric bass, and there was a one-off innovation – Berry's younger sister Martha joined him on vocals for several of the tracks.

Judging by the matrix-number order, Berry played his trump card first. 'Come On' starts with a most unBerry-like guitar phrase and Davis's saxophone gives a wonderfully sleazy feel to the backing as Berry pours out his catalogue of frustrations: 'Ev'ry time the phone rings, sounds like thunder/Some stupid jerk tryin' to reach another number.' When The Rolling Stones nicked this song as their first Decca single somebody must have thought that the word 'jerk' was somewhat vulgar. In Jagger's line he's a 'guy', a tiny change that weakens the resigned, end-of-my-tether cast to this lovely song. Martha chirps away at the chorus and on a second take the tempo quickens and the sound has a thicker texture, but the drawl of the best-known version suits the mood better.

The quality control is then switched off for 'Adulteen'. 'Love and live your life as an adulteen,' exhorts Berry, using one of his less successful made-up words. The track has never been released, and, alas, 'The Man and the Donkey' is barely an improvement. To the tune of the New Orleans classic 'Junco Partner' Berry sings a silly little story about, yes, a man and a donkey. There's a speeded-up guitar dubbed on and, to make matters worse, in the most familiar version this is one of those tracks given the *On Stage* audience treatment.

Fortunately, inspiration returns with the third part of the 'Johnny B Goode' saga, although in one version 'Go Go Go' is also burdened with grafted-on cheering. To a romping rhythm Johnny is now 'duck walking on his knees, pecking like a hen', which makes his actual identity fairly clear. This and 'Come On' were rushed out as the next single but yet again Berry failed to make the chart – until two years later, when the same coupling was released in the UK. The record climbed to no. 38, marking the revival in Berry's career, with The Rolling Stones in pursuit – the cover version won out by peaking at no. 21, but Berry was back on track.

Martha Berry lends a hand once again on the dreadful sing-along 'Trick or Treat'. Once more it was buried by an unjustifiably enthusiastic crowd for *On Stage*, but it deserves to be buried full stop. The crowd were cheering again for a reworking of 'Brown Eyed Handsome Man', which is now set to a vaguely Bo Diddley beat, but cannot compete with the inspired original, and the enthusiastic mob are there yet again on what is to date the only released version of 'All Aboard', which consists simply of a list of all the stations on a railroad journey between Newburgh, near New York, and Oklahoma City. Without the tongue-twisting dexterity of 'I've Been Everywhere' it is simply a musical timetable, although it grooves along pleasantly enough. So, these back-to-back sessions lacked consistency, but for a man with the world bearing down on him Berry did well to add two great songs, 'Come On' and 'Go Go Go', to his catalogue.

On 5 August Berry was returning to St Louis from a no-doubt-welcome booking in Houston, Texas, when his wife Toddy gave birth once more, to a boy. He was named Charles Edward Anderson Jr, and Toddy declared that the family was complete. In the extraordinary language Berry adopted for his autobiography he commented: 'It wasn't too hard to tolerate the diminishing bedroom festivals with the trial and legal expenditures always interfering with a romantic mood.' I think he means to say that worry is an effective contraceptive, but he comes over like a character in Dickens trying to 'sound posh' and failing. For most of their marriage the Berrys have led parallel lives, with the rock 'n' roller travelling the world and getting up to no good, and Toddy happy to remain at home as long as the bills are paid. In the autobiography, therefore, she is a shadowy, elusive figure, and presumably has the patience and forgiveness of a saint.

On 28 October the *Post-Dispatch* reported the almost-inevitable under the headline 'Singer Charles E. Berry's Morals Conviction

Upheld'. 'The court ruled that a lower court did not err in its instructions to the jury nor by not allowing the defence to inspect grand jury testimony of the complaining witness . . .' So Judge Harper's sentence stood, Berry was given until after Christmas to sort out his affairs before reporting to prison, and the *Post-Dispatch* once again saw fit to remind its readers that 'Berry is a Negro'.

If Berry's recollections in his autobiography are accurate, there still seemed to be a racist element to proceedings. When his secretary Francine took the stand one of the questions she was reportedly asked was: 'Did you tell your people you work for a Negro?' The Negro in question seemed to have lost faith in his lawyer, who failed to challenge such unwarranted curiosity.

If Berry had been a white lodge member, a personal friend of the police chief, then associating with an underage prostitute would simply have confirmed in the eyes of the establishment that he was a lucky old rogue. Furthermore, he claims to have been convicted of doing something that he only *intended* to do, though this does stretch one's imagination somewhat.

Although he recounts this period in his autobiography with philosophical resignation, there can be little doubt that he was in reality a deeply embittered man, at odds with white society. Carl Perkins, who knew him before and after his prison sentence, has confirmed as much in interviews. And certainly his feeling that his testimony had been distorted by the press, that damning words had been put into his mouth, prompted a suspicion of journalists that remains to this day. By now he was, he says, 'feeling more black but still intact', a telling phrase that does much to confirm that his reaction to his predicament was a sour one. In his own mind he was a victim of racism, not of his own sexual ambitions.

On 19 February 1962 Berry reported to the authorities in St Louis. Since it was now almost seven months since the last stockpiling recording session, he clearly had nothing creative left to offer Chess Records at this time – his final tidying-up arrangements before turning himself in were purely financial. In handcuffs, he was driven to the Federal Penal Institution near Terre Haute, Indiana, 210 miles east of St Louis towards Indianapolis.

Just two months later, on 22 April, Berry and several other prisoners were bussed to Leavenworth Federal Prison, a saddening experience since the journey took him through St Louis and on down Interstate 70 past Wentzville, tantalizingly close to Berry Park. He was only held here for two weeks, however, during which time he headlined at the inmates' hurriedly organized Leavenworth Rock Festival, before he was once more transferred, this time to the Federal Medical Center at Springfield, Missouri, 225 miles south-west of St Louis.

Berry devised a programme of self-improvement to occupy his spare time that, significantly, included studying business management, business law and accounting. Meanwhile, he swabbed the floor and washed up in the canteen. After six months he began work as a medical orderly, but unfortunately for him he was assigned to 'an arrogant and belligerent paraplegic' patient. Wiping an ungrateful arse must have made his former kitchen-porter duties seem like the pinnacle of his career, and after much lobbying he was appointed as secretary of the physical therapy ward and was relieved of nursing chores.

Once he had settled into the routine of prison Berry's inspiration returned, and he began writing again – 'Nadine', 'No Particular Place to Go', 'Tulane', 'You Never Can Tell' and 'Promised Land', each one a solid gold Berry classic. Having decided on the theme of 'Promised Land', that of a journey by the 'po' boy' from Norfolk, Virginia, across the continent to Los Angeles, he hit a predictable problem. He needed a road atlas to check the route and find place names to adorn the lyric, and the prison authorities were somewhat suspicious of an inmate who needed a map.

Among those who heard him working on the songs with his guitar, incidentally, was the Birdman of Alcatraz, and on one occasion during Berry's prison term Springfield was visited by Burt Lancaster, preparing to play the role of the Birdman in John Frankenheimer's 1962 movie about his life. It seems, however, that the two stars did not meet. Berry also worked conscientiously at his studies, receiving a diploma in business administration, and found himself eligible for parole at the first attempt. His father, Toddy and brother Hank collected him on 18 October 1963 in his own Cadillac, which he drove back to St Louis.

Francine had been holding the fort at Berry Park all this time, and Berry himself was anxious to get back to work. The problem was that he needed permission from his parole officer to travel outside the St Louis area, and his plans were often frustrated either by bureaucratic delays or simple refusal. Chicago, for example, was forbidden. So Leonard Chess pulled some strings, succeeded in getting Berry's parole order transferred from Missouri to Illinois, and in an attempt to put his career back on course Berry moved temporarily to Chicago, where his assigned officer was far more lenient and only required retrospective details of his travels.

One early gig, in Flint, Michigan, teamed him with a backing group of Motown musicians. It was intended to cull a live album from the evening, but disagreements with Motown boss Berry Gordy over a royalty for the musicians froze the project, which has remained unissued. From there Berry moved on to The Cow Palace in San Francisco, and to San Diego for a performance at the naval base. Marshall Chess, Phil's son, had been assigned to Berry to ease him back into civilian life, accompanying him on shopping trips for clothes, and acting as his road manager.

In Nadine Cohodas's *Spinning Blues Into Gold*, Marshall complains that Berry never wished to take meal breaks when on the road, driving past restaurants even when his passenger had told him he was hungry. One evening Marshall saw Berry heating up some tinned food on an electric hotplate he carried around with him. 'Too cheap to buy a meal,' was Marshall's verdict. This would fit perfectly with Berry's penny-pinching character, so there's probably some truth in it. However, Berry had experience of restaurants where as a black man he had to eat at the back door off a paper plate, and he'd been turned away from whites-only lunch counters, so there is likely to be another reason. It was animatedly explained by Bo Diddley, talking to George R. White in *Bo Diddley: Living Legend*.

When I was goin' through the South, I used to cook *all* the time. The reason for that was: here am I, gotta go in some white dude's *back door*, an' I've got ten, maybe 15 thousand dollars in my pocket! So I said: "To hell with your *back* door! I'll go and buy me some chicken an' put it in the trunk, get some utensils, put it all on the bus, an' I'll do my *own* cookin'! I *ain't* goin' to your daggone *back door*! You got a *black* cook sittin' up there cookin' up all this shit, an' gonna tell me I *can't come in* the front door? I gotta go round the *back* an' get a *hamburger* because of the colour of my skin? *BULL-SHIT*!

> So, people in the South lost a *lotta* money . . . we'd go in a grocery
> store, buy all our stuff an' stick it in our little cooler on the bus . . .
> Chuck Berry did the same – he always carried a little electric hotplate
> with him, you know.

The only difference is that, while Bo's fried chicken is a celebrated
delicacy, his label-mate was limited to opening a can, but the reason for
self-catering could surely have been the same in both cases.

The most urgent need now was to create new studio product, and
since Berry had a folder full of prime cuts a Chess session was fixed for
15 and 16 November, four weeks after his release. The drummer this
time was Odie Payne, Elmore James's longtime sidekick. Johnson and
Davis were available, together with a second saxophone player James
Robinson, though the studio records do not identify the bass player.

Berry brought along 'Nadine' and 'You Never Can Tell' from the
great prison songs, together with another original, 'The Little Girl
from Central', also known as 'The Girl from Central High'. The tune
is 'Sweet Little Sixteen' revisited, and the way that Berry ends a couple
of verses by singing 'tweet-deedly-do' as a rhyming phrase suggests perhaps that it wasn't fully fashioned.

In order to get a stock of tracks laid down quickly Berry also dipped
into his blues repertoire. He makes a good stab at Guitar Slim's 'The
Things That I Used To Do', with a loping Jimmy Reed beat, but this is
more a compliment to the quality of the song than to anything fresh that
Berry can bring to it. Slim (Eddie Jones) was one of the great originals
of the blues, flamboyant, manic and innovative, a pioneer of expressive
feedback and the use of a long guitar lead which would sometimes
allow him to wander out of the hall, and this impassioned piece was his
finest moment. Born in Mississippi, he died of drink in 1959 at the age
of thirty-two.

In fact this was the only blues from the session to be released, initially as the B-side to 'Promised Land', though Berry also cut Elmore
James's 'Dust My Broom', T-Bone Walker's 'Mean Old World' (the
familiar staple of Berry's live act) and his own substandard 'I'm in the
Danger Zone'. Of greater interest is the obligatory instrumental, 'O
Rangutang'. Even if it does simply wander through the Elmore James
phrasebook it riffs along to a greasy bass rhythm and never lets up for
a second.

He also turned to the country songbook for the dreadful 'Fräulein', a sentimental old warhorse that was familiar to him from childhood but which had been successfully revived by Bobby Helms in 1957, when it reached the top of *Billboard*'s C & W chart. Better, but similarly pointless, is his reading of 'Crazy Arms'. This had been a hit a few months previously for Marion Worth, and so was fresh in his mind, but between them the original 1956 no. 1 by Ray Price and the precocious version that marked Jerry Lee Lewis's debut later in the same year say all that can be said about this classic country ballad.

However, in matrix order Berry laid down his two new masterpieces at the beginning of this two-day session. The little guitar phrase that introduces 'Nadine', and the supple rhythm that is immediately established, are quintessential Berry, and over the top is laid one of his wittiest lyrics, with the singer's frustration echoed in a repeated saxophone wail. 'As I got on a city bus and found a vacant seat, I thought I saw my future bride walking down the street.' An immediate tension is created – is she his 'future bride' in that they are already engaged, or is he simply smitten with love and determination at first sight? As the lyric develops the former seems most likely. The humour Berry extracts from the frustrations of his desperate chase after the girl, by bus, on foot and in a taxi, is strangely reminiscent of one of the greatest pieces of comic writing in the English language – the agonizingly slow bus journey undertaken by Jim Dixon at the end of Kingsley Amis's *Lucky Jim*, also in pursuit of a girl. The Amis passage and the Berry song are both taut, hilarious narratives on the same theme, with Berry offering the precision of poetry, the feel-good mood of comedy and the excitement of rock 'n' roll in one three-minute package.

In total contrast Berry moved on to 'You Never Can Tell', with Johnnie Johnson turning in one of his finest, bell-like piano performances to decorate the charming story of a teenage wedding between 'the young monsieur and madame'. Everything about the performance is joyous, a wonderfully innocent celebration of the young couple's marriage and their setting up home together, with the 'Koolerator jammed with TV dinners and ginger ale'. Pictures taken at this session and published in Fred Rothwell's book show a relaxed, smiling Berry, dapper in crisp white shirt, slim leather tie and plaid waistcoat. He may have emerged from jail with a grudge against the wider world, but back in the studio he was in his element.

'Nadine' was chosen in February 1964 as the first post-prison single, backed by 'O Rangutang'. 'Back Again with another "Chart Buster" . . .' announced a full-page Chess ad in *Cash Box* launching the record. Back again from what was of course not discussed, even in magazine features about the reborn star.

Four years after 'Let It Rock' had dropped out of the chart 'Nadine' climbed to no. 23 in *Billboard*, 32 in *Cash Box*. But in the UK the Berry revival had begun while he was still in jail, with 'Go Go Go', 'Let It Rock' backed by 'Memphis Tennessee', and 'Run Rudolph Run', all part of the new and energetic distribution deal with Pye International, whose rights to Chess made them ideally placed to capitalize on the British blues revival. 'Nadine' reached no. 27 in February, disappeared and then reappeared for a week in April.

# Britain
# takes to
# Berry

T HE 'NADINE' SESSION launched a six-month peak of creativity, culminating in Berry's first trip to the UK, where he travelled the country as a conquering hero. But before that came a monthly sequence of recording sessions, designed to capitalize on his new popularity. He was back in the studio on 20 February without Johnson (Lafayette Leake is listed as being present for part of the evening), with Odie Payne on drums and, so reported English record man and fan Guy Stevens, who was present at the session and wrote about it for *Jazzbeat*, Willie Dixon on bass. If so, he was playing an electric instrument that sounds like a Fender bass and he had adopted a style similar to his protégé Reggie Boyd, so the jury is still out on this detail.

The first effort, 'Big Ben', is a reworking of 'School Day', but the song is concerned with the frustrations of the working day rather than those of school, from the intrusive ring of the alarm clock to the whistle marking the end of the shift, followed by another night's sleep to prepare for the same dull routine once more. Its similarity to the far more original concept of 'School Day', the trailblazing teenage song, meant that it didn't appear in America until the 1990 *Rarities* set, though it came out on a 1964 UK album, which is presumably when it was given its 'tourist' title. The Westminster bell of Big Ben makes no appearance in the song, but as Roger Miller was to point out in the following year with such success, England was swinging in those days.

'Promised Land' was of course the evening's highlight, an irresistible rhythm urging along Berry's account of an epic journey across America in search of California's 'promised land' by Greyhound, train and plane. Berry introduces the song with a brief but characteristic guitar phrase before chugging straight into a complex lyric that never trips over itself, studded with catchy phrases like 'taxi to the terminal zone', which British pub-rockers Ducks Deluxe nicked as an album title. This is a John Steinbeck novel in three minutes of pure rock 'n' roll genius, Woody Guthrie on speed, a road movie in song.

In 1976 a Louisiana schoolteacher called Johnnie Allan cut a version for Jin Records in Ville Platte, produced by label owner Floyd Soileau, which rocks even harder. Like the Capitol sessionmen who helped create Wanda Jackson's stunning version of 'Let's Have a Party', accordionist Belton Richard and the band set up a groove that simply could not be bettered. In the UK Charlie Gillett picked up the track for his Oval label, and Allan was able to lay down his chalk and duster for a brief promotional tour. Oval reissued the cut in 1982, this time with Tommy McLain's aching version of 'Sweet Dreams' on the other side – two slabs of cajun heaven.

Guy Stevens wrote that 'Promised Land' was the first song cut at the session, but since he fails to mention 'Big Ben' it may be that he arrived at the studio after the start. He gives some insight into Berry's working method in the studio when he says: 'Chuck himself supervised entirely the musical side of things . . . Chuck sang the lyrics from his own music sheets, and the rest of the musicians soon fell in with him. [Promised Land] turned out to be so amusing that the studio engineers and Phil Chess himself frequently grinned and laughed during the recording . . . After about an hour and a half about 20 takes of this song were in the can . . .'

Berry was on such a roll at the time that 'Promised Land' could be held back for single release until December. The February session also included a jazzy shuffle called 'Brenda Lee'. Although the lyric, another portrait from Berry's gallery of girls, is rather twee, the song moves along delightfully, and is one of his more successful attempts to step out of character and adopt the persona of a nightclub smoothie. Asked about the song by *New Musical Express*, he called it 'the story of a girl's progression through the various stages of high school . . . It never occurred to me that people might think of the song as a tribute to the singer Brenda Lee', which he described simply as 'a rhythmic name'. Stevens reports that, listening to the playback, 'Chuck expressed his dissatisfaction with "Brenda Lee", but Phil Chess seemed very pleased with the results.'

Five weeks later Berry was back at 2120 South Michigan Avenue, and this time he brought in 'No Particular Place To Go'. Payne was again on the drum stool but Johnson was still unavailable, his place being taken by an unknown pianist called Paul Williams, who may well have taken over from Leake on the previous occasion, and who turns in a job Johnson would have been proud of. Although Berry cheekily raids 'School Day' once again for the melody and structure of the song, this time the subject matter and even the tone of his guitar are so different that one hardly notices.

Cruising along in the car with his girlfriend beside him and the radio playing, the singer's excitement turns to frustration when the lady's seat belt gets stuck. This cautionary tale was rush-released in April and gave Berry his biggest hit since 'Johnny B Goode' six years earlier, reaching no. 10 and no. 9 in *Billboard* and *Cash Box* respectively. It was also his biggest hit to date in the UK, climbing to no. 3 on the wave of publicity that preceded his long-awaited tour, and no Teddy Boy could be without a copy.

The flip side came from the same session, one of Berry's coy, jazzy little throwaways called 'You Two'. But it shuffles along pleasantly, with a nice interplay between piano and guitar, and the lyric is slightly less cloying than, say, 'Vacation Time'. In the UK, however, we were spared the ditty in favour of the third and last result of the evening's work, a far superior cut that, like 'Big Ben', was given a Brit-friendly title – 'Liverpool Drive'. This is a sprightly instrumental, more jazz than rock 'n' roll, and Berry's fluid guitar works its way through his entire bag of Carl Hogan riffs, and builds its way towards a finger-busting climax before the fade. Much of Berry's hugely influential guitar playing is in fact hewn from fairly straightforward elements, but this is a virtuoso display.

There was one more session before Berry took off for the UK, an unscheduled affair in April. Bo Diddley and his band were in the Chess

The lean, mean machine in one of the
archetype rock'n'roll poses, sweating over
his phallic guitar, slowly doing the splits,
chicken-clucking a classic solo that his
fans know note for note.

(Michael Putland, Retna)

Above: Just down the street in St Louis from where Chuck Berry was born on Goode Avenue stands his parents' church, still thriving i a now-deprived area. Left: the young Chuck ir his darkroom. His early fascination with photography was later t prove an embarrassment.

Left: Leonard Chess, the founding father of the legendary Chicago blues label Chess Records, hit the commercial jackpot for the second time when the rock'n'roll of Berry and Bo Diddley challenged the roots music of Muddy Waters and Howlin' Wolf. (Michael Ochs, courtesy of Redferns)

Above: Pianist Johnnie Johnson, seen here in 1997 at the Colne blues festival in Lancashire, was integral to the Chuck Berry sound but, while his partner hoarded his millions, Johnson sank into alcoholism and poverty. Now, thankfully, he is sober and receiving the recognition that he deserves. (Brian Smith)

Right and below: Berry
relaxes, with female
company as ever, backstage
at Bolton Odeon in 1964,
before accepting a lift in
a Ford Popular - a somewhat
more modest vehicle than
the Cadillacs, Jaguars and
Thunderbirds that he
mythologizes in song.
The driver is Neil Carter,
editor of pioneering British
blues magazine R´n´B
Scene. (Brian Smith)

The Ford delivered Berry safely to a Chinese restaurant, where
he celebrates another successful gig on his first UK tour over
dinner with his fans, some of whom have travelled up from as
far away as South Wales. The picture, says the photographer,
´belies the notion of Berry being aloof - at least, he never
was with us in those days´. (Brian Smith)

Above: The Chuck Berry duck walk had its birth when, as a child, he discovered that he could scoot under the table to fetch his rubber ball, thus amusing rather than annoying his mother and her friends from the church. The backing horn section is from King Size Taylor and the Dominoes. (Brian Smith)

Riffing away (above) at Sheffield City Hall in May 1964 - the sax player appears to be Howie Casey - and (right) backstage at Bolton on the same tour. (Brian Smith)

Above and right: Berry's
early LPs mixed hits and
throwaways, but 1972's <u>San
Francisco Dues</u> had a
cohesive feel that took him
into the album era.
Meanwhile (right) he is
always happy to let the
audience do the work.
(Andrew Putnam, courtesy of Redferns)

<u>Hail! Hail! Rock'n'Roll</u> was a 60th-birthday celebration of Berry's
career that drove musical director Keith Richards (left) to
distraction. Eric Clapton, who was struck by Berry's meanness, is
right of picture. (Universal, courtesy of Kobal)

Chuck Berry has always been keen to show off his ding-a-ling, in particular to young white girls. This home movie reached a wider audience than he would have wished.

The Southern Air restaurant was briefly part of Berry's property portfolio, until he was found to have installed video cameras in the ladies' lavatories.

Once an idealistic dream as an inter-racial country club, Berry Park in Wentzville is now off-limits to strangers.

At the age of 75, Berry in concert at
BB King's Bar and Grill, New York City,
in June 2002. (David Atlas, Retna)

studios when Berry arrived. He strolled into the studio and casually borrowed a surplus guitar. Bo Diddley tells the story: 'All that happened was, Chuck came into the studio, an' I asked him how about me an' him doin' a tune together. So, we did somethin'. Then, he had to be down there the next day, so I came down, an' we did another tune.'

Berry recalled the session in a 1969 interview in *Rolling Stone*. 'As I walked into Chess Records' recording studio to do a session at one o'clock, Bo Diddley was still setting up twenty minutes for his new album, which went over into 2 o'clock, and at 1.30 that was still not enough, he needed another five or ten minutes, and so I was asked to sit down and play some stuff to give Bo some ideas . . .'

Bo scotched a rumour that he was often an uncredited presence on Berry's recordings – a rumour that takes no account of the fact that he had an instantly identifiable amplified identity on guitar, and it cannot be heard on any Berry classic. Berry sometimes stole his rhythms for songs like 'Jo Jo Gunne' and 'Brown Eyed Handsome Man', but seemingly never with the great man in attendance. 'It's been said that I played with Chuck Berry on a lot of his recordings, but I never have. I would have *liked* to – because I think Chuck is a *superb* musician – but we only ever did this one thing.'

This one thing turned out to be two long, improvised instrumentals, rambling but energetic, one on each day. 'Someone yelled "Take one" and all of a sudden it was a Bo Diddley–Chuck Berry session,' says the sleeve note to the resulting patched-together album, *Two Great Guitars*. The jams were given the name 'Chuck's Beat' and 'Bo's Beat', though Bo's shimmering guitar leads into the first and his patented rhythm is the basis of the second.

These two rock 'n' roll pioneers, the saviours of Chess Records at a time when the commercial force of old-fashioned urban blues began to weaken in the mid-1950s, had a lot of respect for each other, and have shared a stage several times over the years, so it is appropriate that at least once they should have played together on an album. But of course these long work-outs, 10 minutes 40 seconds and 14 minutes 8 seconds respectively, are a friendly, unstructured swapping of riffs, not compositions, although no true rocker can be without this clash of the Titans. Apart from the full versions which, together with individual instrumentals (Berry's was 'Liverpool Drive'), made up *Two Great Guitars*, they were issued as a Checker single pruned to less than three minutes each, while in the UK Charly Records, during the period of their disputed and ultimately discredited rights to the Chess catalogue, put out halfway-house versions.

The tour to England, with one diversion north of the Scottish border, was promoted by Don Arden. The April edition of the fanzine *Blues Unlimited* was devoted to Chuck and Bo, and announced that the first gig would be at the Finsbury Park Astoria on 9 May. This art deco masterpiece, formerly a cinema and later renamed the Rainbow, was while it lasted the most humane of the big London venues. Berry was scheduled to move on to the Hammersmith Odeon before travelling the country – Birmingham, Nottingham, Stockton, Carlisle, Bradford, Bournemouth, Liverpool, Southampton, Plymouth, Exeter, Croydon, Manchester, Newcastle, Leicester, Cardiff, Glasgow, Bristol and Southend. The package was successful enough for a second Hammersmith show to be hastily added to complete the schedule.

Whoever booked that itinerary for Arden didn't seem to have access to the office road atlas, in days when the motorway network was in its infancy. But at least the trains worked back then, and the tour mixed road and rail as it crisscrossed the country. Early on his journey, probably en route to the Midlands, he was asked by *NME*: 'The first two nights of your tour were very wild. Were you expecting anything like that?' In his distinctively stilted conversational style he replied: 'It was presented to me that it might be this way and I hoped for it. I was surprised in a way that it did happen.'

The groundwork for the tour had been laid a year earlier, with the formation by Mike Bocock in Bolton of The Chuck Berry Appreciation Society. Soon Guy Stevens, who ran the Sue label in the UK, took over, and at the same time Pye Records began their programme of Chess releases. So by the time he arrived we were ready for him. Reviewer Chris Roby was struck by the contrast between his on- and off-stage personality. 'On stage Chuck is constantly on the move, gyrating acrobatically on his long legs and swinging his guitar like a sub-machine gun. His humour is infectious . . .' Meeting him later Roby observed: 'He seems a rather quiet person, courteous and relaxed but not particularly communicative unless pressed, and at times his manner appears a little sad, as though he were remembering harder times.'

It was 43 miles up the A38 from Taunton to Bristol, which admittedly doesn't have quite the same ring as a journey along Route 66 or Highway 61, but we made it to the Colston Hall in good time – one of my art-school friends had a car, a late-teens rarity in those days. The Animals were on the bill with their current hit 'Baby Let Me Take You Home' and a preview of their summer smash 'House of the Rising Sun', The Nashville Teens were plugging 'Tobacco Road', The Swinging Blues Jeans were on a roll with 'It's Too Late Now', 'Hippy Hippy Shake', 'Good Golly Miss Molly' and their new one 'You're No Good', and Kingsize Taylor and the Dominoes did their considerable best to turn the venerable concert hall into a German bierkeller.

The Taylor band were one of that generation of Liverpudlians who, led by The Beatles (and including The Swinging Blue Jeans), cut their teeth in marathon sessions along the Hamburg red-light strip. The Nashville Teens had also been there, even recording with Jerry Lee Lewis at The Star Club, though their origins were in the slightly less funky surroundings of Weybridge in stockbroker Surrey. The Kingsize outfit had started in the 1950s as a skiffle group and never scored a hit, but their storming 'Stupidity' was a cult success, and their blue-eyed British version of R & B was well-honed from those long German nights, sleazy and noisy.

But much as we enjoyed the home-grown talent that warm night, we were really there to worship two kings. Carl Perkins, whose career up to that point had been a stumble through an alcoholic haze, closed the first half. I remember that he had tears in his eyes when he realized how much we loved him. 'The tour lasted four weeks, and during that time I never once got drunk,' he later recalled in his book *Disciple in Blue Suede Shoes*. 'I was experiencing a rendezvous with God each time I walked on stage. For the first time since [his brother] Jay's death, I felt there was still a place for me in music . . . I nearly jumped through the stage many nights from pure excitement.' The tour was the start of his long haul back from addiction, completed when he joined ex-Sun stablemate Johnny Cash as his featured guitarist and they weaned each other off their habitual booze and pills, watching each other for signs of weakening.

And when the top of the bill appeared, lighted cigarettes flew past our ears from the Teddy Boys at the back of the circle, causing God knows what mayhem down in the stalls. Berry rubbed his hands on the dusty stage – 'My daddy told me always play with dirty hands' – and he rocked like a dream. The Kingsize men, along with The Nashville Teens' bespectacled piano player John Hawken, gave him energetic support, and Carl and Chuck had in turn given us a night to remember. Yet all Berry has to say in his autobiography about this historic night is that, in the overnight bus to Southampton, he was treated to a voyeuristic lesbian display by the tour's two dancers. It seems likely that he was actually en route to Southend, the final date of the tour as originally arranged, since Southampton could have been reached after breakfast, and in any case had been visited earlier.

After the Nottingham show Berry made the obligatory visit to *Saturday Club*, one of the BBC Light Programme's two qualified nods towards rock music (the other being Sunday morning's *East Beat* – 'your Sunday best'). This added yet more retraced miles to the itinerary, since he was due in Stockton-on-Tees on the same evening. With Kingsize Taylor and the Dominoes as his backing group he recorded his contribution five days prior to transmission at the BBC's theatre in Northumberland Avenue, south of Trafalgar Square.

Berry was on his best behaviour when interviewed by compere Brian Mathew, describing audience reaction as 'superb' and his musicians as 'great'. He played his first top-tenner 'School Day' followed by 'Memphis Tennessee', which had given his career in the UK such a fresh kick-start, two of his anthems in 'Sweet Little Sixteen' and 'Johnny B Goode' together with the current 'Nadine'.

A glance at the early recordings of both The Rolling Stones and The Beatles is confirmation of the huge influence of Chuck Berry on the bands that were to cause the next revolution after Berry's rock 'n' roll. The young Stones covered 'Come On', 'Bye Bye Johnny', 'Memphis Tennessee' and 'Roll Over Beethoven' (these two for a BBC Radio session), 'Route 66' (learned from Berry, not Nat 'King' Cole), 'Carol', 'You Can't Catch Me', 'Confessin' the Blues' and 'Down the Road Apiece' (again from the Berry versions), 'Around and Around', 'Don't Lie to Me', and 'Beautiful Delilah' (for the BBC). Of their first 100 recordings, one-fifth was taken from Berry. Add in Bo Diddley and the rest of the Chess catalogue and the proportion is one-third.

By contrast, The Beatles wrote their own songs from the outset, and were more eclectic when it came to choosing songs to cover. However, they included their masterly version of 'Roll Over Beethoven' on their second album, *With the Beatles*, 'Rock 'n' Roll Music' appeared on *Beatles for Sale*, and their early stage act included such Berry classics as 'Johnny B Goode'. Lennon's 'Come Together' was a Berry song in spirit, and he always acknowledged his musical debt to Berry above all other influences.

In June 1964 The Rolling Stones made their first visit to the USA. Later Keith Richards recalled their excitement, saying, 'America was fairyland'. Inevitably the trip included a pilgrimage to 2120 South Michigan Avenue, where they were booked for two recording sessions. On the second visit, as Bill Wyman recalls in his autobiography *Stone Alone*, they were stunned to see Muddy Waters outside the building – and even more so when he helped to carry in their guitars.

'We first cut two tracks,' wrote Wyman,

Chuck Berry's 'Confessin' the Blues' and 'Around and Around'. Berry himself walked in and stayed a long while, chatting to us about amps and things. 'Swing on, gentlemen!' he told us. 'You are sounding most well, if I may say so.' This was the nicest I can remember him ever being, but then we were making money for him! I do remember feeling pleased when, while we were recording 'Down the Road Apiece', he said to us: 'Wow, you guys are really getting it on!'

Wyman's recollections capture Berry's habit of speaking English as a second language.

Back in Chicago on 16 August Berry cut his sequel to 'Memphis', 'Little Marie', but it is too similar to the startling original to sound anything but second-hand, and of course it inevitably lacks the twist that gave structure to 'Memphis' – we now know that Marie is a little girl. The day was completed with a characteristic but utterly routine rocker, 'Go, Bobby Soxer', and the two tracks were released in the following month as his next single, reaching no. 54 and 51 in *Billboard* and *Cash Box*.

In November Berry flew back to London. Such had been his success six months earlier that the impresario Robert Stigwood booked him in a hurry to replace P.J. Proby as headliner on a nationwide tour, because he had sacked Proby for his unreliability. Berry, as usual, delayed signing the contract until he was sure that he had squeezed every possible dollar from the deal, but since this was an emergency

Stigwood lost patience and aborted the negotiations. He did, however, nail down Berry to an agreement to return after Christmas for a January tour.

Berry makes no mention of this disagreement in his autobiography, referring only to a brief visit to France at the same time. In Paris he went to bed with 'a five-foot, two-inch, hazel-eyed, frosted-blond girl around twenty-eight years old', an encounter that lasts for two pages, but of the gigs he has nothing to say! Back home again, with 'Nadine' selling strongly his career was at its highest peak since 1958, and he was now averaging $2000 for a night's work – some three times his fee before he went to prison.

On 15 December Berry reported to the Chess studios for his next session. Backing was this time provided by a St Louis club quartet, The Jules Blattner Group, who most unusually for a Berry session did not include a pianist. The evening started with 'Lonely School Days'. Berry was still exploring teenage angst – in fact, he re-recorded this song in 1966 at the age of thirty-nine, in a superior up-tempo version that eventually appeared on the *San Francisco Dues* album – but he is as effective as ever in his description of classroom jealousy, even if the dragging tempo doesn't work. A less familiar theme (although sung to a melody very similar to the previous number) is the subject of 'His Daughter Caroline', which he also speeded up two years later. Berry now plays the role of a father reluctantly giving away his daughter in marriage, and while the sense of loss is well conveyed the effect, as with this version of 'Lonely School Days', is somewhat maudlin.

As was so often the case Berry pulled one pure pedigree rabbit out of the hat during the session, in this case 'Dear Dad'. The topic is a Berry standby, cars, and once more he shed twenty years in thinking himself into the role of a teenager, writing to his father for money to replace his slow and unreliable motor. And as with 'Memphis' there's a twist to the story when he signs his letter 'Henry Junior Ford'. 'Dear Dad' is a straight-ahead rocker showing all the Berry hallmarks – an intricate, witty lyric bolted firmly to a joyful chunka-chunka rhythm, decorated with a couple of characteristic guitar breaks.

The energy is maintained for 'I Want to be Your Driver', a marriage of Memphis Minnie's 1941 double-entendre hit 'Me and My Chauffeur' and the tune of 'Good Morning Little Schoolgirl'. It's a lively addition to the songs in which driving a car is a euphemism for sex, and Berry's vocals are engagingly frantic.

One cut from the session, 'Spending Christmas', has never surfaced, 'The Song of My Love' is one of Berry's awkward and tedious lapses into cod Spanish, and 'Butterscotch' is a routine instrumental with a touch of the twist about it. But the session was par for the course – a very strong addition to the catalogue in 'Dear Dad', one in 'Lonely School Days' that revealed its own charms when later revived as a mid-tempo rocker, and fillers of varying quality. Everything but 'Lonely School Days' was included on an album called *Chuck Berry in London*, which of course it wasn't, and 'Dear Dad' was released in the following March as the follow-up single to 'Promised Land', but it only nudged into the Hot Hundred at no. 95.

On 9 January 1965, though, he really was in London to complete the album. He had launched his new tour on the previous night at Lewisham Odeon, a now-demolished temple of cinema and rock 'n' roll in south-east London. Pye, his UK label, had their own studio in their offices near Marble Arch, and they teamed Berry with one of the support acts on the tour, The Five Dimensions, whose CV included a stint with the 'second' Sonny Boy Williamson. Their programme note says enigmatically that they 'have played at all but one of London's R & B clubs,' without revealing which one stubbornly refused to book them.

'After It's Over' is a bluesy instrumental number giving prominence to The Five Dimensions' new harmonica player Peter Hogman, with Berry happy to play a supporting role apart from one languid solo. The tempo and mood are maintained for the melancholy 'Why Should We End This Way' before Berry moves up a gear to croon 'You Came a Long Way from St Louis'.

It is ironic that Berry should wait until he was in London to sing an anthem to his home town, a 1940s big-band number that was later revived by Bill Jennings, formerly Louis Jordan's guitarist. The city connection apart, it is not really a Berry number, and for some reason he chose to decorate it with shouted 'olé's from the backing group. Far more in character is a straightforward 12-bar rocker called 'She Once Was Mine', with Berry playing the guitar half in his own style and half in tribute to Elmore James. The session was completed by Berry's impersonation of Harry Belafonte on 'Jamaica Farewell', as pointless an exercise as his Spanish practices.

It is noticeable that, on posters and the tour programme, Berry was billed as 'The King of Rhythm and Blues', not as a rock 'n' roller. The programme proclaims: 'The recent British beat group boom producing world famous stars such as The Beatles, The Animals, The Rolling Stones etc. is based on Chuck Berry's original commercial Rhythm and Blues and he is the idol of these and all other R & B groups and their multitude of fans', and the assessment was spot on. It also noted that his favourite hobby was photography, something that would come back to haunt him in later life, and that his favourite colours were white and blue.

He and The Five Dimensions, who opened the show, shared the bill with Winston G (a twenty-year-old solo singer recently signed by Robert Stigwood), The Graham Bond Organization, Long John Baldry and The Moody Blues (still thankfully in 'Go Now' mode at the time rather than in their 'Nights in White Satin' reincarnation). However, a review of the opening night in *Disc* by Rod Harrod suggests that Baldry pulled out at the last moment, since there is no mention of him but Harrod does refer to a singer called Simon Scott.

Harrod was not overwhelmed by Berry's performance. 'Perhaps it was the poor first house audience not providing sufficient atmosphere for him to perform with the accepted gusto,' he reports. 'Or perhaps . . . he is getting too old!' Harrod identified a problem that too often affects Berry gigs: 'One couldn't help but get the feeling that he was just playing the same notes that he has been striking for the last ten years.' According to this reviewer, Berry only turned on the energy for his finale of 'Johnny B Goode' and 'Go, Johnny, Go'.

There is a striking record-company portrait of Berry in the souvenir programme with his head inclined slightly forward, the trace of a mocking smile on his lips and his huge eyes gazing up challengingly at the camera. Just occasionally, and this is one instance, formal studio shots of Berry probed beyond the dapper exterior and illuminated something far more disturbing, deep behind his eyes.

The Five Dimensions had recently parted company with their lead singer and harmonica player Jimmy Powell, and barely survived this tour. Rod Stewart had been in the band for a while but he and Powell were constantly falling out — 'musical and personal differences' was a common euphemism in the pop press of the day. Powell later recalled: 'After the Chuck Berry tour, that was it, and it was a pretty disastrous tour. It was the time when Chuck was shouting abuse to people all over the country – the thing closed down short of where it should have done.'

During the May tour Berry had seemed to be on his best behaviour, affable if reserved with the press, and working hard on stage. It is said that when The Rolling Stones knocked on his dressing room door at Finsbury Park Astoria he sent out a message: 'I'm sorry but I am very busy right now and I don't wish to see anybody.' However, this was just before he was due on stage, so maybe it was more professionalism than discourtesy. But now a darker mood had taken over.

The first indication was his refusal to sign with Stigwood until it was too late to take part in the November tour, a typical Berry perversity. The St Louis group who backed him on the December session at Chess reported that he was surly and uncommunicative, even though they had been booked on his initiative. And as he made his way around the UK in January his behaviour worsened. One celebrated quote, when asked about The Five Dimensions, was, 'Forgive them, for they know not what they do.'

Did Berry really see himself as Jesus Christ, being crucified by his colleagues? It seems more likely that a pretentious way of insulting them floated into his mind, and he wasn't too bothered about its provenance. At gigs he was now more concerned not to play for a minute longer than the contracted time than he was about what the audience thought of him. At Cardiff the crowd turned violent, angry at being cheated by a lacklustre performance. This was in sad contrast to a promise made to *Record Mirror* writer James Craig just before he flew to London. 'On Mr Stigwood's tour . . . I'm gonna make that audience jump like they've never seen a rock 'n' roll show before.' At Cardiff they weren't just jumping, they were hopping mad.

Berry was better behaved when talking to Peter Meaden, also of *Record Mirror*. 'In my songs I try to convey what I have observed, experienced or imagined at one time or another,' he pronounced. 'You'll see that if you listen to the words . . . The melodies I use in my songs are my own. As for treatment, I sometimes regard it necessary to inject an atmosphere into a song . . . say traffic noises, or train noises, for instance. Incidentally,' he concluded, 'the tour is going just great.'

In spite of the 'Forgive them' insult The Dimensions were back at the Pye studio with Berry on 31 January to complete the London album. He began with two rewrites: the listless 'My Little Love Light' is an adaptation of the religious favourite 'This Little Light of Mine', and the slow, effective blues 'I Got a Booking', with Hogman again excelling on harmonica, is the Big Bill Broonzy standard 'Key to the Highway' in all but name. So much for his original melodies. He saved the best until last, however, once again serenading his home town from 6000 miles away. His vocals and chiming guitar solo on 'St Louis Blues' are full of energy and attack, and belie the ill-tempered manner in which the tour was unravelling. On the following day, according to Fred Rothwell's detective work, Berry taped 'Nadine', 'Promised Land' and 'No Particular Place to Go' for transmission the following Saturday afternoon on the BBC Light Programme's *Top Gear* before flying home.

The contrasting atmospheres of the May 1964 and January 1965 tours set a pattern for the remainder of Berry's career – sometimes sublime (Wembley 1972 springs to mind) but too often mechanical, out-of-tune and grudging. His lifelong rival Jerry Lee Lewis is also capable of short-changing his audience, but his contemptuous command of the keyboard is mesmerizing even when he is sleepwalking through a performance. Berry's witty, joyous rock 'n' roll simply collapses when he feels like offering neither wit nor joy.

Johnnie Johnson, whose fear of flying was the other reason, along with Berry's meanness, for the latter to work mainly as a solo act, noticed the change in Berry's mood. 'He wasn't too much different with me, we always got along good,' he says in his biography. 'But I could see him, how he acted with other people, and I knew he had a chip on his shoulder. He was angry at how the law had treated him and he thought everybody wanted to cheat him . . . He was definitely a different person after he got out of prison.'

# goodbye to Chess Records

THE DAYS OF the package tour were not yet dead, and Berry was back on familiar ground with 1965's *Biggest Show of Stars*. Doo-wop group Little Anthony and the Imperials, formed in 1958 with Alan Freed himself suggesting the 'Little Anthony' tag, looked back to the golden age of such caravans while The Shangri-Las reflected the current vogue for all-girl groups. However, the majority of the acts confirmed that the black mainstream had moved on from rhythm-and-blues to soul.

The bill included Florida-born Walter Jackson, a smooth-voiced balladeer currently hot with 'Suddenly I'm All Alone' and 'Welcome Home' on the Okeh label, the ebullient Texan Joe Tex, who was to score in the Hot Hundred no fewer than seven times during that year, Philadelphia's Solomon Burke, a chart fixture since 1961, and the sophisticated Dionne Warwick, who began 1965 by charting with 'Who Can I Turn To' and the defiant 'You Can Have Him'. Were it not for his post-jail renaissance, Berry could have looked a little out of place in such company, a rock 'n' roll has-been. But 'Nadine' had kept him hot.

The commitment to the tour and other live work resulting from his new popularity meant that Berry stayed away from the Chess studios until 1 September, and for the first time since the 'Nadine' session Johnnie Johnson took leave from the steel company to travel to Chicago. The long absence meant that Berry was booked in for three successive nights, with Jaspar Thomas back on drums and a new electric bass player in Chuck Bernard.

He began with a 1948 Louis Jordan hit, 'Run Joe', but apart from the obvious nod to one of his main influences he can bring little to this Caribbean calypso. The same is true of his reading of the 1943 song 'One For My Baby'. Although he makes a brave, melancholy and echo-laden stab at the number, with an unusual interplay between piano and bass, it is indelibly linked with Frank Sinatra, half-sitting on a stool with his jacket draped over his shoulder, porkpie hat tipped back, with a cigarette smouldering on the bar, and the silent barman Joe drying glasses in the background. Berry is not a barfly, and cannot destroy memories of the world-weary Sinatra image – nor, for British fans of a certain age, of the hilarious parody of Sinatra performed by the music-hall comic Dickie Henderson, struggling with stool, cigarette, drink and peanuts.

Berry's own 'It's My Own Business' is an improvement, with some sharp lyrics – 'If I go and buy a Cadillac convertible coupe and all I got at home to eat is onion soup, it's my own business' – together with a catchy blues melody and some spiky guitar work. There is clearly an autobiographical element here, given Berry's penchant for Cadillacs and his habit of heating up cans of food on the road to save money – it's his choice, his business. The standard then droops a little with 'Every Day We Rock and Roll' because, in spite of some more energetic guitar fills, the lyric does little to develop the bland, anthemic title.

All was not lost, however. Almost all the notes Berry plays in 'My Mustang Ford' are familiar, as is the theme (yet another car story, naturally), and yet the energy level, the unusual, treble-heavy tone of the guitar, with Berry making a Gibson sound more like a Fender Telecaster, and his occasional avoidance of the obvious in the guitar breaks salvage the evening.

The second night was less productive – a daft, nursery-rhyme throwaway called 'Merrily We Rock and Roll', a respectable attempt at the Spanish ballad 'Vaya Con Dios' (more successful than most of Berry's journeys south of the border, but one still wonders why he bothered), and a smoky slow blues called 'Wee Hour Blues', on which

Johnnie Johnson stretches out beautifully but cannot disguise the fact that this is simply 'Wee Wee Hours' effortlessly revisited.

The third evening produced the highlight of this extended session, and marked a departure for Berry in that 'It Wasn't Me' was later overdubbed by two of the young white musicians in Chicago who had chosen to 'cross the tracks' into the blues clubs. Given that Berry did not dub on his own guitar lead at the time this may well have been the intention from the start.

In the late 1950s a talented teenage harmonica player, Paul Butterfield, began to sneak into gigs by his hero Muddy Waters, and once he had persuaded Muddy to let him sit in he was regularly invited up on stage. Although he was only seventeen at the time, four years underage for the licensed clubs, he was tall and solidly built enough to get away with it. Guitarist Mike Bloomfield, however, was only fourteen, and had no chance of getting through the door until a few years later. In *Michael Bloomfield: The Rise and Fall of an American Guitar Player*, Ed Ward quotes him as saying: 'From two blocks away you'd hear that harmonica, and then you'd hear Muddy's slide, and I'd be like a dog in heat.'

The book title refers to a 'rise and fall' because Bloomfield ended his life a disillusioned man, laying down soundtracks for porn films before dying of a drug overdose in 1981. But back in the 1960s he and Butterfield, along with University of Chicago graduate and guitarist Elvin Bishop, took the commercially fading art form of the Chicago blues and, like their British counterparts, breathed new life into it by taking it to a mass white audience. And, unlike the British revivalists, they had actually served their apprenticeship at the feet of the masters.

In 1965 the three combined with a former Howlin' Wolf rhythm section, drummer Sam Lay and bassist Jerome Arnold, together with keyboard player Mark Naftalin, as The Paul Butterfield Blues Band, making an eponymous album that launched the home-grown blues revival in America. In that year, with Billy Davenport replacing Lay, they took part in a moment of musical history when, as Bob Dylan's backing band at the Newport Folk Festival, they unveiled the 'electric Dylan' and hastened the next rock 'n' roll revolution. Naftalin continued to play regularly with Berry for several years.

And Butterfield and Bloomfield were also hired by Chess to dress up 'It Wasn't Me', after Berry had launched this rocker with a familiar intro owing much to 'Johnny B Goode'. The lyric is a strong one, with Berry denying knowledge of a whole catalogue of misdemeanours. Butterfield's harmonica drives the song along while Bloomfield adds spiky slide decorations, *Blonde on Blonde* style.

Berry returns to Louis Jordan for a rollicking version of 'Ain't That Just Like a Woman', although for the most part he rewrites the lyrics, and as mentioned earlier he avoids the 'Johnny B Goode' introduction initiated by Carl Hogan's original lead guitar introduction. The mid-tempo 'Right Off Rampart Street' has an effective New Orleans strut to it, while 'Welcome Back Pretty Baby' is a routine West-Coast style blues. 'Sad Day, Long Night' is exactly the same thing in instrumental form, with Butterfield's harmonica replacing Berry's vocals, while the evening's last effort, 'Forgive Me', has never been released in any form. 'It Wasn't Me' was selected for the next single, backed with 'Welcome Back Pretty Baby', but after 'Dear Dad' Berry returned to chart limbo until 1972.

In November he took a three-day break in Hawaii, and as with his European trip a year earlier he travelled with Francine – platonically, it is implied – rather than his wife Toddy. It was, he says, his first-ever vacation, and the first time he had 'stayed overnight in any city without working or playing music'. Clearly holidays made no economic sense to him, but he passed the time pleasantly enough by gazing at the girls on the beach.

Berry's time at Chess Records was soon to come to an end, and what turned out to be his last session at 2120 South Michigan Avenue for over three years was convened for 13 April 1966. With Thomas on drums and Bernard on bass, Johnnie Johnson was for the first time featured on organ as well as piano. 'Ramona, Say Yes' is about the lady's choice of dress – 'the neckline's down south and the hemline's way out west', 'Viva Rock & Roll' is an enjoyable anthem, not without interest in its reference to sister Lucy's classical leanings, and Berry's speeded-up revisit to 'His Daughter Caroline' has never been released.

There was one success to conclude the evening, however: the similarly rethought version of 'Lonely School Days', with its characteristically insistent rhythm track, avoids the maudlin cast of the original and trucks along engagingly. It also suggests that Berry was beginning to experiment with the various foot pedals and special effects that were coming onto the market at the time. His overdubbed lead guitar is not only soaked in echo but has a 'squelch' added to it to give it a sound unlike anything he had tried before, but which he was to take much further on such albums as *San Francisco Dues*. In fact, along with 'Viva Rock & Roll', this version of 'Lonely School Days' was to be included on that 1971 album, but in the meantime it was teamed with 'Ramona, Say Yes' as a June single release, at precisely the time that Berry was preparing to jump ship and leave Chess. A couple of months later, with no new singles coming on stream, Chess reissued the record with 'Ramona' as the A-side and the old 'Havana Moon' on the flip. Neither attempt revived Berry's chart life.

Berry Park, though, was thriving. An admiring piece in the UK fanzine *Soul* noted: 'The task of designing this huge amusement centre was done by Chuck himself – throughout the three years that the Park has been under construction he has never used an architect.' *Soul* puts the construction costs by this stage at $80,000. Sounding like a television travel show, it continues: 'The lake covers most of the front section of the Park, and as you drive up into the picnic/swimming area you can see the guest house, and off in the distance the new lodge, consisting of ten bedrooms, each with private bath, the whole building being centrally heated and air-conditioned. Each room has its own TV set and radio.'

The piece goes on to describe the guitar-shaped pool with its 180,000 gallon capacity, overlooked by the clubhouse with its games room, bandstand, bar and restaurant. At the rear of the clubhouse Berry had built dressing rooms, locker rooms for guests, kitchens and a 'conference room'. At its peak, Berry Park was clearly an impressive facility, and Berry proved to be a pioneer. Later such country stars as Dolly Parton would adopt the idea and develop star-branded amusement parks on a bigger and, to be fair to Berry, a more vulgar, scale. His resistance to white-knuckle rides and fairground attractions may have been prompted by an unwillingness to make the capital investment, but it meant that Berry Park remained true to its 'country club' ideal. If only he had been a golfer (ironically, he now lives in an exclusive golf-club development in St Louis), Berry Park could still be thriving.

# the Mercury
# years

UNKNOWN TO LEONARD Chess, Berry had been in discussions with the major label Mercury for some time. He seemed to sense something that Mercury clearly didn't – that his career was on a downhill slope. Of course this had happened before, but it was now over a year since the very modest chart success of 'Dear Dad', a full eighteen months since he had cut it, and in spite of the occasional second-division track, since then he had largely turned out forgettable material.

Mercury came to him – in the person of one of their senior executives, the musician, arranger and producer Quincy Jones, later to turn Michael Jackson from pop star into commercial phenomenon – and so Berry could guess that top dollar might be involved. The nitty-gritty of the negotiations, however, were conducted by another refugee from Chess, executive Johnny Sippel. Two figures are commonly quoted as the guaranteed advance offered by Mercury for a three-year contract: one is the trumpet-blowing $150,000, a huge amount in the years before the 'rock explosion' of the late 1960s led such executives as Clive Davis at CBS to start hurling millions into the pot. The other figure, the one that Berry usually owns to, perhaps in the knowledge that the taxman might be listening, is the still-handsome $60,000. However, talking to Greil Marcus in 1969 he also quoted $150,000 ('. . . it's spent now'). The contract was signed on 17 June 1966.

'You'll be back in three years,' said Leonard Chess confidently and correctly, though, alas, he died just too soon to know how accurate his prediction was. He was a businessman and so was Berry, and Chess could see that the money was the only reason for the move – and also that the creative control he had allowed his stubborn star would be denied him at Mercury. A spokesman at Chess was quoted as saying: 'Leonard was strictly business . . . [he] wasn't about to give Chuck any more money. He didn't think that Chuck was worth it any more. Mercury obviously did.' In 1967 Berry told Norman Jopling of *Record Mirror*: 'There were no bad feelings. We just shook hands and they wished me good luck. The changeover was just a business deal.'

Historically, the choice of the Mercury label might well have made sense to Berry. Although it was a major imprint in that it had its own national distribution set-up, its home was in Chicago, where it had been founded in 1947 – the same year as Leonard Chess took control over Aristocrat, the forerunner of Chess. One of Berry's heroes, Jay McShann, had been on the label along with other R & B names like Illinois Jacquet and Buddy Johnson, and it was also home to some of the smoother singers that Berry professed an admiration for, like Dinah Washington, Brook Benton and Sarah Vaughan. Above all, Louis Jordan had signed with Mercury in 1956, after his long association with Decca.

And yet Jordan's experience should have been a warning to Berry, since Mercury's main interest was in getting Jordan to recut his Decca hits so that they too could exploit the titles. Although Berry could hardly have been innocent of the fact that Mercury would require the same of him, maybe the money muffled the alarm bells. Certainly he later came to regret such meaningless recycling. In 1987 he told Tom Wheeler of *Guitar* magazine, somewhat wistfully: 'Mercury just wanted me to re-record my hits so they could have masters of their own.' And he dismissed the tracks. 'They were not as good,' he said tellingly, 'because I couldn't get them [his backing musicians on the Mercury sessions] to play like Johnnie.'

And this in spite of the fact that Johnson was actually playing on most of them – though he claims never to have bothered to listen to the results. In fact, he denies being there at all! 'I've never heard what Chuck did at Mercury, but from what I've been told, they ain't too good,' he told Travis Fitzpatrick. 'I don't know why he didn't want me to play on them albums, and I wasn't 'bout to ask him his reasons. That's one thing 'bout Chuck — he don't like to be asked a lot of questions 'bout his business.' The Mercury session files confirm Johnson's presence, so he has contracted either professional or alcoholic amnesia.

With the arguable exception of The Everly Brothers, who moved from Cadence to Warner Brothers and beautifully recreated their early hits with the help of Nashville's finest, these retreads have never equalled the originals, and no one would claim that even the Everlys *surpassed* the early versions. Did anyone seriously think, for example, that Little Richard could ever recapture the revolutionary flame of those 1950s Specialty sides? Undoubtedly not, but Richard had cash in hand and several companies have titles they can call *Greatest Hits*, to be found these days on the counters of corner shops and garages. At least Berry was in good rock 'n' roll company.

Anxious to please their new signing, Mercury arranged for Berry's first batch of sessions to be held conveniently at Technisonic Studio in Clayton, St Louis, setting dates for 20 and 21 September, 26 and 27 October. The first day produced the usual instrumental warm-up, in this case a lively work-out called 'Campus Cookie', followed by a fragment of family discord, 'Mum's the Word'. Berry also recreated the 'Wee Wee Hours' mood with an effective slow blues, 'Laugh and Cry'. Finally there came 'My Tambourine', Berry's first variation on the 'My Ding-a-Ling' theme.

The song first surfaced in the 1950s sung by Dave Bartholomew, Fats Domino's bandleader and a New Orleans recording artist in his own right, although this is the type of song that probably has a long and obscure folk pedigree. Bartholomew cut it twice, as 'My Ding-a-Ling' and 'Little Girl Sing Ding-a-Ling', but few were listening. It resurfaced as 'Toy Bell' by The Bees before being rewritten by Berry. His version is perhaps most notable for the line, 'I was talking to a girl in the vestibule,' an unusual place for a conversation in a pop song. The tambourine of the title clearly belongs to the singer, although its appearance in the equally rude song about a virginal Salvation Army girl who 'broke her tambourine' would seem to make more anatomical sense.

Either way, this childish ditty can now be forgotten until its fateful reappearance in Coventry six years later.

On the following day the retreads began – 'Maybellene' (though now spelt 'Maybelline'), 'School Day', 'Sweet Little Sixteen', 'Johnny B Goode', 'Memphis', 'Roll Over Beethoven' and 'Rock 'n' Roll Music'. If you went to a Berry concert and he and the pick-up band put on a show like this you'd feel that you'd got your money's worth. On record, though, they have the air of a confidence trick. A great record has a charisma that goes beyond the song itself, beyond the performance and the production. It still has the spontaneity of its creation (even if it's the thirty-sixth take before Leonard Chess is satisfied), it will have little accidental moments that help to define its unique character, and it has its place in history. Particularly if it is a song like 'Maybellene', which re-routed the flow of popular music. The Mercury cuts are 'greatest hit titles', not 'greatest hits'.

On 26 October 'Around and Around', 'Back in the USA' and 'Thirty Days' got the new treatment. Berry also cut a badly produced narrative about a football match, 'Oh Captain', which Mercury turned into gibberish by editing it so that the game starts in the middle before going back to the beginning, and an up-tempo rewrite of 'Don't You Lie to Me' called 'Misery'. The most useful result of the day was 'Club Nitty Gritty', about a country bar that sounds made for Johnny B Goode to play in, with Berry putting some welcome muscle into his voice. With 'Laugh and Cry' as the flip, it was his first Mercury single in January 1967, but it didn't threaten the charts. On the following day, for the fourth Mercury session, 'Carol', 'Brown Eyed Handsome Man', 'Let It Rock', 'Reelin' and Rockin'' and 'Almost Grown' were led to the execution block. Berry had fulfilled the first and main requirement of his lucrative contract, with more skill than enthusiasm.

If the Alan Freed packages, riots or no, were a reminder of Berry's earliest days on the road then a gig on 24 January 1967 and a three-day booking for 17–19 February were pointers to the future. For the first, at Soul City Club in Dallas, he was supported by Janis Joplin, a full eighteen months before she and her new band Big Brother and the Holding Company broke through with 'Piece of My Heart'. 'I thought she was rather bold to appear on stage with a drink in her hand,' was Berry's prim comment. He was then billed with The Grateful Dead at

San Francisco's temple of hippiedom, Bill Graham's Fillmore Auditorium. The Dead had only just assumed the name that was to carry them through as one of the most successful live acts in rock music for decades to come, having previously traded as Mother McCree's Uptown Jug Champions and then The Warlocks, still pretty much R & B in spirit.

Berry noted in his autobiography a change in his audiences. 'During my concerts in the middle of the 1960s, multitudes of young university students and festival-goers were indulging in smoking grass. There seemed to be a unanimous acceptance of the use of marijuana as opposed to liquor. I was being offered joints at the foot of the stage . . .' One such occasion was at a religious college, of all places, in the presence of nuns and police officers. To great applause Berry accepted a toke, but says that he soon realized that he should be setting an example, and refused further such opportunities.

On 21 March Berry had a three-day recording date at the Royal Recording Studios in Memphis, Tennessee, and the improvement in quality after the re-recorded hits was remarkable. The city's finest were there in support – guitarist Reggie Young, pianist Bobby Emmons, bass player Tommy Cogbill and drummer Jerry Arnold were augmented by a horn section of Gene Miller, James Mitchell and one half of the legendary Memphis Horns, Andrew Love.

All twelve cuts were made use of on the album *Chuck Berry in Memphis* (although his reading of the Benny Goodman/Lionel Hampton classic 'Flying Home' had to wait for the 1989 CD issue) while 'Back to Memphis' was a natural as the second Mercury single. The band set up a characteristically tight, driving riff over which Berry sings about his new-found home, the lines punctuated by spiky little guitar figures. Admittedly it has a similar feel to the debut single 'Club Nitty Gritty', but it is a superior song.

The flip of the single was a slow, melodic blues, 'I Do Really Love You', the tune of which is largely based on Jimmy Reed's 'Honest I Do' with just a hint of Alvin Robinson's 1964 New Orleans strut 'Something You Got'. The first day also produced perhaps Berry's finest nod to Nat 'King' Cole, a sparsely produced revival of 'Ramblin' Rose', and a characteristic rocker, 'Check Me Out'. Although Berry brings nothing new to it, the shared guitar break with Reggie Young makes for an intriguing contrast in styles – black country and white soul, in fact.

Day two saw another return to Nat 'King' Cole, not the superstar of 1962's 'Ramblin' Rose' but the trio pianist–singer of 1942's 'Bring Another Drink'. Berry's version slinks along nicely to a restrained horn backing. His revival of The Spaniels' 1954 classic 'Goodnight, Well It's Time to Go' has long been part of the climax to Berry's stage act, here complete with excruciating verses in French. Far superior is Ruth Brown's 1949 hit 'So Long'. Berry is the first to admit he's no soul singer, but this is at the slow, bluesy end of the pre-soul spectrum, and with its beautifully judged backing it is the highlight of a day that was completed with a chunky version of Elmore James's 'It Hurts Me Too', which naturally lacks all the desperate passion of the great original.

On the third day, 'My Heart Will Always Belong to You' is probably one slow blues too many for a balanced album, but Berry plays an ace when he gets to the guitar solo, pulling out a number of surprise variations on his familiar runs. He then makes a fair stab at the big-band swing of 'Flying Home' but clearly not to his satisfaction – he was to surpass it at the second attempt during his next session. The Memphis visit concluded with OK revivals of 'Sweet Little Rock 'n' Roller' and 'Oh Baby Doll', slightly rethought rhythmically, but to little purpose. Nevertheless, *Chuck Berry in Memphis* undoubtedly has its moments.

Berry celebrated by indulging in what had now become an annual ritual, buying a new Cadillac. He says that he had discovered that the trade-in price was not worth having, and so by this time he had about six such cars, handed on to family or employees. This looks forward to the amusing scene in the film *Hail! Hail! Rock 'n' Roll* where he peels back the plastic covering from a fleet of exotic vehicles, saying that he refuses to sell them because he cannot get what he believes to be the right price. This indicates something about his character, surely – he has his notional price for everything, including his services, and will not drop below it, even if it means a garage full of ghost automobiles. Similarly he has said that if the going rate for his forty-five-minute live act ever drops below $1000 he will have no option but to retire.

So he holds to his price, even if it means turning down the invitation to appear at the Monterey Pop Festival on 16–18 June 1967. He could not get the fee he wanted, and so missed out on the gaudy, exhilarating occasion that made stars of Jimi Hendrix and Otis Redding among white fans, and in many ways launched the new age of rock. Berry was already known to them, of course, but as something from the past. His stubborn way with a deal sacrificed the opportunity to re-establish his credentials at a dangerous moment in his career.

Instead, a week later found him back at the Fillmore Auditorium, backed by a group that was beginning to build a local reputation, The Steve Miller Band. They *had* been at Monterey, and went on to a career that reached its peak with 'The Joker'. The booking was for a week, with Eric Burdon (familiar to Berry from the 1964 UK tour) and his New Animals in support. Mercury taped two of the gigs to use on the album *Chuck Berry Live at Fillmore Auditorium*, its cover in the swirling, colourful graphic style that came to epitomize West Coast rock poster design.

'Rockin' at the Fillmore' is a revival of Berry's 'Rock at the Philharmonic' and here it is eventually transmuted into a stomping version of 'Everyday I Have the Blues'. The elderly blues 'C.C. Rider' had been turned into rock 'n' roll in 1957 by Chuck Willis, but Berry's shuffling version is in a lower key. Next up was a third-rate revisit to Charles Brown's 'Drifting Blues', followed by a guitar–organ instrumental called 'Feelin' It', chosen in November as the B-side to the next single behind a new version of 'It Hurts Me Too'. The last track cut on the first night at the Fillmore was Berry's brisk return to the Goodman–Hampton classic 'Flying Home', and it is a considerable improvement on the Memphis take.

Two nights later Berry started with a second-best version of Willie Dixon's great Muddy Waters hit 'I'm Your Hoochie Coochie Man', now with modish reference to marijuana. It was followed by a far superior stab at 'It Hurts Me Too', chosen as the single to follow 'Back to Memphis', and the 'first' Sonny Boy Williamson's 'Good Morning Little Schoolgirl'. An improvised 12-bar called 'Fillmore Blues', another version of Big Joe Turner's 'Wee Baby Blues', a dire revisit to Nat 'King' Cole's 'Bring Another Drink' and a decent 'Worried Life Blues' came next. Although it was not released at the time, Berry moved on to a rude rewrite of 'Reelin' and Rockin'', the first example of what has been a concert staple ever since, and then to a tentative middle-period 'My Ding-a-Ling', before rushing through a 'Johnny B Goode' finale. Mercury culled the ten-track album from the two nights for November release.

Just before Christmas Berry was back in San Francisco for an unproductive meeting with The Sir Douglas Quintet, the Doug Sahm–Augie

Meyers Texan band now resident in the city and signed to Mercury. Only two cuts were ever released and they're not bad, the up-tempo 'Soul Rockin'' and the blues 'I Can't Believe'. But the Quintet's collective mind wasn't really on the job, according to Berry.

'The whole quintet would go off into the corner of the room in a huddle for eight to twelve minutes.' After three of these interruptions Berry discovered that they were worshipping at an altar of 'neatly placed herbs'. When he went into the control room to complain about this he found that the producer and engineer were similarly engaged. This working routine was soon to reward the Quintet with their second big hit, after 1965's Beatles-inspired 'She's About a Mover', in the glorious country groove of 'Mendocino'. But it wasn't a method that appealed to the business-like Berry. The tracks did appear a year later on the fourth Mercury album, *From St Louie* [sic] *to Frisco*, a ragbag of the sessions to date.

At around this point in his autobiography Berry confirms where his heart really lies. Having detailed the stages whereby agency, national taxes, state taxes and on-the-road expenses hack away at this earnings, he says: 'There is no such tax on real estate, which attracted me to investing in property. When my bank account arose to a height that half of it could purchase 75 per cent of a building I had chosen, I'd buy it.' Such mathematical precision contrasts with the throwaway comments on a catalogue of songs that have provided a soundtrack to so many lives.

Berry stayed out of the studio until 1 July 1968, when he returned to San Francisco in the company of his then seventeen-year-old daughter Darlin Ingrid and an unidentified band, although the pianist's style suggests that it is Johnnie Johnson. The highlight was a return to the wistful 'Song of My Love', previously recorded for Chess but spoilt by Berry's insistence on singing in cod Spanish. Now, duetting with Ingrid, he finds some simple beauty in the song. He also cut 'Ma Dear', with its New Orleans groove; a very brief but promising rocker in 'Rock Cradle Rock'; a slow blues 'The Love I Lost'; the up-tempo 'Louie to Frisco'; the six-minute love song 'I Love Her, I Love Her'; and an uneasy number called 'Little Fox', where Berry sings somewhat inappropriately to his daughter. 'Louie to Frisco' and 'Ma Dear' were briskly issued as the next single.

In August 1968 Berry bought the cinema building in Wentzville, and since the burden of actually running it inevitably fell on Francine, she moved her office from Berry Park into the cinema. The venture failed, however, something that Berry puts down to small-town racism. Some of the townspeople, it seems, were not willing to accept a black employer and a white secretary in their midst, and hinted that 'secretary' was in any case a euphemism. When a brick came through the office window Francine moved back to the park, and with the bigotry causing falling attendances the cinema was soon uneconomic, so Berry closed it down. Undeterred, however, he invested in another Wentzville property, renting out the ground floor with the intention of using upstairs as an office, and also installed another secretary, Rona Pfeffer, at Berry Park, buying a huge trailer for her to live in. Later she moved into the main building.

Before long a girl fan, Candy, was also living at the park, together with casual workers who would earn room and board by working around the estate. This was the peak of the Berry Park experiment, now open to the public with dances in the music room every weekend and a constant feeling of activity, although just a year later a catastrophic fire was to damage the dream. However, from 6 January 1969 the community no longer included Francine, who suddenly decided to quit and return to Pennsylvania. She would not stay away for long, suggesting that this strange friendship, though basically a business relationship, had an additional element of emotional interdependence.

# back home

**I**N THE MEANTIME, however, one of the key features of Berry Park, the recording studio, was up and running. A session in January 1969 was the first time that tracks were produced there for release, and Berry had recruited a new band including St Louis guitarist Billy Peek, who is still playing around the city. For live work, Peek could perfectly reproduce Berry's trademark rhythm, leaving the bandleader to concentrate on the singing and solos, and Peek could also play piano and blues harmonica. This was the first time that Berry had taken musicians on the road with him since the early days. The band was completed by bassist 'Kermit' Eugene Cooley and drummer Dale Gischer.

In the mid-1970s Rod Stewart, having seen Peek backing Berry on a television show, lured him away from Berry to play on such rockers as 'Hot Legs', and so Peek transferred his loyalty from one notoriously tightfisted employer to another. But throughout the early 1970s he was a regular in Berry's band.

The results of the Wentzville sessions made up what was to prove a farewell package to Mercury, the disappointing album *Concerto in B Goode*, which sold poorly. 'Good Lookin' Woman' is based on the Elmore James riff but there is too much going on in the background, including a squelchy wah-wah guitar out of keeping with the drive of the song. 'My Woman' is a pleasant slow blues, 'Put Her Down' less so, since it is yet another variation on 'It Hurts Me Too' – in fact, it's plagiarism. The most original song, a narrative about a girl who is afraid of the dark called 'It's Too Dark In There', which causes the same sort of frustration to her suitor as the jammed seat belt in 'No Particular Place To Go', is also compromised by Berry's new-found fascination with guitar gizmos.

Side Two of this take-it-or-leave-it set was devoted to the title track, more than eighteen minutes of guitar doodling over a bustling bass line. There are some effective chord changes but this is little more than Berry demonstrating what sort of noises his studio can achieve. It is a concerto without any structure and little virtuosity, just a lot of quacking guitars and wah-wah pedals. Various other tracks, including a slow version of 'Concerto in B Goode', remained mercifully in the can. Mercury, with little option, chose 'It's Too Dark in There' as the August single, backed by 'Good Lookin' Woman'.

Meanwhile in May Berry fulfilled an unusual double booking on the university campus at Berkeley, California – an evening gig preceded by a lunchtime 'lecture' in the Students' Union to a standing-room-only crowd. *Rolling Stone* writer Greil Marcus fed Berry the questions and the transcribed session made the cover feature of the magazine on 14 June, a notable tribute to the veteran rocker from the fortnightly bible of long-haired hippiedom. As was noted earlier, Berry churlishly claimed to have forgotten the names of the 'jive musicians' who helped him with his first demo tape, and said that 'Maybellene' was cut with 'some Chicago musicians'. He was, however, consistent in naming the trinity of Charlie Christian, T-Bone Walker and Carl Hogan as the main influences on his guitar style.

When asked if he would have written songs without a commercial incentive, Berry disappoints any artistic idealists in his audience. 'No, I wouldn't have had time. The commercial value in songs is a great instigator.' Later, he says: 'The dollar dictates what music is written.' In spite of this, he claims not to know the extent to which The Beatles had assisted his royalty earnings. Naturally no reference is made to his time in prison, although Berry alludes to 'a lull in recordings' as the reason he wanted people to make a link between his comeback song 'Nadine' and his first hit 'Maybellene' to re-establish himself in their minds. He also claims that the similarity of the 'No Particular Place to Go' and 'School Day' melodies was deliberate, for the same reason.

Berry tells a story that illustrates the unique catering arrangements necessary in the racist south. 'Bobby Charles [Louisiana writer of such hits as 'See You Later Alligator', 'But I Do' and 'Walking to New Orleans'] and I had a tour once of eleven days and we had a swing thing goin' – he would go in the front door and I would go in the back door; he would come and bring me the warm meal, and incidentally he likes sandwiches. We'd switch out front because I ate meals and he ate sandwiches. We even got stopped for riding together . . .'

It became clear during the course of the conversation that Berry regretted the move to Mercury, apart from the advance. 'Since I have been with Mercury, things haven't been going too well . . . I have kept in constant contact with Chess Records. I like little companies because there is a warmer relationship between the artist and the executive. I shall be going back soon, to Chess Records . . .' He was to find out that it wasn't the Chess he had left, the Chess of this wistful memory, but in his own mind he was going home.

The problem with referring to a 'rock 'n' roll revival', as with a revival in the blues itself, is the implication that the music could have spent time in a comatose condition, or forgotten, or even as dead as Lazarus. But this is the music that has nourished everything that has since happened in pop. As Berry himself put it: 'Rock 'n' roll never had heart trouble and thus did not need to be revived.' Maybe, though, a generation that thought of rock stars as being long-haired and white needed reminding occasionally.

Just after Christmas 1968, the Miami Pop Festival found Berry in top form. The three-day bash, 28–30 December, assembled an eclectic bill that included hard rockers Steppenwolf and Iron Butterfly, The Grateful Dead, Procol Harum, Fleetwood Mac, The Paul Butterfield Blues Band, harmonica bluesman James Cotton and Booker T and the MGs. Berry's flared-trouser transformation from package-tour star to the elder statesman of the festival scene was complete. His longtime Beverly Hills agent, Dick Alen of the William Morris Agency, diversified Berry's bookings in an attempt to maintain relevance in a rapidly changing music industry. To the traditional diet of concerts and cabaret appearances he added college and festival bookings.

Nineteen sixty-nine was the climactic year of the rock festival. It reached its height at Woodstock and then the smiling, stoned, free-wheeling, shambolic spirit of the rock festival came to an end in the same year, on 6 December, at a stock car track called Altamont, 15 miles from Berkeley. The Rolling Stones wanted to play a free concert and after endless hassles a site was provided. Disastrously, control of security was given to the Hell's Angels, in the hope that getting them 'on side' would keep violence under control. The experiment failed disastrously when Meredith Hunter, a black man with a white girl-friend, was stabbed and kicked to death by the Angels.

Berry, meanwhile, missing out on Woodstock and no doubt grate-ful to have nothing to do with Altamont, appeared at the less notorious Seattle and New Orleans pop festivals instead. And there was also Toronto, which became rather hijacked when John Lennon chose it as the launch pad for his first post-Beatles venture The Plastic Ono Band, complete with shrieking Yoko and bemused Eric Clapton, but it had started out as a celebration of rock 'n' roll. Indeed, it used that con-tentious term for its banner – Toronto Rock 'n' Roll Revival. It was held at the Varsity Stadium, a huge sports arena attached to the University of Toronto.

This was Lennon's first appearance on stage since The Beatles' Candlestick Park farewell in San Francisco three years earlier, and what had been intended as a rock 'n' roll spectacular was hurriedly rebranded the Toronto Peace Festival. But it was still the rock 'n' roll acts that gave the day its identity, even though Chuck Berry decided to wear a huge Ban the Bomb medallion and kept shouting 'Peace'.

Promoters John Brower and Ken Walker invited film-maker D.A. Pennebaker to record the event. His subsequent footage has undergone various edits, including a version as *Live Peace from Toronto*. Once it was accepted that Yoko screaming from inside a bag, accompanied by feed-back from Clapton's abandoned guitar, was not the best way to send an audience dancing into the streets, and probably did little for world peace, the film began to concentrate on its rock 'n' roll heart.

Brower and Walker booked the best imaginable bill – Berry, Jerry Lee Lewis, Bo Diddley, Gene Vincent and Little Richard. They sur-rounded them with a compendium of late-1960s acts – jazz-rockers Chicago Transit Authority, the swampy Tony Joe White, cajun virtuoso Doug Kershaw, Britain's music-hall rock 'n' roller Screaming Lord

Sutch, 'revivalists' Cat Mother and the All-Night Newsboys and the extravagant Alice Cooper.

Of the rock 'n' roll legends, Bo was elected to open the show, in the company of the latest in the line of his female singer-musicians, Cookie. Later Jerry Lee Lewis stormed into 'Mystery Train' and kept up the tension, determined to make life tricky for the act to follow him – Berry – just as he had whenever the running order insulted him in this way.

Lewis turned in a dynamic set, but Berry had nothing to fear in Toronto – it was his sixth appearance in the city that year, surely making the 'revival' tag redundant. Later still, Gene Vincent picked his way onto a stage that had been recently vacated by Alice Cooper and his squawking, feather-shedding live chickens. Alas, Vincent had been waiting in the heat too long, quenching his thirst. Although he provoked the first dancers from the crowd to take to the stage he was tearfully drunk, and his set was omitted from all but the very first cut of the film. Little Richard won back the crowd with his usual mix of camp, hammed-up rock 'n' roll and striptease, before compere Kim Fowley got the audience to light matches and cigarette lighters to greet The Plastic Ono Band. Berry took note of the effect, and lit up Wembley three years later. Nowadays, presumably, too many of us are lapsed smokers for this home-made light show to be spectacular.

Writing in *Music Now* Roy Carr caught the tone. 'This wasn't just a cavalcade of tired, outdated, half-forgotten old-timers, quite the reverse; here were the true heroes, the original trend setters, who between them had written and waxed hundreds of all-time hits of rock 'n' roll. Each a headliner in his own right performed in the much-copied style that had made him a living legend.' In writing about the Ono band Carr noted: 'It was only when John and Eric started to belt out "Blue Suede Shoes", "Dizzy Miss Lizzy" and "Money" that it was obvious that when you've scraped away all the commercial tags, labels and trappings it's still just good old rock 'n' roll . . .'

The point is well made. Lesser talents than Berry, if they are to keep working, are limited to small-scale cabaret appearances seeded with occasional nostalgia packages – if you put enough minor-league names like Brian Hyland and Little Eva together they will attract a crowd, but the music will inevitably be frozen in time, a mere trigger for middle-aged memories. But Berry goes on being 'relevant' because he started it all – he is a living, guitar-toting confirmation that rock 'n' roll has a culture and a history to be cherished. During the festival era he was as capable as ever of being embarrassingly bad, but not embarrassingly old – the cult of youth could not diminish his stature.

He had now caught up with the times in terms of gents' outfitting. Amid the psychedelic swirls of the Fillmore album cover, two years previously, his slim brown suit had been an anachronism. By Toronto he had adopted the sartorial style that has, by and large, served him ever since, in this case a billowing white shirt trapped beneath a gaudy waistcoat, with matching tight trousers. His hair was getting a little longer, too.

Backed by local group Nucleus, the Berry set started chaotically with 'Rock 'n' Roll Music' and there were further occasional moments of non-communication between maestro and terrified hired hands, but in general he was in good and good-natured form. And, as Fred Rothwell reminds me, he even did an encore! In various permutations, this performance has been frequently available on record as well as in Pennebaker's film.

On 21 November Berry anticipated the end of the Mercury deal by recording in Chicago's Ter-Mar studio, with the clear intention of reviving his career on Chess. The drummer is not known but Lafayette Leake was there on piano, while the bass player was Phil Upchurch. He is still best known for his 1961 combo recording 'You Can't Sit Down', an exhilarating organ-led instrumental that reached no. 29 in America and no. 39 in the UK, and later he was retained by Chess as a session musician. Completing the band was a St Louis musician, Bob Baldori, on harmonica – he would have played piano had Leake not been around, and he had supported Berry in Detroit on the previous evening.

Baldori, with or without his club band, was to become a regular Berry sidekick for many years – including a celebrated 1994 gig at The White House at the request of President Clinton. He has always juggled two careers, as Boogie Bob the musician and as Robert Baldori, member of The National Association of Criminal Defense Lawyers. More relevantly he has often turned his legal expertise towards the negotiating of show-business contracts, and worked for both Chess and Tamla Motown on their distribution deals. His CV as a lawyer includes the statement that 'clients have included . . . Chuck Berry', who repaid him in his autobiography by getting his name wrong. Reminiscent of his response to a question at the Berkeley forum: 'Not to my knowledge have I talked with this person of whom you spoke – Dick Jagger?'

Wearing his Boogie Bob hat Baldori and his band The Woolies had a hit in March 1967 when their cover of Bo Diddley's 'Who Do You Love' reached no. 95 on the *Billboard* chart, and the album of the same title included covers of Berry's 'Back in the USA', Magic Sam's 'Easy Baby', Willie Dixon's 'Little Red Rooster' and Buster Brown's 'Fannie Mae'. The Woolies, including Bob's brother Jeffrey on guitar and Bee Metros on drums, have played hundreds of dates with Berry in the course of thirty-five years, and they get a name check in Berry's song 'Festival'. It's certainly a band with stamina, since their relationship with Berry continues. It began at the time that 'Who Do You Love' was still being played on the radio.

Bob, who always refers to Berry as Charles, recalls: 'I walked into The Dells, which was a roadhouse in Haslett, Michigan, not knowing what to expect. There was a pretty weird band opening the show. Sort of an Alice Cooper imitator, making ear-splitting noise. Then Chuck takes the stage. He is electrifying. But the band doesn't get it. Like recalcitrant teenagers. After the show Joe Oade, the owner, catches up with me and asks what it will take to get me to work with Charles. This is a five-day engagement. In retrospect, sort of an amazing fact – what would it take to get Charles to play anywhere for five nights? Of course, it doesn't take much to get us to work the gig.

'Next night we show up for a sound check. He comes into the dressing room and barely communicates. What do I remember? Bomp, ba bomp for the bass. Don't drop down to the four on turnarounds. That was about it! We were so worried about Spyder [The Woolies' bass player at the time] collapsing on us, and he was so scared, that I played bass for the first set. Chuck kept staring at the piano. After the set he asks: 'Who plays that?' When I told him it was me he says: 'Shame on you!' and makes me play piano on the second set. After that we were off and running . . .'

As Baldori recalls it, Berry seemed to be an enthusiastic communicator on stage, although he was clearly a private person off it: 'Charles had that twinkle in his eye. He didn't miss the irony of four white kids from Dearborn being soulmates with the founder of rock 'n' roll. We fitted together as tight as you could fit, even with Spyder on bass.

'I don't recall a lot of interaction with Charles off stage during that week, although we did get to know one another and had dinner together several times. Breaking bread with Charles was always an event . . . No matter what the subject, he had a different take on it. It was never what you might expect.

'He could be sociable, but he could also turn into a lone wolf. It was my first experience of him disappearing into a crowd, becoming almost invisible. Then he would turn up at your elbow . . . Amusing himself by drifting around and turning up in places you would never expect to find him. Enjoying the surprise his appearance created . . .'

As soon as Berry knew he was going back to Chess, he called on Baldori to add some harmonica to that November session in Chicago. The session began with Berry's final masterpiece to date, 'Tulane', and its sequel song 'Have Mercy Judge', a natural pairing for the first single of his new Chess period the following August. Tulane and her partner Johnny are drug dealers, not vulgar street-corner merchants but proprietors of a 'novelty shop', and as Johnny is carted away by the police he shouts advice to Tulane about how to keep herself in the clear. The song has the drive, wit and freshness of Berry at his finest – the 'Nadine' period, for example.

It is on Berry's assertion that I earlier included 'Tulane', along with 'Nadine', among the remarkable clutch of songs written during the prison sentence following 'the Indian trial'. Stylistically it makes sense – from here on Berry could rarely see a wah-wah pedal without switching it on. Creatively it makes sense – he still had a few great songs to come, but none so clearly in the 'Johnny B Goode' tradition that he was still working with in 1963. And it's hard to know why Berry, such a determined liar on so many subjects, merely careless or absent-minded on others, should want to *pretend* that he wrote 'Tulane' in 1963 and not 1969.

But there is something that doesn't quite make sense, quite apart from the fact that Berry recorded so much dross in the intervening years that, even in unfinished form, he must have been tempted to pull this one out of the drawer – unless he had deliberately tucked it away as a homecoming gift to Chess, always knowing that he'd be back. The main problem is his chirpy, sympathetic attitude to drug dealing, his identification with Johnny, who could be Johnny B Goode in a later career. His distaste for alcohol remained constant, but he was now admitting to the occasional indulgence in grass, and this was made explicit in the 1971 monologue 'My Dream'. And beyond that, he was consciously attempting in many songs to write for his new hippie audience.

Even if he remained resolutely anti-drugs in his private life, he would presumably be content to write a song with harmless, happy, hippie drug dealers as heroes if he thought it would sell, or increase his credibility in the new market. He could not have felt this so easily in 1963 as six years later, when 'recreational' drugs were commonplace. Maybe there is a halfway house, with 'Tulane' indeed being sketched out in jail, perhaps inspired by a real-life dealer in Springfield, to be reworked later.

In 'Have Mercy Judge' Johnny faces the inevitable, and with the prospect of jail his main concern is that Tulane will presumably not take a vow of celibacy during his absence. He takes a magnanimous view towards this. Berry then moved on to the latest incarnation of 'My Ding-a-Ling', now in 3/4 time. This version remains unissued, along with a warm-up instrumental and a song called 'That's None of Your Business', a rewrite of the 1965 cut 'It's My Own Business'.

On 1 December 1969, just days before the murder at Altamont, Berry had his own tragedy to contend with. A fire broke out at Berry Park, probably caused by a careless cigarette. Berry is convinced that when the fire department did attend, they deliberately attacked the fire from the upwind direction, simply chasing it as it moved across the entire property. All but the basement was destroyed. Once the loss adjuster had been and gone Berry hired contractors to start work on a new building. His plans received a boost when the faithful Francine returned to the fold in January.

As soon as he had fulfilled his Mercury contract Berry re-signed with Chess, and was 'back home' on 9 May 1970. However, it turned out to be no longer the home he had pined for. Leonard Chess was dead, and during the last year of his life had progressively transferred his enthusiasm from records to radio. 'The recording sessions became more foreign than ever,' Berry notes, 'full of red tape and requirements for permission from other departments of the company for any changes, as opposed to the family-type, small-business settings of the earlier sessions.'

And there was also the question of royalties. Berry eventually won an admission from the company that they had not been paying song-writer royalties on his Chess sales while he had been at Mercury. He also discovered that he had been receiving the same songwriter percentage for an album as for a single, and that foreign royalties had been piling up in the country of origin, earning interest not for Berry but for the European and Japanese publishers. These discrepancies came to light as a result of the hiring of a New York music-business attorney, Bill Krasilovsky, who was charged with putting Berry's affairs into order. Berry's do-it-yourself approach, prompted mainly by his suspicion that the world was trying to rip him off, had extracted a price. His love of a deal had not included the necessary paperwork and vigilance.

The changes at Chess Records were hardly surprising – a family company, dependent for its success on the intuition and energy of Leonard and Phil, had been flogged off. The decision had been made by the Chess brothers towards the end of 1968. Leonard saw his future in radio, perhaps even TV, both of which he regarded as less stressful than the day-to-day business of selling records. The Chess lawyer he turned to for advice, Allen Arrow in New York, also represented a Californian company whose core business was manufacturing tape cassettes and cartridges, General Recorded Tape (GRT). The GRT boss Alan Bayley had recently mentioned to Arrow that perhaps he should expand by acquiring his own roster of artists, since the day would surely come when record companies would set up plants to produce their own tapes. Arrow put the two parties together, and eventually GRT bought Chess. It would prove to be the death of the label.

As reported in *Billboard*, GRT paid $6.5 million and 20,000 GRT shares for the Chess catalogue, their pressing facilities and the Chicago building, although the deal did not include Arc Music, the publishing arm. Negotiations were protracted and often conducted with mutual suspicion, and were concluded in January 1969. The old Chess Records, the one where Leonard Chess could be sitting foul-mouthed in the control room mixing it with a truculent Howlin' Wolf, was dead.

As Marshall Chess, who had expected to take over the company he had known since he was a child, told Nadine Cohodas: 'They were changing the organic nature of the company without knowing it, trying to make it more businesslike because they were a public company.

They bought a family company that was making black music, and they tried to turn it into a suits and tie corporation.'

And so the Chess Records that Berry returned to was no longer a small family business in Chicago. It was diffuse, dispersed, and run by accountants. And Leonard, its mainspring, was dead. But house producer Ralph Bass was optimistic about the prodigal. 'Chuck came back to Chess because an artist doesn't forget the people who found him. Anyway, they didn't understand him at Mercury.'

A further British visit in summer 1970 was cancelled due to poor ticket sales, but Berry's popularity was undiminished elsewhere. In Sweden he topped the bill at the Festival of the Midnight Sun, illuminated by a huge red moon on one horizon, the glow of the sun on the other. According to *Blues & Soul*: 'From the first note of "Maybellene" the audience were on their feet, throwing off their coats and bopping madly. Sweden's equivalent of the grease – older and drunker than the rest of the audience – moved up to the front. Berry had them in his hands . . .'

By 28 August 1970 Berry Park was sufficiently restored to hold a one-day festival, with Berry topping the bill accompanied by Bob Baldori. Music continued to be promoted at the park for a few years, until an argument between two members of the crowd led to one firing a gun at the other. The injured teenager's mother sued Berry Park for $100,000, and although she was only awarded the cost of her medical bills, a sum exceeded by her court costs, it brought an end to the days of concerts in the park in 1974.

Since the 'Tulane' session had only produced two acceptable cuts Berry was well short of a homecoming album, to be called *Back Home*. He returned to Ter-Mar on 27 April, with Baldori and uncredited guitar, bass and drums, and it almost seems that he stayed in the studio (or returned after a night's sleep), working until he had an album's-worth regardless of quality. And, since nothing from the session can match 'Tulane' or 'Have Mercy Judge', the result is a patchy album collection. In more inspired days, much of the material would have simply been regarded as warm-ups.

The baldly titled 'Instrumental' would sit well in a road movie soundtrack, since Berry runs energetically through his repertoire of 'Johnny B Goode' riffs with sterling support from Baldori on harmonica and dubbed piano. Dynamic though it is, however, as a composition it is simply Berry selling his talent by the metre. 'Christmas' is another blues about seasonal loneliness, but compared to Charles Brown's 'Merry Christmas Baby' or Elvis Presley's 'Blue Christmas', to name but two, it adds nothing to the genre.

'Gun' is an instrumental showcase for Baldori's crisp harmonica, while 'I'm a Rocker' is so similar to 'Reelin' and Rockin'' that Berry doesn't even bother to rewrite some of the lyric lines. Baldori also takes the lion's share of yet another instrumental, called 'Flyin' Home', though it is not the Lionel Hampton number that Berry had earlier recorded twice. Its jazzy melody and departure from Berry's usual style, however, give it a pleasant groove. 'Fish & Chips' also has an intriguing melody, but the words are quite awful – as perhaps you would expect of a rock song about fish and chips – and 'Some People' only comes alive for the guitar breaks, since the lyrics have Berry haltingly and unconvincingly expressing a hippie philosophy of give rather than take.

So, Berry was back home but with only 'Tulane' to show for it, and inspiration in the studio would have to wait until the following January. Although Berry was feeling out in the cold as far as the new-look Chess Records was concerned, he had certainly struck up a friendly working relationship with Baldori and The Woolies over the previous two years, and it was to come to fruition on Berry's great album, *San Francisco Dues*.

# San
# Francisco
# dues

**B**OB BALDORI OFFERS some more memories of getting to
know Berry. Musically, he says, they hit it off right away.
'Charles and I were on our way to a wonderful dialogue. For
some reason, he was really hearing whatever it was I was playing.
Maybe it wasn't really the playing, but the listening. That's always been
the hardest thing to find in a musician. It's no problem finding players
who can play their ass off. But almost impossible to find a player who
can listen. And Charles is all ears. He hears everything. There's no
question that part of our relationship has always been based on that dialogue, the ability to listen. The ability to hear one another all the time.
It seems to be built in to Bee Metros as well. So we really had something going right from the start.

'And it got better every night. I was started on my advanced degree in
rock 'n' roll! I remember Charles coming over at one point, giving me a
lead and chopping away with his guitar on the off beats. Syncopate, he
started shouting. Smiling at me – syncopate! We started having fun with
that and never stopped. He was hitting on the up beat, in unexpected
places. But keeping that merciless beat rocking at the same time.' It was
a musical relationship that reached a creative peak with *San Francisco Dues*.

In the good old days at Chess Records they didn't make albums. A great album has a cohesiveness of purpose, and represents a statement of the point the artist has arrived at. Think of the exhilarating procession from *Bob Dylan* to *Blonde on Blonde*, or the same artist's 1997 suite *Time Out of Mind*. These are the real 'concept' albums. As a thematic device, something that could be more than a collection of singles, the album was perhaps born when Frank Sinatra cut his first 12in LP for the Capitol label in 1955. *In the Wee Small Hours*, inspired by the crumbling of the singer's marriage to Ava Gardner, is a meditation on melancholy by a loner 'uneasy in my easy chair'. He wrote another long-playing suicide note three years later, *Only the Lonely*, interspersing these despairing epics with the jauntier themes of *Songs for Swingin' Lovers* and *Come Fly with Me*. Naturally Sinatra 'wrote' not as a songwriter but as the filter through which various composers built up a specific tone.

By contrast, all Chuck Berry's albums for the first part of his Chess career were either compilations of singles or an arbitrary mix of hits and fillers. It was with Chess's jazz arm Argo that the company first exploited the thematic potential of the 12in disc, in particular with 1958's *Ahmad Jamal Live at the Pershing*, a phenomenal crossover success that rose to no. 3 on the pop chart. Meanwhile releases like *Chuck Berry's Greatest Hits* or *Bo Diddley's 16 All-Time Greatest Hits* were wondrous, dross-free collections, but they were built from individual and isolated fragments.

So *San Francisco Dues* could be seen as Chuck Berry's first and last truly great album. He remained constantly accessible to the public through his schedule of live work, from clubs to stadiums, up to 200 gigs a year, and at this time his regular association with The Woolies was some guarantee that the experience would be worthwhile, however much crap the promoter might have had to crawl through to get his temperamental star on stage. Meanwhile his huge catalogue of rock 'n' roll classics meant that his place in rock history was secure.

But he was in his mid-forties before he exerted enough creative control over his own imagination to produce a wholly satisfying set. Admittedly, for the purposes of the album a relaxed five-day session was bulked out with two songs from his final pre-Mercury session in 1966 — but 'Viva Rock & Roll' and above all the fast version of 'Lonely School Days' are decent cuts, not fillers, and symbolically they bridge 'the wilderness years' and forge a link with those more fruitful mid-1960s sessions.

Given limitless time Berry will fiddle around in his studio playing with gadgets and gizmos, overlays and double-tracks. His youthful fascination with the workings of cameras and radios has never left him. It was a privilege for me to hear early, fragmented stabs at a new song, 'Big Boys', courtesy of Dave Torretta in St Louis (in the Italian quarter, naturally), during autumn 2001. But it was clear that, for the song really to work as a new Chuck Berry anthem, he would have to work his way through all the studio effects and emerge at the other end with a leaner, meaner song. On *San Francisco Dues* Berry does play with some of the studio toys, but with discretion. The cohesiveness comes from the overall quality of the new material, not because every track has been squeezed through a fuzz box.

And the fact that he didn't have limitless time, just five days with responsive musicians, focused his mind wonderfully. Later Johnnie Johnson added his keyboard caress to 'Festival' and 'Your Lick', and there were of course those earlier tracks tacked on, but the core of the album is right there, from raw ideas to multitrack tape, in a week.

Perhaps the closest a previous session had come, admittedly in the one-day, cut-it-and-press-it days, was the one that produced, among lesser material, 'I Got to Find My Baby', 'Don't You Lie To Me', 'Worried Life Blues', 'Bye Bye Johnny' and 'Jaguar and Thunderbird' in February 1960, but only the last two are Berry originals.

Bob Baldori is based in Okemos, Michigan, where his main law office is established, and on 8 January 1971 Berry went to Baldori's own Lansing Studio there to start work. Chess was represented by Esmond Edwards, credited on the album as 'supervisor', but with Berry as producer. As Berry recalled nearly two years later in *Melody Maker*: 'I was there for a gig and I heard that the studio was really good . . . I didn't finish the recording so I went home and just finished it in a small studio.' But the aural evidence suggests that the basic work was done during the five days in Michigan.

The first track, both on the album and by matrix number, is unlike anything Berry had attempted before. 'Oh Louisiana' (engagingly pronounced 'Loozanna') is languorous, nostalgic and melancholy, built around Jack 'Zocko' Groendal's throbbing bass line, with Jeff Baldori contributing pulsing and restrained wah-wah licks to counterpoint

Berry's own guitar phrasing. The vocal tone is affecting, and the song is as steamy and lazy as a Louisiana swamp.

'Festival' is Berry's most successful attempt to marry his old style with the new age of rock. Johnson's dubbed piano is a joy, and the lyrics are expertly stitched into the driving rhythm, as he describes the biggest fantasy festival ever, with 'The Grateful Dead, Little Richard and The Rolling Stones' and fifty more artists for every taste. Bob Baldori contributes electric piano to 'Let's Do Our Thing Together', which skips along to a speeded-up Jimmy Reed beat out of which jumps Berry's reverb-laden solo. 'Your Lick' would be an instrumental, following a slow, southern Slim Harpo groove, were it not for Berry's close-to-the-mike grunts and groans that make it clear what sort of licking is going on, and it is followed by a wistful, bluesy country song, 'Bound To Lose', adorned by a beautifully straightforward guitar solo, with The Woolies noodling along pleasantly in the background.

The southern feel returns with a straight Hank Williams rewrite – 'Bordeaux In My Pirough' is 'Jambalaya' with new but similar lyrics. Jeff Baldori's wah-wah guitar, commendably restrained until this point, is now beginning to quack rather, and this is the slightest number on the set. Even then, it does show the chameleon nature of Berry's writing skill – he's no more a cajun than Williams was, but they could both think themselves into the heart of a Louisiana Saturday night.

The melding of Baldori's wah-wah and Berry's own guitar lines is more effective on 'San Francisco Dues', a slow, contemplative blues with the rhythm staying just a necessary skip ahead of a plod, some lovely Berry guitar phrases, and an effective use of echo. Berry then makes a rare move to the piano stool (an acoustic model, not the electric keyboard that Bob Baldori plays on most tracks) for 'My Dream', a poem narrated in an intimate voice that flirts with pretentiousness but gets away with it, except for the verse when he is 'feeding his dog and playing with his little cat'. This six-minute meditation on Berry's dream house is held together by Groendal's flatulent bass line, although the limitations of Berry's piano technique are exposed before the end, and the melancholy feel to the dream is explained in the pay-off verse – the idyllic domestic routine is meaningless if there's no one to share it with.

*Back Home* had been a worrying set – the great 'Tulane', the strong blues 'Have Mercy Judge' and seven fillers. But Berry's week in Okemos, Michigan with The Woolies, four years into their working relationship, proved that the creative embers were still glowing brightly. The cohesive feel to the album was stressed when Chess did not pick out a track for single release, but this must mainly have been because the most obvious candidate, 'Lonely School Days', had already had two 45rpm outings in 1965 and 1966, in the slow version and this faster take respectively.

A month after the *San Francisco Dues* session, journalist Fred Stuckey described in *Guitar Player* the frustrations of attempting to interview Berry, and having finally pinned him down the difficulty of persuading him to say anything illuminating. 'It proved to be a trying and fruitless experience,' he says. 'A number of unreturned phone calls and unkept appointments.' Finally Stuckey tracked down where Berry was staying in San Francisco – revealingly 'a tawdry, rundown place where wrinkled, shabbily dressed men sit in the lobby staring at the linoleum floor,' – and checked in. Discovering that Berry had gone out, he walked the streets until he bumped into his quarry. Berry ignored him before changing his mind with the warning, 'When it comes to my personal life, I'd cut you off right there.' Even his date of birth, it transpired, came into this category.

During the interview the reason becomes clear – Berry is in one of his rewriting-history moods. Asked about how he could relate to kids sufficiently to write songs like 'Sweet Little Sixteen' he says: 'Don't forget I was pretty much of a kid myself. When I started going out in front of people I was nineteen. I was out of school, but I wasn't like thirty, you know.' No, he was in fact thirty-one when he recorded 'Sweet Little Sixteen'.

He is, however, revealing about an influence on his guitar style. 'You won't believe it, but [it was] my mathematics teacher . . . I keep the basics on 4/4 time, and I take the deviations, dotted quarter notes and so forth. So I teach the basics and take the versatility, as I should I suppose, myself. That's the reason why I'm out there seeming to deviate from the basic beat.' In reality, surely, this lesson was taught him by T-Bone Walker and Carl Hogan, with their records as Berry's textbook.

# my
# ding-a-ling

**W**HILE THE ON-STAGE Berry found some stability and reliability
in The Woolies; without them his gigs were too often still
patchy. Shay Healy, reporting for the *Melody Maker* from
Massachusetts early in 1972, caught the mood of this creative lottery.

The concert raged inside, exposing us to two of the worst groups in the
western hemisphere. The committee raged in the back room. Chuck
was already a half-hour behind schedule. Chuck raged quietly in his
dressing room. They were trying to cut his fee of three thousand
dollars. In the hall, the crowd of High School kids raged vociferously.
They wanted the great man and quick.

At ten past ten, without having rehearsed with his backing group,
Chuck Berry hit the stage. At twenty past he began and went into one
of his less popular [sic] numbers 'Nadine'. It was just passable. Then
with a wiggle and a shake he sang the familiar words, 'Up in the
morning and off to school,' and half of the crowd of about one thousand
kids were on their feet waving their arms from side to side . . .

. . . The sweat ran down his face in gallons. He began to gyrate
more, moving back and over the stage. Slowly he was becoming the
legendary Chuck Berry, the king of rock 'n' roll . . . The stage was full

of musicians all joining in for a jam. The kids were dancing on stage. Swarthy cops were moving in threateningly. The music went on for 15 minutes and the hall was jumping so high. And then it was over.

That seems to encapsulate so many Berry gigs over the years. The mediocre support bill and the unrehearsed, inadequate backing musicians. The surly Berry locked away arguing about money. The listless start. The effortless ability to give the crowd a glimpse, a timed, controlled glimpse, of his greatness. And the brisk departure. Afterwards there was a fitting coda to the evening as Healy conducted his 'three question' interview.

Me: Chuck, do you mind if I ask you a few questions?

Him: No, as long as it's a few (one gone).

Me: How do you react to playing in front of kids, teenagers all the time through all the years?

Him: I don't. I have a sort of immunity to it now. I'm not really conscious of them. It's just something that's there or isn't there. But I don't think about it.

Me: Did you ever feel that rock 'n' roll would come back around you, the way it has in the last two years?

Him: I never thought about it further than the end of the year. That's the time the taxman is around and I have to worry about him.

Me: When you were writing . . .

Him: Now, man, we said a few, right?

In February 1972 John Lennon was in Philadelphia to be a guest co-host on five taped editions of an afternoon chat show, *The Mike Douglas Show*. He and Yoko clearly had some say in the choice of guests, because they included Chuck Berry. This was when Lennon, in introducing Berry, said the often-quoted line: 'If you ever tried to give rock 'n' roll another name you might call it Chuck Berry.' They jammed through a somewhat chaotic 'Memphis Tennessee' and 'Johnny B Goode', interspersed with Yoko Ono's screeching in the name of art and some very awkward sofa chat. What did come over, though, was Lennon's genuine awe at meeting his hero – although they had shared the Toronto bill in 1969, Berry was on the way home before Lennon arrived.

In 1998 Rhino Home Video issued a completists-only video box of all the Lennon–Mike Douglas shows in their entirety. 'Beatles fans expecting an all-out jam session will be disappointed,' said *Billboard*, 'but Berry and Lennon performing "Johnny B Goode" and "Memphis" are great. The only sour note is Yoko singing "Sisters O Sisters", and there is a laughable spoken-word performance by Douglas.'

The next day, five years after his previous visit to the UK when he played Brian Epstein's brief West End adventure, the Saville Theatre, Berry was back in London en route for Coventry University in the Midlands. He had been booked to play at the university's Lanchester Arts Festival. Pink Floyd were the headliners, but before them there was an early show featuring Slade, Billy Preston, The Roy Young Band and Berry. The venue was the Locarno Ballroom in the city centre.

The *New Musical Express* coverage was headed 'One of the Most Adventurous Bills Ever', but to reviewer Tony Stewart, Berry offered his usual mixed bag.

> Without a doubt, the highlight of the first house was the appearance of Chuck Berry. A tall, mean-looking man, and one of the world's greatest showmen. He had the whole thing sussed out. He'd play the first bars of any of his famous numbers, do a little on vocals, and leave the rest to the audience . . .
>
> But it was nostalgic: he's no ace on guitar, and his voice has a hollow quality. But he is Chuck Berry . . . He ain't got that much musical ability, but he's got feel.

Of course, Stewart didn't know at the time that one of the planned encores was about to rewrite Berry's career, but he does offer an intriguing definition of subtle wit. 'On one of the encores, "Ding-a-Ling", with females taking one part and guys the other, his wit was subtle but effective.'

Berry doesn't do encores, but this one was a candidate for an upcoming album to be called *The London Chuck Berry Sessions* – at least Coventry is in the same country as London, unlike Chicago, the source of some of the 1965 *Chuck Berry in London* tracks. The Pye mobile studio had been set up for the gig, with Esmond Edwards on hand, but there were technical problems with the feed that meant that most of the gig has remained in the can.

Roy Young, one of the more effective British rock 'n' rollers of the day with a fine Jerry Lee Lewis pastiche, donated his rhythm section to

Berry for the evening. Guitarist Onnie McIntyre and drummer Robbie McIntosh were soon to move on to the London pubs and hence to the international charts as part of The Average White Band. Nick Potter played bass, and replacing Young on piano was Dave Kaffinetti, late of Rare Bird. This was a seasoned outfit well capable of dealing with Berry's non-existent set list and disdain for rehearsals.

When Berry finally got on stage he went into 'Roll Over Beethoven' – a good choice, since anyone in the audience who didn't know the original certainly knew The Beatles' cover – and the crowd were with him straight away. Berry was pleasantly surprised at the reception, and leading up to the extraordinary climax of the set he ran through 'School Day', 'Back in the USA', 'Maybellene', 'Around and Around', 'Sweet Little Sixteen' and 'Nadine', with a break in the middle for an ad-libbed, underachieving version of Big Joe Turner and Pete Johnson's 'Roll 'em Pete' and a familiar standby in 'It Hurts Me Too'.

Then Berry went into a long, dirty version of 'Reelin' and Rockin'' which had now turned into 'Fuck Around the Clock', followed by the audience-response 'My Ding-a-Ling' and a red-hot finale in 'Johnny B Goode'. Berry's biggest ever hit consists of a chorus saying 'I want you to play with my ding-a-ling' interspersed with verses that describe various adventures involving the eponymous organ. The audience loved it, and sang lustily.

By now the organizers were getting agitated, desperate to clear the ballroom and set up for Pink Floyd. The expectations of the crowd had been built up by the support acts and they were ready for Berry, ninety minutes late. To his credit, for once giving the lie to the indifference he expressed to Shay Healy, he responded. The gig was one of the defining points of his career, not just because it produced his only no. 1 hit and a huge follow-up in the carefully edited 'Reelin' and Rockin'', but because he worked harder and harder as the set progressed, revelling in the reception and repaying the crowd's enthusiasm.

The last part of the show may have consisted of two vulgar and childish songs followed by yet another 'Johnny B Goode', but they also showed a master working a willing audience, many of them born after that phone call from Johnnie Johnson to Berry twenty years earlier. The NME's Tony Stewart, unimpressed by Berry's musicianship, nevertheless called him 'one of the world's greatest showmen'. This was one of those nights I'd bracket with the 1964 UK tour and Wembley later in 1972, the occasions when he deigned to prove it. And with 2000 angry, cold and drenched Pink Floyd fans waiting outside, the set only ended when organizer Ted Little eased Berry from the stage.

The excitement was captured by Charles Shaar Murray, writing in *Cream*.

> . . . There, four or so feet away was Chuck Berry with his clean cherry red Gibson and his psychedelic satin shirt and his immaculate white trousers and his two-tone sharpie shoes. He looked good . . . Then he started to sing 'Roll Over Beethoven' and the packed room full of people just started to bounce in perfect time and they yelled the words right back at him at his own machine-gun pace, with his own intonations. They all knew all the words and a few of them were putting on harmonies . . .

> Chuck couldn't believe it . . . He kept looking over to the side of the stage and pointing out over the audience, grinning in ecstatic disbelief, his face tracked with what could have been either sweat or tears . . . We sang loud enough to wreck the tapes being made for a live album. When the mike blew he played an instrumental blues . . .

> The duck walk still gets 'em going. Knees together, legs bent, strutting across the stage in Egyptian profile with the Gibson proudly facing us like a banner, an emblem, a symbol of his power . . . Was Chuck Berry celebrating the realities of the rock 'n' roll experience, or had he simply formed our future in his image?

At this point in his autobiography, Berry does a little personal stock-taking. Four grandchildren from the marriages of Ingrid and Melody. Nineteen nieces and nephews, all living in St Louis. A total of twenty-nine cars over the years, mostly new and mostly Cadillacs. A property portfolio of twenty-three purchases costing $677,000. A savings account just $50,000 short of a million. And a pair of red stage trousers that cost $8.

As for 'My Ding-a-Ling': 'I can't deny that it turned out OK but it would have been better for the band and myself to know if and when the recording was being made.' It is of course inconceivable that Berry was unaware of the Pye truck parked outside, and of the presence of Esmond Edwards. Edwards has since challenged Berry's assertion that he did not know that he was being recorded. Even with a no. 1 hit, Berry had to find something to complain about.

Two days later, on 5 February, Berry was back at Pye's London studio. He was joined by pianist Ian McLagan and drummer Kenny Jones from The Faces, ex-Artwoods guitarist Derek Griffiths and Ric Grech, late of Blind Faith, on bass. Only half an album was salvageable from the flawed Coventry tape but in five hours – including, Berry recalls, a lunch break – they cut a further five tracks, live and into the can.

'They could have been just anybody,' he said in *Melody Maker* of his eager backing musicians. 'It could have been some guys on the corner. I really didn't know one from the other . . . It was a pure accident that we got those guys on the record. Esmond [Edwards] asked some of his friends over there to direct him to some musicians and that was that . . . I hope that their addition has no influence on the record . . . because I hope that the record stands on its own, in that I will be completely responsible for my own work.' This is a graceless dismissal of one of the more successful alliances between a Chess artist and white English musicians.

'Let's Boogie' is a solid mid-tempo 12-bar number to a four-square Jimmy Reed beat, a minor piece of work. Matters improve when Berry returns to one of his on-stage stand-bys, T-Bone Walker's 'Mean Old World'. The tempo is slowed down almost to the point of disintegration, with McLagan filling the gaps with well-judged piano frills and Berry turning in an imaginative lead guitar. The standard is maintained with a rocker, 'I Love You'. Although the lyrics are so repetitive that one assumes this was virtually an ad lib, the band strikes up a tough groove and Jones enjoys himself on the turnarounds.

The melody of 'I Will Not Let You Go' is stolen from 'I Shall Not Be Moved', and the guitar introduction quotes 'Johnny B Goode', but the raw energy carries it through, and the afternoon ended with a six-minute jam, 'London Berry Blues'. It may only be a catalogue of Berry licks, but once again the band's commitment and, one assumes, sheer enjoyment at the chance to play with the man shines through. So, although the session adds nothing particularly new to Berry's discography, with the exception of a fully achieved version of 'Mean Old World', this was a productive five-hour session.

It was also hugely profitable. The first royalty cheque Berry received after 'My Ding-a-Ling' was for a quarter of a million. At the end of the year he was sent a royalty statement showing sales of 1,295,075 for the single, 187,975 for the album. As a bonus, his own Isalee Music

Company published 'My Ding-a-Ling', now somehow credited to Berry as well as Dave Bartholomew. In America the song, with the Coventry version of 'Johnny B Goode' on the flip, entered the Hot Hundred in August, reached no. 1 and remained in the chart for the rest of the year. It was released in the UK in October with 'Let's Boogie' as the B-side and also climbed to the top, selling strongly well into the New Year. In November 'Reelin' and Rockin'' (confusingly backed by 'Let's Boogie') came out in America and peaked at no. 27. Held back until January 1973 in the UK, with 'I Will Not Let You Go' on the reverse, it passed 'My Ding-a-Ling' on the way to the no. 18 slot. Berry's chart career was over, ironically with his most successful back-to-back hits ever. In Esmond Edwards's estimate, 'My Ding-a-Ling' increased Berry's gig fee tenfold.

It is a huge irony that in commercial terms this song is the peak of Berry's career. It is the sort of sing-along piece that, in a perfect musical world, would be left to a club folk-singer given his one moment of hit parade glory. Berry milks his audience beautifully, of course, and the call-and-response technique gives the playground smut of the lyrics the feel of a Christian Fellowship rally. One thing is for sure – even if Berry knows that 'Johnny B Goode' is a far superior piece of work, as far as he is concerned the vindication for 'My Ding-a-Ling' is in the royalty statements.

While still on the crest of a commercial wave he could negotiate an improved contract with Chess, and in future would receive 10 per cent of an album's recommended retail price, rather than a maximum of 21½ cents. In addition, the company agreed to absorb the first $15,000 of recording costs for each album, and to schedule two albums a year. This was something of a Pyrrhic victory, though, as the Chess owners GRT Corporation was in severe financial trouble – as they had feared, with tape sales increasing all the time as a percentage of the total market – the record companies were now manufacturing and distributing their own, rather than leasing the rights to GRT.

A month after the Lanchester Festival Berry was on tour in Europe, and on 29 March he returned to London to tape a performance for BBC2's *Sounds for Saturday*, an early-evening series of 'as live' concerts. The studio was done out as a little club, with the audience seated at tables around the stage, rather like a smaller version of

Jools Holland's in-the-round *Later . . .* shows. Berry was backed by ex-Merseybeat Billy Kinsley's band Rockin' Horse, and it was far enough into the tour for the band to be at ease and help to produce an excellent performance. Among the obvious hits, climaxing with the necessary 'Johnny B Goode', Berry also sang an old Memphis Slim blues, 'Beer Drinking Woman', 'Mean Old World' once again and his rude rewrite of 'South of the Border' ('south of *her* border'), which became the UK single after 'Reelin' and Rockin''. By this time, though, Berry's new-found fans had had enough of his playground smut, and it sold poorly.

During the BBC visit he agreed to a group interview that was attended by Rob Mackie of *Record Mirror*. Someone asks: 'Do you always take your wife along on trips?' to which Berry responds: 'I don't think I can answer that question unless you rephrase it.' And so it is rephrased: 'Do you take your wife along on trips always?' Berry's shrewd change from suspicious, defensive attitude to laughter at the joke diffuses the awkward atmosphere, and of course avoids the need to answer the question.

He also talks about the time he once kicked Keith Richards off stage. 'The backing was too loud. So at the end of the first number I said: "Slow down, it's too loud." But there was no decrease in volume, in fact the guitar and piano seemed to get even louder on the second number. I said: "If you're gonna play with me, play with me, not agin' me." I just had to finish it after that number – I thought they were doing it for spite. When I got off stage, my secretary said: "That was Keith Richards on guitar."' If he had been true to form Berry should have asked who Keith Richards was, but instead he insisted of The Rolling Stones: 'I love 'em.' Of what was to prove the historic gig in Coventry he claimed: 'I don't remember that especially.'

The concert invaded by Keith Richards had been a prestigious affair at the Hollywood Palladium, graced by two of Berry's heroes, T-Bone Walker and Big Joe Turner. Berry followed Turner: 'About midway through my show,' he wrote, 'another musician appeared on stage and exchanged places with the guy on guitar . . . It was getting too loud but going good until the sound man working the stage monitor turned the guitar up even more, causing him to miss the breaks in the song . . . I terminated the selection, turned, and asked for my guitarist to return to the stage.'

In *Sounds*, Martin Hayman noted of Berry's press-conference performance: 'He is particularly chary about questions on the business or on his personal life. He has things too well figured out to want to attract any aggravation, and anyway why should anyone expect the whole truth and nothing but?' As for Berry, so often in interviews he uses specious similes to hide his unwillingness to say anything at all, and his contributions quoted in *Sounds* were fairly typical. Referring to the London sessions, he states: 'There were some things which really gassed me which perhaps had never happened before. But in a session, it's like this, you see – strawberry shortcake is far out, and peach melba is far out, but which one is better, you know . . . every session has its highs, but there are some hassles in every session as well.'

Berry's European flirtation continued when, on 16 June 1972, he appeared at the sixth annual Montreux Jazz Festival. He was part of a Chess package along with Bo Diddley, Muddy Waters, Willie Dixon, Koko Taylor, Lafayette Leake, Fred Below, guitarist Louis Myers and drummer Dave Myers. All the Chess artists were taped and some of the results appeared on the album *Blues/Rock Avalanche* but they did not include Berry, whose set has remained in the can. This in spite of the fact that at one point he was joined by his hero T-Bone Walker, who was also on the bill. The Chess records discography shows that matrix numbers were issued for eight Berry tracks and that two of them, 'Let It Rock' and 'School Day', were originally listed for inclusion in the album.

Back at Berry Park, Bo Diddley put in an appearance for an Independence Day concert before Berry returned to the UK yet again. On 5 August 1972 history was made when the shrine of English football, Wembley Stadium, staged a concert for the first time. The London Rock 'n' Roll Show started around midday with a roster of British artists, notably Billy Fury, who as the best of the home-grown performers was not best served by performing while the stadium was still slowly filling up. Other acts included The Houseshakers, Heinz, the bottle-blond bass player from the Tornadoes, Screaming Lord Sutch and Gary Glitter.

In late afternoon the copyists gave way to the greatest-ever bill of rocking originals – Bill Haley and his Comets, Bo Diddley, Jerry Lee Lewis, Little Richard and Chuck Berry. Haley was not out of place among his raunchier successors, responding well to a warm reception and producing his familiar and thoroughly professional western-swing version of rock 'n' roll. Bo Diddley provided the day's first excitement – he was to become a regular visitor to the UK, notably on a wonderful double-header with Carl Perkins, and had already played a club tour in the mid-1960s, but this was the first time that most of his audience had seen him. Even viewed from half a stadium away, he was a formidable and dignified presence.

Jerry Lee commented that he might be getting old, but he wasn't as old as some people thought he was. He proceeded to prove it. He was probably not best pleased with an early-evening slot with two of his rivals still to come, but as at Toronto he simply tried to make life difficult for them. Little Richard, not helped by microphone failure at one point, seemed to be flying somewhere high above Wembley. As the band riffed gamely on, he spent more time standing on the piano removing gaudy items of clothing than he did hammering out the hits, but when he did get down to work the voice was as manic and powerful as on the treasured Specialty sides.

Richard recalled the event in Charles White's *The Life and Times of Little Richard*. 'There wasn't nobody topping the bill over Little Richard, and the "old black Berry" had to believe it. Why, it would've been Ann-Margret being over Queen Elizabeth. I was the undisputed King of Rock 'n' Roll and that's what the whole world knew.'

He also explained some of the stories that had appeared in the tabloid press in the build-up to the show.

The promoters had told me that ticket sales were a bit sticky. I told them I would start a Cassius Clay–Sonny Liston-type feud with Chuck Berry. It was all done tongue in cheek, just to publicize the show, 'cos Chuck is my friend. It worked. But it turned some people against me. When we arrived at the stadium there was some bad vibes in the air . . .

I believe that somebody had it in for me that night because I said I was the King of Rock 'n' Roll, which is the undisputed truth. When I went on stage the microphones were really high for the other stars, but for me the microphones were down . . .

According to his biographer White, Richard was asked by Berry to go back on stage for a jam session, which he refused, saying: 'When we get back to the States.'

This was not exactly the recollection of one of the organizers, Jeremy Beadle, who later abandoned the fraught world of rock 'n' roll promotion for a career as a TV prankster. 'We paid Chuck Berry in used teenagers,' he joked to Q magazine.

Jerry Lee Lewis arrived really late and I was trying to get him into a dressing room and he said, 'Just tell me one thing, boy: you ain't put me next to any niggers, have you?' . . . I'd actually put him next to bloody Little Richard. And then Little Richard overstayed his welcome. He just played on and on. Meanwhile, Chuck Berry's waiting to get on and he's getting more and more agitated – the show has to end at twelve and it's twenty to. Little Richard finally comes off and Chuck Berry's so furious, he comes to me and says, 'You take me down to Little Richard's dressing room now!' and we walk in and Little Richard's sitting there with this fur coat – it's got to be thirty grand's worth of mistreated animal – and he's obviously totally out of his head, shouting, 'They *love* me! They *love* me!' And Chuck Berry says, 'Fuck you, boy. Love *you*, boy? They're waiting for *me*! You ever eat in my town, boy, you're gonna eat my shit!' And I'm going, 'Ah, yes, well, very good, Mr Berry. Can we get on stage now, please?'

With time running out, and eaten into even further by Berry's fury at Richard, the crowd was very restless by the time he did appear. With the adrenaline-level still high from his outburst he was clearly in a mood for work, to blow Richard out of the crowd's memory, and the catcalls subsided immediately. Inevitably, however, a jobsworth from the Greater London Council came onto the stage with the warning that the show was overrunning, and that he was about to turn off the power.

Berry instructed the crowd to light matches and cigarette lighters, creating a vast illuminated shrine to rock 'n' roll. He completed his truncated set to what must have been one of the biggest ovations of his career. Although the mugging glances into the wings noted by Charles Shaar Murray at Coventry, feigning pleasurable surprise, are just part of the pantomime of Berry's act, he was genuinely bowled over by both the warmth and the knowledge of his songs that his young audience showed. When he got to Wembley, 'My Ding-a-Ling' was yet to be released. He still had work to do, and even though the audience had been short-changed by Richard's antics, he sent them home happy.

The Wembley extravaganza was filmed by Peter Clifton and within the last year or so it has been made available on video and DVD, though the picture and sound quality are poor. On CD, the performances by the big names have been issued on Magnum.

On 16 December 1972 *Melody Maker* published a long feature by Patrick William Salvo, referred to several times earlier, which was pieced together from various snatched interviews with Berry, and balked by such helpful comments from acolytes as: 'Berry won't understand how these interviews can help his career.' There were, however, moments of insight to be gleaned from the reluctant interviewee.

Looking back, it is easy to see how landmark events in rock history happened because the time was right – the white Elvis sounding black; Berry (sounding white), Fats Domino and Little Richard hammering down the gates of the pop charts as white kids discovered the rebellious values of espousing black music; Bob Dylan emerging from the new-found social awareness of the early 1960s; The Beatles reintroducing a rude rasp of rock 'n' roll just as things were getting too polite. Berry rightly reminds us that such events are accidents, when asked about the timing of his emergence in 1955.

'What timing? I didn't time myself to go into the music business. I just happened along. See, I did not know what people expected – I don't think anybody knows. I never plotted anything before I started playing music.' He also insists that the music didn't just appeal to the white market. 'They [the blacks] were buying everything . . . the only reason that they weren't buying more . . . is because there weren't as many blacks as whites.'

Berry also makes depressingly clear just why so many of his live performances are disappointing in their perfunctory, playing-by-numbers attitude. 'I just go up there on stage and go through it. There's really no thought involved and when something doesn't have to register in your mind and you don't have to think about it, it doesn't mean as much to you . . . When I go up on stage and play "Maybellene" it's just second nature and I don't have to think about it.'

Every Chuck Berry fan will have got that impression many a time, and wondered whether it wouldn't be best to stick with those wonderful records rather than risk another feeling of being short-changed by the live article. It is ironic, though, that Berry made this observation at the end of the most successful year of his career, the year of Coventry and Wembley, the year he gave the impression of trying hard.

# Bio and beyond

**A** CHAPTER OF musical history had come to an end in 1970 when cash-strapped GRT shut down the Chess office in Chicago and moved everything to their New York headquarters. By this time, though, it was just another stage in the slow death of the label. 'Well, they sold out,' said Berry. 'That's business . . . Frankly, I don't think about these things.'

The future of Chess Records had first been threatened by the death of Leonard Chess, but almost equally significant was the fact that he had died without leaving a signed, notarized will. This meant that there was no provision for the continuation of the company, since his assets would eventually be split between the tax man and his widow. Said Phil's son Marshall: 'It was like a cancer from the moment GRT arrived, eating away at Chess Records.' The situation was made even worse, as Nadine Cohodas points out, by the fact that the GRT executives clearly had no idea of Phil Chess's central importance to the spirit of the company, seeing him not as Leonard's creative partner but as his errand boy.

And so Phil found himself effectively sidelined, selling most of his assets and turning to property dealing and ranching in Arizona, and in

1970 Marshall Chess also decided to leave. Ironically, after a failed attempt to set up a label to record an artist he had just come across in San Francisco, Boz Scaggs, Marshall was invited over to London to run Rolling Stones Records. And so the last family link with the Chess label had now left to work for its most famous fans.

The fact was that an organisation whose business was manufacturing tape cassettes had no idea how to run a record company, and certainly not one whose chief asset consisted of a quarter of a century of America's cultural history. The Chicago building was finally sold in 1973, and vast stacks of this history – boxes of records – were sold off or even destroyed. Chess 'cut-outs', original albums with one corner of the sleeve snipped off to indicate that they were being sold as surplus stock, were available at a knockdown price.

In an unsuccessful attempt to stave off bankruptcy, GRT sold its Chess masters to the All Platinum Record Company in 1975. They in turn sold off the act who were the label's last real creative and commercial force, The Dells. All Platinum had no more success than GRT in keeping Chess alive, and the catalogue was acquired by MCA in 1986. In the UK, the independent label Charly claimed the rights to release Chess product, but after a long and bloody court battle MCA, now part of Universal, successfully asserted their ownership.

Ironically Chess had been very well served by Charly, and MCA also began a coherent programme of re-releases. Many of the treasures of the Chess label are now easily available. But in the process of being mishandled by GRT and All Platinum, Chess Records inevitably died as an ongoing, evolving concern, and became instead an archive of Chicago blues and soul. The value of the label is now recognized, and the legendary studio at 2120 South Michigan Avenue was thankfully preserved, eventually becoming the home of Blues Heaven Foundation, a venture started by the late Willie Dixon.

Meanwhile, though, Chuck Berry was still a contracted Chess artist during this sad decline. He returned yet again to the UK and mainland Europe early in 1973, now with his St Louis band led by Billy Peek. And as far as the press were concerned, he was as cold and distant as ever. For *New Musical Express*, Charlie Gillett travelled to Birmingham for a prearranged interview. 'If Berry himself knew of the arrangement, he forgot or ignored it,' reported Gillett. After watching a lacklustre first-house performance he tried again. 'He gave me the famous icy stare that had frozen other people in the past. He was beat, had to eat. I shut the door, with me outside it.'

Martin Hayman of *Sounds* fared better, but Berry was studiously unrevealing in the course of a long interview, except when Hayman asked him about 'the band you were working with'. 'I'm not working with them,' replied Berry sharply and precisely. 'They're working with me.'

Just before Berry returned to America Gillett was at last granted an audience, but as with so many long features on the man, he had to weave columns of words around the thin gruel of a few first-person quotes. What Berry did deign to say, however, was self-effacing in the extreme. 'They call me the father of rock, but that's not me. There is such a person somewhere, but whoever it is, it isn't me. I've never really created anything. I just re-expose what I hear.' This act of humility remained consistent. Fifteen years later he told the *Sunday Express*: 'I don't want to be the king. Little Richard always said he was the king and I said: don't tell me, show me. Kings come and go. Me, I want to be known as prime minister of rock.' In groping for an image he overlooked the fact that prime ministers come and go even more frequently.

In London he played at The Rainbow, and seemed to do his best to dissipate all the goodwill he had built up the previous year. He had been billed to appear at 9.30 – ideal, allowing for a quick sprint across the road to the Sir George Robey for a couple of pints before closing time. No such luck by the time he did take to the stage, after what seemed like hours of slow handclapping, 'last orders' had already been called. He played for precisely an hour, left abruptly and as always ignored the clamour for an encore. 'The audience,' commented *Blues & Soul*, 'was left wondering if it had all been worth it.' At Coventry he had ignored the pleas of the promoter to wind up his act and had played on and on, to the delight of the crowd. A year later he set the pattern for the rest of his career – keep them waiting, give them an hour and then leave. A subsequent edition of *Blues & Soul*, giving a warm reception to the UK release *Chuck Berry's Golden Decade Volume 2*, warned: 'On stage these days it appears that he may be in danger of becoming a parody of himself. But this album demonstrates the real thing.'

On the German leg of the tour, according to his own account, his late appearance on one occasion was not his fault. Berry was sitting in his rented car waiting to top the bill on a concert that had overrun beyond midnight. His eternal support act Jerry Lee Lewis was drunk and running way over time, so Berry invaded the stage to jam through the climax of Lewis's act before playing his own early-hours set.

Immediately on his return to the States, on 1 March, Berry cut a session at Technisonic Studio in the St Louis suburb of Clayton, accompanied by the Peek band. 'Rain Eyes', the day's highlight, is effectively the third episode of 'Memphis Tennessee', but now with a happy ending. Berry overdubs an attractive harmony vocal, and adds piano to the jaunty mix. For the amusing 'Sue Answer', with stuttering vocals again overdubbed, and the meandering, lightweight rocker 'Got It and Gone', he stays on piano and leaves the Chuck Berry guitar licks to Billy Peek. The latter is another variation on 'Johnny B Goode' but with a fraction of its energy. The session's final offering (with the exception of the unissued 'You and My Country') is 'A Deuce', one of Berry's more successful moves towards jazz. It's a slinky little saunter about sharing a joint, effectively a marijuana rewrite of Nat 'King' Cole's 'Bring Another Drink'.

Berry's future problems with the taxman, which would come to a head in 1979 with yet another prison sentence, had their origins at this time. The Internal Revenue Service claimed that his long-standing company, Chuck Berry Music Inc., was simply a holding operation and had to be closed down, with its assets redistributed. In its place Chuck Berry Communication Systems Inc. was created, but in the meantime Berry's 1973 income was boosted by $150,000 in assets from the defunct company.

Berry's arrangement with promoter Richard Nader also came to the attention of the IRS. Nader was a rock 'n' roll fan who began to stage 'revival' shows featuring the stars of the 1950s. On the sleeve note to the 1973 album *Let the Good Times Roll* he described the birth of the idea, when he was serving in the army and talking to fellow soldier Jim Pewter. 'Jim and I were sitting in Korea selecting artists for our make-believe rock 'n' roll shows, arguing for hours about billing and who would close the show. I decided then that the rock 'n' roll artists of the fifties were not to be forgotten, and that some day I would get them back to centre stage again.'

It didn't take him long. On Berry's forty-third birthday, 18 October 1969, Nader staged his first concert, at New York's Felt Forum. It starred Berry, Jimmy Clanton – the Louisiana artist who had co-starred with Berry in *Go, Johnny, Go* – The Coasters, Bill Haley and his Comets, The Platters and The Shirelles, and was the first of some one hundred such shows that Nader put on in the next three years.

Even though he was trading under a 'nostalgia' banner, there is no doubt that Nader gave a shot in the arm to many floundering careers. Bo Diddley, for one, was grateful. 'They're beginnin' to find out there are cats like myself, Chuck Berry, Little Richard, who were there, who laid the groundwork, an' are still *alive*,' he told Max Jones of *Melody Maker*. However, Nader's book-keeping wasn't straightforward.

He came to an arrangement with Berry that a small payment would be quoted in the contract, with the bulk of the fee being handed over in cash, in a metaphorical brown envelope. Effectively Berry was working for a lower fee than usual, trimmed by the amount he should otherwise have paid in tax. But the arrangement suited both parties – he had cash in his pocket, Nader had his services for less than the going rate, and claimed that without such a manoeuvre he couldn't afford to mount the shows.

He couldn't in any case. Nader soon went bankrupt and confessed the scam. Berry learned that the promoter of his recent UK tour had also gone bankrupt, and had inflated the amount he paid to his head-liner. To top all this the IRS decided to audit Berry's accounts. These and a number of other discrepancies eventually led them to indict Berry on a charge of tax evasion.

Berry's excuse for his underhand deal with Nader was that he was tantalizingly close to owning a million dollars in 'caressable, cold cash', and that the arrangement would hasten the day he reached seven figures in the folding stuff. Of course with his ever-growing property portfolio he was already a millionaire, probably a couple of times over, but it was the dollar bills, not bricks and mortar, that he truly loved. Perhaps only a very greedy man could shamelessly present his greed as a mitigating factor for financial misdealings.

But the end result of these problems – more time in jail – was still way in the future as Berry worked on his next album for the ailing Chess label. Even with all four useable Clayton tracks as candidates he was still way short, and there was no stockpile as there had been in more creative times. With GRT now based solely in New York, that is where

Berry went on 3 June 1973, and John Lennon's backing group Elephant's Memory were booked to accompany him.

The album was built around a song that set Berry's biography to Elmore James's most familiar lick, a song suitably called 'Bio'. Its quality and energy would not have disgraced Berry's 'golden decade' and it provided the theme for a handsome gatefold album sleeve, sporting snapshots from his childhood up to the present. The fascinating cover photo, of Berry posing on the street at maybe ten years old, shows that his knowing smile and cold eyes were already fully formed.

'Rain Eyes' and 'Got It and Gone' from the previous session were combined with four other results of his day in New York for July release. 'Talkin' About My Buddy' is a long narrative on seduction, with his friend's exploits clearly those of the randy Berry himself, ending with a protestation of future fidelity. It is set to a rather plodding version of the tumbling melody that Doc Pomus and Mort Shuman used for their Ray Charles classic 'Lonely Avenue'. 'Hello Little Girl, Goodbye' adds nothing new to the Berry catalogue but it fires along well, with Stan Bronstein's saxophone solo an unusual feature in a Berry rocker.

'Aimlessly Driftin'' is a lengthy, pleasant-enough retake on Charles Brown's 'Drifting Blues' and finally 'Woodpecker' is a fine jazzy instrumental to a funk beat that gives evidence of being more than a warm-up filler. While *Bio* does not display all the resourcefulness of *San Francisco Dues* it was surely good enough to satisfy all the new fans gained by the success of the Coventry–London recordings.

An amusing story from around this time illustrates a rare occasion on which Berry got the worst of a situation, one in which he behaved with unapologetic selfishness. But, then, he shouldn't have offended the mighty Howlin' Wolf. The tale comes from Emery Williams Jr, better known as Detroit Jr, and it must date from somewhere between 1972, the year that Emery joined the Wolf's band, and 1976, when the Wolf died of cancer. Emery related the incident to *Living Blues* in 1996, although there are no specific details of time or place, except that the venue was called The Aragon.

> I went out of the lobby to go across the street to get a sandwich. I see Chuck Berry pull up in his white Cadillac, top down. He start runnin' in. He's late. The Aragon is packed with people. Chuck didn't have any guitar. He picked up Wolf's guitar and played it. That was a mistake.

When he got through, he come back from the stage and Wolf's sittin' up there. He set it right by Wolf, didn't say nothin'. Oooh, that was the mistake he made!

Now, when we went back on stage playin', Wolf got in front of all them people talkin' about Chuck. He say, 'You know, Chuck Berry. Here he come to work with no guitar. He played my guitar. He come by me, didn't ask me to play it. Then he come by me, don't even say thank you. Now, big and black as I am sittin' here, ain't no way he could miss me.' Chuck had to come back out on the stage and apologize to Wolf before he'd shut up!

But he probably didn't learn his lesson. Rejecting a fetishistic fan's request for his guitar strings in 1988 because he thought the idea was silly, he said, 'I will use anybody's guitar.'

Although 'Bio' was released as a single with the Coventry track 'Roll 'em Pete' on the B-side, Berry soon became frustrated by the apparent lack of activity on the part of the record company. 'It was getting so GRT wasn't releasing any selections from my sessions at all,' he wrote, an observation confirmed by a gap of almost two years before another, final Berry single appeared on Chess. This was the time that GRT, unknown to him, were negotiating with All Platinum with the intention of offloading the label.

But Berry ploughed on, returning to New York in August for a four-day session that was intended to produce a double album. In the event, as if to confirm his suspicion that the company's interest in him was waning, eleven of the tracks remained in the can – half of his output over the four days. The remaining eleven, together with 'A Deuce' and 'Sue Answer', were to make up Berry's last Chess album, given the imaginative title *Chuck Berry*. In the UK it was pinpointed a little more accurately as *Chuck Berry '75*. The session musicians were locals, Wilbur Bascomb Jr on a throbbing electric bass, pianist Ernest W. Hayes and drummer Earl C. Williams (replaced by Jimmy Johnson Jr after the first day), and Berry's daughter Ingrid sang harmony vocals. Later Esmond Edwards stressed the country feel of much of the material by overdubbing Elliott Randall's steel guitar on several tracks.

'I'm Just a Name', a wistful original written from the point of view of a groupie, is pleasant second-division Berry. It is also the only Berry composition that surfaced from the four sessions, which suggests that Berry could see the writing on the wall and had no intention of putting in more effort than necessary. The first cover, 'Too Late', is a run-of-the-mill 1940s country song revived in 1957 by The Louvin Brothers.

In 1964 Chess had leased a New York recording for their Checker imprint, Tommy Tucker's 'Hi Heel Sneakers', a wonderfully sly, pulsing 12-bar that was a big hit on both sides of the Atlantic. Although it became an instant standard, included in the repertoire of every blue-eyed British R & B band – who solemnly sang 'Put your wig hat on your head' as if it was a perfectly natural thing to say – nobody has touched the three minutes of inspiration by organist Tucker and his band. Berry turns in a convincingly lazy vocal but the song goes nowhere for four and a half minutes, with Berry throwing in the 'Good Morning Little Schoolgirl' guitar lick and ad-libbing meaninglessly, while the rhythm section increasingly sound as if they are wading through mud.

'South of the Border' is clearly a favourite of Berry's since it has long been a staple of his stage act, with its smutty rewritten lyrics and his awful Mexican accent, but I doubt if any of his fans has ever been convinced by his enthusiasm. Far better is his rocked-up version of Stephen Foster's 1851 song 'Swanee River', which sounds like nothing Foster could possibly have envisaged. Another dinosaur, 'You Are My Sunshine', is of interest only because Berry often screams the lyric, an extraordinary and unprecedented contrast to his usual clipped, mellow tone. Maybe he was demob-happy. However, a funked-up revival of Tampa Red's 'Don't You Lie To Me', which Berry so adeptly covered in 1960, is a meandering mess.

'My Babe' would be more enjoyable if one could block out the memory of Little Walter's marvellously slinky 1955 shuffle, and Berry's revival of Muddy Waters's 'Just Make Love to Me' (now more logically called 'I Just Want To Make Love To You') is chiefly of interest because he appears to be impersonating Mick Jagger. Far better is a storming, good-natured version of 'Shake, Rattle and Roll', eventually released in February 1975 as Berry's farewell Chess single, but the last surviving song, Jimmy Reed's 'Baby What You Want Me To Do' (with Ingrid taking the lead vocal and her dad mumbling in the background just like Mama Reed used to do), is a rather pointless pastiche of the great bluesman's drunken style, although Ingrid is in good voice and Berry's very last Chess guitar break is a strong one. Of the tracks that have remained on the shelf only one demands to be heard, for its curiosity value if nothing else – Berry's take on The Band's pseudo-biblical epic 'The Weight'.

With Chess Records imploding Berry went to court seeking a break with All Platinum, on the basis that they were not in a position to honour their obligations to the artists they had inherited, and he was released from his contract – which in any case had been with the late Leonard Chess. Eventually he would sign a deal with Atco, which resulted in the 1979 album *Rockit*. By which time he was in jail again.

In the mid-1970s Berry spent a lot of time working at his Wentzville studio, laying down tracks for what he intended to be a double album provisionally and modestly called *The Second Coming*. Fred Rothwell notes that at one point he spoke of a specific release date, 26 March 1976, and that it would appear on the Warner Brothers label. There is no doubt that he was talking to various record companies about a deal, probably without any great sense of urgency, but none of the Berry Park tapes materialized until Atco put out *Rockit* in 1979, and that proved to be a one-off. Atco was a subsidiary of Atlantic Records, who by then had been frontrunners for some time in seeking his signature.

His fans were beginning to accept that the fire was dying down, in any case. Writing in *Blues & Soul* in 1976 Spencer Leigh said: 'These days Chuck spends a lot of time at his amusement centre Berry Park in Wentzville, Missouri. There are no pressures on him to come up with new material and he can trade on his former glories from now 'til kingdom come. I doubt if he'll be responsible for any more stylistic innovations but he is to be commended for staying true to rock 'n' roll and not turning himself into a cabaret artist . . .'

In the meantime Berry was out there on the road, often now with bass player Jim Marsala, another St Louis musician who accompanies him on close-to-home gigs to this day. When he visited the UK and Europe, promoters sometimes teamed him with one of the bands riding on the current rockabilly craze, some of whom, like Matchbox, had emerged from the pubs and teddy-boy clubs into the pop charts. In May 1976 he was back in the UK yet again for ten dates. 'We weren't expecting him,' said a record company spokesman when Berry suddenly turned up two days early. 'He's a bit of a law unto himself.' But the performances this time rarely achieved the heights of 1972, the year of his second career revival. Like William Wordsworth, Berry has spent most of the second half of his career on autopilot – although fortunately not always, as the final chapter of this book attests.

In his mid-seventies, it is enough that Berry can put on a show at all. What is sad is that the real creative fire, the desire to tear up a room and not rest on his well-earned laurels, had died by the time he was fifty. And yet, strangely, he kept on keeping on, when he could surely have settled for a quiet life of property dealing and extramarital sex. He has claimed in interviews that he has no need of inspiration, simply going on stage to do his job and collect his wages, and as we have seen he has occasionally denied his originality and played down his rock 'n' roll status. And yet it must be ego that drives him, that forces him to haggle the next appearance fee, put the Gibson into its case and head for St Louis Lambert airport. For all his denials, he *is* Chuck Berry and he never forgets it.

This is the central enigma of Berry the performer. Of the truly great rock artists, Bob Dylan is the only one who engages in a never-ending world tour. But he differs from Berry in two significant aspects. One is that he constantly reinterprets his material, to keep it fresh for himself as a singer and writer, and the other is that he seems to have no burning reason to stay at home. The road and his life have become as one. He does not go fishing. Nor, it seems, does he have Berry's passion for business, expressed particularly in real estate. And so it makes sense that Dylan is out there somewhere in the world, on stage. B.B. King is similar.

It must be, surely, that Berry's expressed indifference to his art is yet another smoke screen, perhaps born out of a defensive awareness that, to most of the world, rock 'n' roll is an irrelevance. He cares much more than he lets on, proud of his contribution to American culture, recognized by presidents like Jimmy Carter, flattered that he can express it to an audience ever younger than himself. But alongside this there is a devil inside him that says, 'If it ain't broke, break it.' His customary, though not invariable, bad behaviour when being interviewed is too easily explained as arising from a suspicion that he will be misquoted. Beyond this, he does seem to take pleasure in the discomfort of others.

But then, just to prove that human beings are much more complex than that, there is Berry the charmer, to whom his personal assistant Francine has remained loyal for decades, who is spoken of with both affection and respect by many of those who have worked with him, who has never wanted for female company, and who occasionally in his autobiography lets slip a hint of vulnerability. Everyone shows changes of mood. In Berry the sunshine and the clouds hanging over his personality are more intense than in most people.

By the mid-1970s all was not well at Berry Park. Following the accidental drowning of an eleven-year-old girl in his pool the police continued to hassle him, and when they raided the Park in 1974 following the argument between two kids, one of whom had a gun, they allegedly found children in possession of marijuana. And then a security guard fired a shot at a teenager in the crowd. As a live venue Berry Park closed down, a brave experiment in colour-blind recreation that failed partly due to lax stewardship, but partly because those in authority were determined that it should indeed fail.

There was a brief, happier period in 1977, when the fifty-one-year-old Berry played himself as if twenty years earlier in the movie *American Hot Wax*, a highly fictionalized but thoroughly enjoyable biopic of Alan Freed, played by Tim McIntyre. Included in the fiction is Berry's performance of the 'rude' version of 'Reelin' and Rockin'', something that would have brought down the safety curtain if he had tried it on a teenage audience in the polka-dot days of innocence.

The film, released in February 1978, brings together three of the originals – Berry, Jerry Lee Lewis and Screaming Jay Hawkins – with fictitious 1950s acts. Joe Esposito, Bruce Sudano and Ed Hokenson, who were actually a group called Brooklyn Dreams, join with the film's musical director Kenny Vance as Professor La Plano and the Planotones to sing 'Rock 'n' Roll is Here to Stay'. Charles Green plays solo singer Clark Otis, performing Dee Clark's 'Hey Little Girl', and The Delights, Timmy & the Tulips and The Chesterfields complete the musical cast.

The film casts Freed as the rock 'n' roll hero battling reactionary forces determined to stifle the music – and of course there is an element of truth in this romantic cliché. Although somewhat hampered by the eleven-piece Big Beat Band led by guitarist Ira Newborn, Berry's contribution – a medley of 'Reelin' and Rockin'' and 'Roll Over Beethoven' – is a spirited affair, and it is preceded by the film's comic highlight.

As Berry stands in the wings waiting to go on stage Freed tells him that the Internal Revenue Service has seized the box-office take, and so there is no money to pay the performers. The saintly Berry thinks for a moment, as the crowd screams for him, and says: 'You know, rock 'n' roll has been pretty good to me. I think I'll do this one for rock 'n' roll.' Screenwriter John Kaye will have enjoyed putting these bizarre words into Berry's mouth.

# back to jail

**O**N 14 FEBRUARY 1979 two of Nashville's top session-men, drummer Kenny Buttrey and bass player Bob Wray, were at Berry Park for the session that resulted in the *Rockit* album. Jim Marsala was also there, and may have replaced Wray on most of the tracks, but above all Johnnie Johnson turned up to add some authentic gloss to the proceedings. Berry says that Ebby Hardy was present as well: although this seems very unlikely, he was certainly around at the time, since he appeared in the television documentary referred to below. Marsala, however, simply recalls 'two local drummers'. He also contests Berry's recollection of a two-day session, saying it was more like two weeks.

'I was surprised to hear from Chuck and even more surprised to hear that he wanted to do another record,' Johnson told Travis Fitzpatrick. 'I figured he was long done with makin' records and that he was just tourin' on his name.' Most of his piano parts were cut at the time, as was Johnson's preference, though some were overdubbed later. 'I just did what they told me to,' he said. 'To be honest, I don't really remember a whole lot from that session 'cause that was at a time when I was drinkin' pretty heavily.'

Berry wasn't too happy about the record-company presence at Berry Park – 'What was an executive producer anyway?' – and in Marsala's view the technical superiority of the recording process over the instinctive methods at Chess was outweighed by a resulting sound that was too cold and clean. Talking to Fitzpatrick, he put his finger on the problem. 'The great thing about Chuck and Johnnie was that neither one of them read music at all, so everything they did together was spontaneous . . . They really needed to capture the live sound because that is closer to what Chuck Berry is all about. He's not a studio musician and neither, I think, is Johnnie . . . So no, I'd have to say I didn't like the album very much.'

As for Johnson, he has little recollection and no considered view of the project. He was at his lowest point, a professional drunk in failing health, a part-time pianist in his mid-fifties living in a slum apartment across the river in East St Louis. He was sinking fast and his rehabilitation was still a few years away.

Unlike his final offering to Chess, this time Berry contributed all the material. 'Move It' is a chunky three-verse boogie and 'California' is a tourist-board tribute to the charms of the west coast. 'Pass Away', an exotic poem recited to Berry's pedal-steel backing, suggests that his recent reading might have included Shelley's 'Ozymandias', a sonnet about the crumbling ruin of a huge statue lying in the desert. The pedestal bears the inscription 'My name is Ozymandias, king of kings: Look on my works, ye Mighty, and despair.' But Berry doesn't read books. In his version the King of Persia recognizes that all his wealth, fame and the pleasures of the flesh are transient.

The strongest cut from the first batch of tracks, though, is 'Oh What a Thrill', a catchy, good-time sing-along driven by Johnson's piano. With 'California' on the flip it was to be Berry's only Atco single. Later he added the blues 'I Need You Baby', a rather silly rocker called 'If I Were', his end-of-show chant 'House Lights', an intriguing meditation on racism, 'I Never Thought', an atrocious remake of 'Havana Moon' and the killer track 'Wuden't Me'. Although it's a relative of 'It Wasn't Me' this is a more carefully crafted song in that the catalogue of frustrations are not isolated, but grow out of a developing narrative, that of a black prisoner in Mississippi breaking out of jail, being pursued by guards and dogs and hitching a lift with a Ku Klux Klan member. If this was indeed a new or comparatively recent song that Berry brought to the session then it seems doubly remarkable and sad that his inspiration then seemed to dry up totally.

The BBC television arts strand *Omnibus* devoted a 1979 edition to *Johnny B Goode: a Film about Chuck Berry*. It showed him working at Berry Park, playing on stage, driving around Wentzville, playing an open-air gig at The White House to an appreciative Jimmy Carter, and breaking into the derelict Club Bandstand building for a nostalgic reunion party with Johnnie Johnson and Ebby Hardy, playing the record of 'Oh What a Thrill' and singing along.

'I can't sing,' he says in his precise drawl. 'I don't have that luxurious voice like Nathaniel Cole, Frank Sinatra. And I imagine I don't play like . . . Charlie Christian. But then I plunk awhile. I get by.' He addresses his reputation for meanness and surliness, in that familiar stilted fashion. 'I have tried to curb the manners in which I have been ripped off so that they don't happen again, and this has given me a reputation of being – cynical, is it? – and distrustful. It's not that I'm distrustful, it's just that if the same kind of dog comes up you think that he'll bite you or move out.'

After this garbled metaphor the shutters come down. In the film's most revealing moment he denies something that has clearly just happened. His hapless interviewer says: 'We were going along the motorway . . . and we met Officer Medley. You said, "That's Officer Medley, that was the guy who arrested me back in 1958 . . ."'

'That's a lie,' snaps Berry. 'I did not say that to you. If you're trying to invoke some sort of response – because I take pictures of an officer does not mean I was arrested by him. Well?'

'Well, you said that was the man, back in '59 . . .'

'You're repeating yourself.'

'That's [laughs awkwardly] . . . that's what you said to me . . .'

Berry speaks in a menacing, singsong tone: 'You're lying again.'

'So you don't want to talk about that area . . . you talked about the Mexican girl . . .'

Suddenly Berry stands up. 'We're finished.' And they are, because he stalks out of the room.

Much as he professes a love of his home town St Louis, Berry had always felt, since his conviction under the Mann Act all those years ago and not without reason, that certain elements in authority would be out to get him. With his trial for tax evasion looming he hired Los Angeles lawyers in the hope of getting the hearing transferred there, on neutral ground. The negotiations succeeded, though as is the way with American law this was only half of the deal – the other half was that Berry had to plead guilty, but to reduced charges. Since he knew he was guilty he saw this as a good result, and agreed to the arrangement, although again one wonders whether his offence wouldn't have been considered a minor financial misdemeanour, an oversight, if committed by an upstanding white Lodge member.

His case came to court on 11 June 1979, by which time Judge Pregerson had made his decision – three years in jail, suspended all but for 120 days that had to be served, with a four-year probationary period to follow, and 1000 hours of community service. Berry was to report to jail in August but in the meantime his passport was returned, enabling him to fulfil a contract for a short tour to France, Germany and the UK.

In London he appeared at the ambitious, six-day Capital Radio Jazz and Blues Festival held on the slopes of Muswell Hill in north London, beneath the massive brick cliff of Alexandra Palace, originally built as a Victorian pleasure dome. Crucially, the weather stayed fine and the setting was perfect for a long, lazy musical picnic. Berry was billed in a tantalizing sequence between Muddy Waters and B.B. King, and he had a seasoned band in Jim Marsala and two British musicians familiar with his awkward behaviour, drummer Rod De'Ath and pianist Lou Martin. He also looked great, leaving the psychedelic paisley swirls at home and opting for a smartly tailored grey suit, shirt and tie.

But his guitar slipped out of tune and as usual he ignored this detail. He did just enough to please the crowd and no more. 'Perfunctory, mechanical and facile in the way that most of his performances have seemed to be for many years,' wrote *New Musical Express* reviewer Paul Du Noyer, before adding: 'And, of course, it all works beautifully.' He brought the crowd to its feet and, not surprisingly, finished with his last hit to date, 'Reelin' and Rockin''. As always he ignored the clamour for an encore while drinks cans rained onto the stage.

In fact before completely disappearing he did reluctantly attend a press conference backstage – 'an elaborate farce,' in the words of the same paper's Nick Kent.

Berry is currently facing somewhere between a four or fifteen-month term of imprisonment for tax evasion, and it's a topic that he adamantly refuses to discuss. Instead he foxes his way out of the tax evasion scam and every other topic broached in this ludicrous affair [the press conference].

He still refuses to admit to the term of imprisonment he underwent in 1960, for example, while other questions he destroys by manhandling their wording or by simply outstaring his interrogator in a fake display of serene misunderstanding.

All who have attended these icy exercises in non-communication will find Kent's words chillingly evocative.

When Michael Watts of *Melody Maker* tried a different approach, tackling Berry as he and a young blonde companion sat in the hotel coffee lounge, he achieved little more. 'Do you have ten minutes?' 'No, I have one, or maybe two.' Watts soon noted a characteristic of Berry's 'conversation', that when an unwelcome subject is raised his voice becomes lower and quieter, the words spaced out and even more carefully enunciated. 'Menacing,' he wrote. 'He is obviously much better at this kind of evasion than he is at evading the US Government.'

By 1982, in *Goldmine*, Berry was ready to admit it was a 'fair cop'. This tax thing that I was in was no bum rap. It was straight, true. It was a bum rap in the sense that it was a little more, it was about 15 per cent that they added on, but that's nothing to kick about  But if I had known that there was more than just payin' it back, if I'd have known that there was a penalty to it . . . Every penny I still had in my safe. I didn't want nobody to find *the* dollar, with *the* number on it. I just thought, 'Well, whenever they catch up with ya . . .' Six years I had it. Six years I held that bread . . . I didn't want it to go through the bank.

Back in St Louis and driving home to Berry Park, he listed in his mind the things that seemed important to him, but would once more have to be put on hold – travel, playing music, 'watching girls', saving his money and writing songs. No mention of his wife and family back in town, just that when he arrived in Wentzville 'the staff at Berry Park was asleep'.

On 8 August Berry flew to Los Angeles for winding-up meetings with the William Morris Agency, his lawyer and his property manager, and two days later he drove north to Lompoc Prison Camp in a rented station wagon. He took with him $260 (precisely the permitted $65 per month pocket money), his guitar, two dictionaries and a stack of typing paper – work on his autobiography was to be his main project while in jail.

'The building resembled a typical old unpainted concrete Holiday Inn three storeys high,' he noted, and welcomed the fact that, unlike the forty-four-bunk dormitory at Algoa in the early 1960s, he was now in a three-bed cubicle. 'The only real bother about prison, to me, is the loss of love,' he recorded, disturbed to find that the late-night head count was often conducted by a female warden, increasing his priapic distress. It wasn't love he was missing – that, of course, could survive a comparatively brief separation. One solution was to alternate work on his autobiography with the penning of erotic short stories, which found a ready readership among the inmates. The problem was compounded when he was summoned to the office of the prison's recreational officer to discuss a concert for the inmates that he had agreed to do. The officer was an attractive woman and Berry found that he had to sit down, uninvited, to disguise the embarrassing wriggle in his jeans.

On 29 October, Berry's thirty-first wedding anniversary, he queued to telephone 'the first and only lady, wife and mother to my children', the long-suffering Toddy, and on 1 November he played a concert for the inmates. One of them, Shane Williams, described the event in *Trouser Press*.

[The] authorities . . . created somewhat of a Catch 22 situation due to Berry's sentence calling for community service concerts. They probably didn't think it right for him to work off one of his 1000 hours playing for his fellow prisoners. Berry didn't view it like that. He just wanted to play because he knew people were looking forward to it.

After Berry started borrowing the Pen's musical equipment to play shows at the Farm, recreation department officials themselves put pressure on the higher-ups . . . Berry forbade cameras. A poster calling for his liberation did double duty as advertising for the 'free' concert.

Five hundred convicts jammed the auditorium . . . The lights were turned down very low (to make sure no photos were taken?) and Berry, accompanied by his band of felons from Camp, came on stage. He started off with a rousing 'Roll Over Beethoven' and kept the pace up during a 75-minute set . . . When I called out something from his latest *Rockit* LP he expressed surprise that anyone had heard it, as the album came out a month before he entered prison.

Berry was freed on 19 November, having served two-thirds of his sentence. Jim Marsala had delivered Berry's own car to the local airport car park on the previous day, and Berry drove back to his Hollywood office to pick up the threads of his business affairs before flying home to St Louis. For some time into the future, benefit concerts would be seeded into his performance schedule to satisfy his community service obligation. As he put it: 'Every mother and trucker was calling Fran to book me at their benefit.'

The November issue of the collectors' magazine *Goldmine* ran an interview with Berry by Dan Fries, who must have found the experience as pleasant as a visit to the dentist. Berry finds it necessary to contradict, deflate or pretend to misunderstand Fries at every opportunity – asked about his childhood, he observes, 'Everyone was a child at some time,' and when Fries says that he has read that Berry sang in a church choir the answer is, 'Truth is whatever you believe, but yes, I did sing in the choir.'

This cussedness leads him to deny that he was ripped off over royalties, in contrast to his confused mad dog metaphor in the *Omnibus* film, simply so that he can contradict his interviewer. 'How can you tell what is "due" someone who creates?' he asks airily. '. . . Did I get money for my records? Yes I did and I do, but I don't say I was ripped off.'

He then denies knowing why Alan Freed's name appeared on 'Maybellene', a somewhat unlikely ignorance that fools no one after his quarter of a century in the music industry, but he is a little more revealing when Fries reminds him that in the movie *American Hot Wax* he makes the unprecedented offer to play for free. 'In the movies,' he says, 'the truth isn't always on the screen.' And so when asked if he's ever played for nothing in real life he simply smiles, strokes a guitar string and remains silent.

'I don't know that story!' he laughs, when asked if he revived his childhood 'duck walk' to hide the wrinkles in his suit – a story that came from Berry himself. He doesn't know anything about the payola scandal that destroyed Alan Freed and led to his premature death, and clams up again when asked about his troubles with the law — a November publication date suggests that the interview was probably carried out while he was waiting to serve his third jail sentence. When thanked profusely, presumably through gritted teeth, for a conversation in which he deliberately said almost nothing, he simply points out: 'I seldom allow people into my dressing room.'

While still fulfilling bookings through his agency in California, Berry now entered a quiet creative period that, in a sense, has lasted ever since. Early in 1980 his energies were directed towards writing the autobiography and into developing Berry Park, where he ran new roads into the woods and created a picnic area. It must be doubtful, after the problems resulting from public access to the site in the past, that he sustained serious ambitions about continuing it as a country club. Rather Berry Park had become a refuge, a Xanadu, where he could plan and dream, drive his tractor and trace out his blueprints. While he worked on his schemes his mother Martha died, in July 1980.

His arm's-length relationship to the all-pervasive television medium, he says at this stage in his book, is because, 'it locks the performance into a schedule, usually with stock music [presumably by this he means playing one of his hits for the zillionth time], and leaves no room for the innovation and spontaneous inventive creation which, to me, are the main glory in the thrill of performing.'

His observations on the limitations of TV performance seem spot-on, but his claim to be an innovative and spontaneous spirit in performance is hard to take. Usually — with the glorious exceptions that, from personal experience, I have often been able to pay tribute to — he is the opposite. He continues to write in his unique blend of bullshit and humility. 'If it wasn't for the feeling I get while performing, I think it would have been impossible for me to have continued as long as I have. It is also difficult for me to conceive what on earth people see in my act that has caused it to linger as long as it has . . .'

If Berry wasn't such a suspicious, self-contained operator, maybe at some stage someone could have got close enough to convince him that, yes, what he says he feels about the joy of performance may be true but, no, he cannot usually be bothered to convey it. Many of the musicians that I have spoken to must remain anonymous because their enthusiastic endorsement of Berry's genius – the mainspring of this book – is tempered by hints of his dark side. And all of them, named or not, would agree with Bob Baldori that 'Charles is a very private person'. The ego demands that he still performs, raking over the embers of a creative fire that, decades ago, changed pop music for ever.

# hail! hail!
## rock 'n'
## roll

ONE STAPLE OF the radio industry in America ever since its first boom in the 1920s has been the syndicated show, on acetate or LP, tape or CD, which can if appropriate be personalized by each local station. In its most extreme form it consists of a series of answers to questions that the presenter reads from a script, in the hope of giving the impression that the celebrity is actually on a whistle-stop visit to Nowheresville, and has stopped by to chat to his old buddy Mickey the Most, Your Afternoon Host.

More substantially, these records can offer a complete show branded by a commercial sponsor who covers the costs of recording, artist fees and distribution. Fred Rothwell has identified a couple of typical Berry examples from the 1979–81 period. The first is a complete documentary produced by the NBC network for distribution to its stations across the country. The connecting commentary is by journalist and critic Robert Christgau while Berry chats about his life to an unheard interviewer, interspersed with music on record from the start of his career up to *Rockit*, and contributions from Bo Diddley and Berry disciple George Thorogood.

The second is a contrast in that it is branded, by Budweiser, and consists of a newly recorded live performance from a dance hall in Reseda, a suburb of Los Angeles, called Wolf & Rismiller's Country Club. Most of the album is devoted to Thorogood, who had a promotional deal at the time with the vast St Louis brewery Anheuser-Busch, purveyors of Budweiser, while Berry contributes an energetic 'Maybellene', 'Sweet Little Sixteen' and his familiar segue of 'Carol' and 'Little Queenie'.

In November 1980 Berry toured South America and in April 1981 he flew to Japan. These were both new territories for him, and he insured himself against a culture clash by taking Jim Marsala and Ingrid Berry with him, although he still had to use local pianists and drummers. Two Tokyo concerts in April, and for that matter a return-visit gig in Yokohama the following year with Japanese backing musicians, were recorded for official release in Japan only, on the local subsidiary of EMI. The Yokohama recording is devoted more to Sam Moore and his Sam and Dave Revue, with Berry contributing just two songs, 'Bio' and 'Johnny B Goode'. It is noticeable that whereas Sam Moore, hardly a guaranteed box-office attraction since his acrimonious split with his soul-duo partner Dave Prater, nevertheless travelled with his own nine-piece band, Berry made do with a Japanese trio.

On returning from the first Japanese trip he and his brother Paul were repairing a roof when Berry jumped to the ground and sustained a ruptured disc in his spine. This required traction in hospital, his first visit 'since my circumcision'. He did, however, manage to fulfil a booking in Chicago almost immediately afterwards, while in considerable pain.

In between the two Japanese trips a further live recording, and a video, resulted from a filmed-for-television performance at the Roxy theatre in Hollywood. While a television special like *Chuck Berry Live at the Roxy* is to be welcomed, particularly with the novel attraction of a 'Rock 'n' Roll Music' duet with Tina Turner, since he hasn't been overexposed in the medium, the live 'greatest hits' packages that appeared in the 1980s are for completists only. Unlike Bob Dylan, Berry tends to play with his eye on the clock, rushing through his songs and happy simply to shout out his trigger phrases while the audience does the work.

Given that Berry has tended to steer clear of the cinema since those early Alan Freed quickies, his decision to appear in *National Lampoon's*

*Class Reunion*, for which he filmed his brief contributions in March 1982, is a strange one. The original movie spin-off by the *Lampoon* in 1978, *National Lampoon's Animal House*, at least had John Belushi as its star and John Landis directing. For the follow-up such laughs as there were in *Animal House* had evaporated, and the lumbering plot involves a killer stalking the fraternity house. Berry is seen in fragments of 'Festival', 'It Wasn't Me' and 'My Ding-a-Ling'.

Backstage at a gig in 1981 Keith Richards had tapped Berry on the arm to say hello. Berry's response was to swing round and punch him in the face. 'Fuck off,' Berry said to his most celebrated fan. A year later, at the Ritz Club in New York City, Berry had the opportunity to apologize when the two shared a stage, and unlike the 1972 occasion when Richards was deemed to be playing too loud they managed to complete the gig in harmony. 'For the boo-boo I did, I publicly apologize. This is my main man,' says Berry. A low-fi bootleg of the occasion eventually surfaced as *Let It Rock*, which also contains live versions of Berry songs by The Rolling Stones.

A UK recording dating from 1983 is of slightly higher quality than most from the 'greatest hits' treadmill, however. Local radio station Hereward, based in Peterborough, promoted a Rock 'n' Roll Spectacular on 3 September, with an undercard consisting of 1960s Mersey band Billy J. Kramer and the Dakotas, the ever-present Screaming Lord Sutch, cockney growler Tommy Bruce, Gary Glitter's backing group The Glitter Band and a singer billed on the poster as 'Billy Davies' – actually Billie Davis, the 'blue-eyed soul' singer who had a handful of early-1960s hits, notably 'Tell Him'.

'Don't miss this chance in a lifetime for "yesterday's" swingers to relive old memories and for today's kids to see "The Master" in action,' shouted the advertising. Alas, the enterprise was dogged with problems. It was intended to hold the concert in a circus tent with a capacity of 5000, and tickets sold well. However, high winds threatened the safety of the Big Top, and with hours to go six of the supporting poles buckled. A last-minute switch was made to nearby sports arena the Wirrina Stadium, the concert started ninety minutes late and only 1250 of the paying customers could be squeezed in, leaving 2000 disgruntled fans locked outside.

This time Berry travelled with Billy Peek as well as Jim Marsala and Ingrid Berry, and they were augmented by British drummer Graham

Hollingworth. One novelty is that the country roots of 'Maybellene' are stressed when Berry segues into the old hillbilly song 'Mountain Dew'. The number was in his repertoire in his early days as 'the black hillbilly', but this is the first time it had been recorded. In 1994 the back-catalogue company Magnum Force, who also re-released Berry's Atco album *Rockit*, issued the set as *Live On Stage*.

In the fraught circumstances, the concert was considered a success. 'It was a miracle we ever got the show together,' said Hereward Radio disc jockey Stewart Francis. 'The switch was done in just four hours.' Some of the supporting bands only had time for a couple of numbers to keep within the midnight curfew and Berry played for his customary forty-five minutes, on better and more energetic form than had become the custom. This seems to be the last time he was recorded in performance or in the studio for three years, when he began rehearsals for the film *Hail! Hail! Rock 'n' Roll*.

Nineteen eighty-six, the year that Berry turned sixty, was a momentous one for him. He was the first artist to be inducted into the newly formed Rock 'n' Roll Hall of Fame, with the citation read by Keith Richards, and he then went to New York to discuss the possibility of making a film about his music. His lawyer Bill Krasilovsky introduced him to a producer, Stephanie Bennett of Delilah Films, and at a further meeting in February, when Berry was back in New York for a concert, what had started as a video project became a full-blown theatrical movie. It was decided to end the film with a concert performance at the Fox theatre on North Grand Boulevard in St Louis, a sumptuous former picture palace where the eleven-year-old Berry and his father had been refused admission to *A Tale of Two Cities* because of their skin colour. Not unnaturally, Berry revelled in the irony of returning nearly half a century later as the star performer.

Bennett approached Keith Richards to act as musical director on the film, and Taylor Hackford (*An Officer and a Gentleman*) was hired to direct. Richards needed no persuading. 'I realized if I don't do it,' he said, 'I'll be kicking myself for the rest of my life . . . It was the offer you couldn't refuse. I went in knowing it wouldn't be a piece of cake, but I figured, "I'm big enough and ugly enough now. I can take Chuck Berry on any time."' During the film he says: 'If anyone was going to do it I wanted it to be me. Not so much a musical director as S & M director.' On another occasion he dubbed Berry 'the most charming cunt I ever met'.

Reputedly, he wasn't the production company's original choice. The MD on Martin Scorsese's *The Last Waltz*, surely the finest rock performance movie ever, was The Band's Robbie Robertson, but Berry's tiresome personality made the proposed gig too much of a chore for Robertson, opening the way for Richards to suffer instead.

Pre-production work and musical rehearsals progressed during the year, with the band being finalized in midsummer and rehearsals at Berry Park beginning in August. Musically, the high spot of the early sparring is a loose, good-natured version of 'Come On' sung by Robert Cray and Ingrid Berry.

Hackford's intention was to cast light on a 'dark, difficult, brilliant guy'. It is questionable whether Berry, the ultimate control freak, foresaw the degree to which the process of film-making takes that control away from the subject. He was given a co-producer credit 'in name only,' according to Bennett, and had no say in the editing of the film. His double personality is clearly on show: sometimes he is warm and approachable, sometimes he is deliberately misleading or simply clams up. And there are times when his voice becomes quieter, more deliberate, and the menace lurking behind his eyes seems suddenly to come into focus. 'Chuck has to control his environment,' said Richards, 'and I think he found it kind of strange that he wasn't in control even of his own house for a few days.'

The film *Hail! Hail! Rock 'n' Roll* begins with John Lennon's 'If you ever tried to give rock 'n' roll another name' quote. Bo Diddley, Little Richard, Jerry Lee Lewis, The Everly Brothers, Bruce Springsteen and the late Willie Dixon pop up to pay tribute to Berry. Springsteen recalls a gig when he was just beginning to make his name, supporting Berry and Jerry Lee. When the promoter said that he had to find a band to back Berry, Springsteen insisted on doing the job. 'Chuck Berry turned up five minutes before he was due on . . . Went straight to the office.' Springsteen understood that he received $11,000 in cash, and the arrangement was that he would return $1000 if the backing band was satisfactory and the equipment worked. This, it seemed, was a common Berry ploy.

When Springsteen asked Berry what songs they'd be playing the answer was, 'Some Chuck Berry songs', and as usual he would simply start playing without calling out the name of the song or the key. Springsteen noted that he played in some difficult keys for guitarists to follow. Keith Richards supplies the answer when talking about Johnnie Johnson. 'He's not playing a Chuck Berry song. It's his riff. Chuck took it and adapted it . . . he's playing in piano keys. Johnnie Johnson's keys . . .'

Hackford managed to get the semi-derelict Cosmopolitan Club opened and spruced up for a relaxed gig early in the film, and as Berry reminisces about his early days he shows total recall of the exact money he was paid for every booking. His obsession with money forms a thread through the film, as when he says that he needs to buy a new guitar about every six months. 'Deductible, you know. Tools.' He is candid about the failure of Berry Park to live up to his original plans. 'I wanted it to be like Disneyland, Six Flags or something. Turned out to be One Flag.' Later he admits: 'Actually we didn't get off the ground with this because I was touring so much.' Nonetheless, the vast acres of Berry Park are clearly seen by him as a tangible symbol of his success.

'I never heard him play in tune,' muses Richards, regretting Berry's casual attitude towards his craft. The film's most revealing high point is the rehearsal of 'Carol' at Berry Park. Richards makes the dangerous suggestion that Berry should concentrate on playing the rhythm part while he supplies the lead fills. Berry seems to deny the fact that he always overdubbed his solos. And so he keeps stopping the song before it can get under way. 'If you want to get it right, let's get it right,' he says, patiently instructing Richards on the finer points of the intro, which Richards knows backwards. When Berry finally condescends to let the song proceed, his slapdash vocal is the weakest part of the per-formance. 'That's Chuck's way of showing who's boss,' Johnson told Travis Fitzpatrick. 'He knows in his heart that he ain't near the guitar player that Keith is, but he always has to be in control. Doesn't matter who it is either. It could be the President of the United States and Chuck would tell him what to do.' 'I wouldn't warm to Chuck Berry even if I was cremated next to him,' was Richards's reaction.

'I was eating bullets, yeah,' Richards later told *Musician* magazine about this ritual humiliation by Berry. 'I figured that if I showed that I can go through that, then nobody else could complain . . . Chuck Berry is the only cat who can do that to me. I had to show the rest of the band that I was serious. They're sitting there thinking Chuck's got a knife in me and I'm going to whack him over the head with my guitar.' But, as he pointed out, Richards had worked with Mick Jagger and Brian Jones. Compared to them and their power trips, Berry was 'chicken feed'. Richards later observed: 'Chuck doesn't give a shit. Chuck only thinks about himself. I like Chuck, but I feel sorry for him. He's a very lonely man.'

The band assembled for the Fox theatre, in addition to Berry, Johnson and Richards, was bass player Joey Spampinato, preferred to Jim Marsala for his ability to get an 'upright bass' noise from his instrument, drummer Steve Jordan, saxophonist Bobby Keys, organist Chuck Leavell and guitarist Robert Cray, with guest contributions from Linda Ronstadt, Julian Lennon, Eric Clapton, Ingrid Berry and Etta James. Jordan, who had known Richards since the late 1970s and had contributed added percussion to The Rolling Stones' album *Dirty Work*, had originally been told by Richards that he wasn't the right drummer for the *Hail! Hail!* project – so Berry made a point of asking for him. Later, referring to Richards' musical debt to Berry, Jordan said: 'It really didn't matter what Chuck put him through, because Keith was going to pay that debt, no matter what it took.'

'I still love his music,' said Clapton later, 'but meeting him in some senses took the edge off it for me. I found out bit by bit that he was so concerned with money and himself, and he is such an ambitious man, that in a way it kind of spoiled the feeling for the music.' 'It may seem mean,' Berry once said, 'but a contract is a contract is a contract and I play what it says in writing.'

'Asshole that he can be,' Richards told *Musician*, 'I still love him. I'm still fascinated by what he does. I wouldn't have missed it for the world.' One of the most dynamic confrontation scenes in the film concerns the setting on Berry's amplifier. Richards and the sound engineer want to alter it because it is sounding dreadful over the headphones. 'That's my amp,' says Berry, 'and that's how I'm setting it.' In *Musician*, Richards revealed how they dealt with this problem when it came to the Fox theatre show. 'He's got to be the loudest guy in the room, so he's always going back to his amplifier and cranking it up. We just couldn't get a good sound off that amp for the film. So we ran a wire off it down to the sub-sub-sub-basement where we put his guitar through a Boogie [amp] that we had set just right. So no matter what he did on stage, we had the right sound recorded for the movie. I think it's probably the best Chuck Berry live you're ever going to get.'

There were two concerts, something that had not been made clear to those who bought tickets for the first show in the belief that it was a one-off gala performance, and Hackford filmed it in the traditional manner – in other words, there were numerous lengthy pauses for reloading the cameras and moving the lights. This further alienated the audience, since not only were they unpaid extras at a movie location, but they had actually paid for their tickets. Meanwhile a crowd was building up outside the theatre for a second house that didn't get under way until well after midnight. A total of 9200 paid $20 each, most of it going to the production company.

Given the inevitable frictions this caused, exacerbated by the fact that Berry did nothing to jolly things along during the breaks, it is perhaps surprising that the event comes over as well as it does, although when it comes to atmosphere the impromptu gig at the Cosmo Club is far more enjoyable. Richards is right about the way his subterfuge improved the sound quality, and although Hackford could surely have learned from the festival films of the late 1960s and early 1970s, above all *Woodstock* or the documentaries of D.A. Pennebaker, that you need enough cameras to keep rolling and preserve the spontaneity, once it was edited the concert does look pretty seamless.

That did not help on the night, however, which was crassly organized with no respect for the paying audience. Susan Hegger of the local *Riverfront Times* took the side of the long-suffering punters. 'Acts that were eagerly awaited didn't appear . . . [and] the filming, not the concert, dominated the evening.' Pointing out that 4000 were waiting outside for a concert that was billed to begin at 9.45 but didn't start until 12.30, she said:

While the anticipation of a memorable evening kept the mood in the lines from becoming too mean and hostile, at least one fight broke out . . .

. . . Not only did the show stretch on for what seemed like infinity, many people left voluntarily before it was even over. 'Rip off' was the word frequently overheard to describe this so-called 'once-in-a-lifetime concert event' . . . While Bob Dylan's absence was officially explained by an illness, rumour had it that Dylan had clashed with Berry during rehearsals.

Having mentioned Robbie Robertson's pointed non-appearance, Hegger also named Paul McCartney, Mick Jagger and Tina Turner as others who had been strongly rumoured to be appearing. She also pointed out that Linda Ronstadt failed to reappear for the big finale, and that Joe Walsh only turned up for the second show. Her thesis was clearly that these no-shows and partly-shows were indications of back-stage tensions.

'Mostly it was a crashing bore,' she said. '. . . but even the long, tedious intervals between numbers could have been made acceptable – had Berry seen fit to communicate in some form with the audience . . . When the cameras turned off, so did Berry.' It took the saintly Johnson to realize what was going on – or not going on – and he began to jam during the breaks, with others gradually joining in.

'I was amazed that Chuck made it,' said Richards. 'He was sixty years old that week. Johnnie Johnson was sixty-eight [Richards acci-dentally aged him by five years]. It was punishing under those lights. We didn't even stop between breaks, because we had to keep the audience in the theatre entertained while they were changing film every couple of songs . . . And you were supposed to look good the whole time. I lost 10 pounds. Our suits didn't fit by the end.'

Of the guest performers, Robert Cray is workmanlike on 'Brown Eyed Handsome Man', 'Johnny B Goode' is wasted on an out-of-place Julian Lennon, Eric Clapton excels with 'Wee Wee Hours', Linda Ronstadt sassily revives her 1978 hit version of 'Back in the USA' and the incomparable Etta James punches her considerable weight on 'Rock 'n' Roll Music' and 'Hoochie Coochie Man'. Given that number-one fan Richards was already involved it was still a strange roster in two respects – Cray, who acquits himself well, has no Berry credentials, and one can only assume that Julian Lennon is simply representing his dead father.

At the backstage party after the concerts Berry dutifully cut his birthday cake but said little, particularly to reporters. Ingrid did speak about him, though. 'He's a dear man inside, though he doesn't often let others see it. He's very private, but very generous and I can tell he is touched by what is happening to him now even if he won't say it himself.'

Richards told of watching the film with Berry at the New York Film Festival, and suddenly realizing that an embarrassing moment was about to come up, when he suggests that Johnnie Johnson, rather than Berry, wrote the melodies for the songs. 'I don't think he ever dreamt up a song or a chord sequence. So I'm sitting there in the balcony and I realize that I want a parachute, 'cause I'm about to suggest that Chuck did not write the songs . . . But he thought it was all great . . . And in the end, he did take Johnnie Johnson with him for a tour of Europe. Not that he paid him. Johnnie told me that. Chuck said to the promoters that he wanted to bring his piano player, but only if they pay him. Chuck's about bucks.'

Richards is also illuminating about Berry's attitude to his own talent. 'He doesn't see it. "If you pay me better than for my carpentry, I'll play my guitar." In a way, that's the beauty of it. He has no conception of his talent, of his stature. That's kind of beautiful. Such a mixture of spoiled, moody brat and innocent, prolific artist. It's almost impossible to fit the two guys into the same frame.' 'I never thought of anything where I could make more money,' is Berry's version. 'Politics, maybe, or show business – or racketeering. I've tried two out of the three.' After a pause he adds: 'I never had no taste for politics.'

Just before Berry started the negotiations that led to the film, the 'sixth Stone' Ian Stewart had died of a heart attack, on 12 December 1985. His piano playing had adorned records by The Rolling Stones since the early days, when manager Andrew Loog Oldham decided that his face didn't fit the image he was creating for the band, and sacked him as an on-stage member. Just before he died, Stewart had reminded Keith Richards that his hero Johnnie Johnson was still alive and playing. That above all was what resolved Richards to involve Johnson in the film. He compared Johnson and Berry to Lennon and McCartney, Leiber and Stoller and, yes, Jagger and Richards. Ever since, Johnson has gratefully pinpointed his involvement in the film as the start of his comeback, and his rehabilitation.

Nineteen eighty-six was also the year that Berry completed his autobiography, seven years after writing the first draft while in Lompoc. It is a strange piece of work in that the creator of some of the wittiest, neatest lyrics in popular music cannot translate this skill to prose, but it is also a revealing book. In the film he refuses to talk about prison and his marriage – he silences the unseen Hackford during a brief appearance by Toddy when he suspects that he may be about to ask an indiscreet question. Maybe he was deliberately saving some aspects of his life for the printed page. The prison terms and the serial adultery are a running thread through the narrative, and he even threatens to write a follow-up devoted exclusively to his sex life.

Because of Berry's stilted style the book is not particularly easy to read, and it certainly cannot be relied on as a chronological source, and yet his determination to be frank on paper where he is evasive in conversation does give some insight into his complex character. His prison memories, notably, seem more detailed than those of making music. They also seem more accurate, although of course this can only be an impression – he is our only source of information regarding his time in Springfield and Lompoc, whereas elsewhere we can weigh his recollections against discographies, and the memories of others like Johnnie Johnson and Marshall Chess.

His accounts of prison life – and remember that up until the publication of the book he was still blithely denying that he had been inside – show a model prisoner, one who took quiet satisfaction in his star status, but also someone determined to make something positive out of his loss of freedom – business studies, songwriting, drafting the autobiography, all determinedly making good use of endless free time. He has nothing to say, however, about the possibility of illegitimate children, and there is no record of any paternity suits. So either he has been extraordinarily careful or he has dealt with the situation discreetly.

A tour in summer 1987 is worthy of note because it saw Berry and Johnnie Johnson playing together in Europe for only the second time, following a one-off performance in Sweden during 1984. However, a bootleg of a performance in Nyon, Switzerland, suggests that Berry was just going through the motions as was his wont, doubly sad since for once he had an all-American touring band completed by bass player George French, drummer Herman Jackson and Ingrid Berry on second vocals.

Meanwhile on their release the film and the book reawakened the interest of the popular press yet again in the elderly rocker. 'They tell stories quietly about Chuck Berry in the corridors,' whispered the *Sunday Express*. 'He made a movie and the producer tells how he can be "incredibly dark and menacing". She says there are stories too terrible to tell. Club security at the New York Limelight, big men, pass his door cautiously; his agent dances frantic attendance. They say his mood can go from springtime to thunder in seconds, that he's unpredictable and wild.'

The book, copyrighted to Berry's own Isalee Publishing Company, was published in the USA by Harmony Books, a division of Crown Publishers, and in the UK it was picked up by the venerable and highly respectable imprint Faber and Faber. Chairman Matthew Evans recalls how the book came to them:

> At that time Pete Townshend was working for us as a consulting editor, bringing in a lot of new ideas and energy, and so for a while we were doing quite a lot of rock 'n' roll books. Chuck Berry came over, theoretically to promote the book. It's unfair to say he was a difficult author, because he was a rock star, not a writer. But he was very difficult indeed.
>
> He was staying in a hotel in Knightsbridge and we all trooped round to see him. Our publicist, a woman, went up to his room and he attacked her. I remember she came downstairs with scrambled egg in her ear! Chuck Berry was very difficult, very chippy. He felt he was being exploited, and he wouldn't do the things we needed to publicize the book. In fact, he was a complete fucking pain in the arse.

Paul Mansfield from the Melbourne paper *The Age* got the full blast of Berry's unique approach to public relations, as he reported on 26 March 1988.

> In a sixth-floor suite at London's Royal Garden Hotel, Chuck Berry is being impossible. He already has a reputation for being difficult, but this is something else. He is in London ostensibly to promote his new autobiography and . . . *Hail! Hail! Rock 'n' Roll*. But then he cancelled all his media interviews without warning. Then he cancelled his photo call too . . . He has, it is rumoured, made a pass at the female head of publicity of his publishing company, and then sulked when it was rebuffed. He has reduced several members of his PR entourage to tears.

'He's a wanker . . . Sod him,' was the tour promoter's verdict.

Eventually, Mansfield is granted five minutes, with Berry pointedly looking at his watch from the outset. His interviewer produces a press cutting that he thinks will be of interest to Berry, who says: 'You want me to read this now? On your time?' Having taken half of his rationed time to read the clipping, Berry's response is: 'Why would I find it interesting? . . . Where's your question?'

Suddenly, the mercurial Berry decides that he is willing to talk, and invites the reporter to his hotel room later. Now that the book is out, he does not deny his spells in prison. He refers proudly to the song-writing he did in Springfield. 'I've always believed that no place or condition can really hinder a person from being free if he has an active, imaginative mind . . . I did cheat the Government of my imprisonment by way of the achievements I accomplished while there.' Similarly, he used his time in Lompoc to work on his book. Berry concluded a long interview by inviting Mansfield and his girlfriend backstage at Hammersmith Odeon, and during the gig he dedicated a song to them. The baffling paradox of his personality – in this case from thunder to springtime – had unfolded in twenty-four hours.

# sex, lies
## and
## videotape

**I**N 1988 BERRY expanded his property portfolio when he bought the Southern Air Restaurant at 1102 Pitman Avenue on the outskirts of Wentzville. It is a handsome neocolonial building below Interstate 70 that had been closed up for a year. After the spate of activity connected with the book, the film and the promotional aftermath of both, Berry retreated to the Park and looked around for a new challenge. When he closed the deal for the restaurant, he put his guitar away whenever he could and busied himself with the renovations, decoration and rewiring of the property in the run-up to its opening on 12 September. It was the rewiring that was soon to put him back on the front pages for all the wrong reasons.

The restaurant seated around 140 people and, as well as the main dining area, had a music room that Berry planned to open each evening, as soon as his liquor licence came through. In the meantime he was in his element, scurrying around with pliers or carpet samples, harrying suppliers and making plans for an elegant addition to the little town's nightlife.

The building dates from the late 1930s and for years it was a convenient stopping-off place for travellers between St Louis and Columbia seeking refreshment. The house speciality was its fried chicken, and regular customers included country stars Loretta Lynn and Barbara Mandrell. Colonel Sanders once ate there, checking on the chicken, and it was particularly busy after football games in Columbia. Its Missouri Room was the only place between the two cities that served cocktails, and because there was no bar in the nearby town of Troy it enjoyed many boom years before its decline in the mid-1980s.

In the early hours of Saturday 25 March 1989, when Southern Air had been reopened for six months, fire broke out at Berry Park for the second time. Berry himself was in his St Louis house that night, and those like Francine who were asleep on the property remained unaware of the danger, but a neighbour happened to look out of her window and drove around to identify the source of the flames. She alerted the fire department just after 2.00 a.m. The firefighters, numbering about fifty and drawn from four local districts, were unable to prevent his recording studio from being completely burned down, with the blaze once more fanned by the prevailing wind, and Berry later said that a master tape containing thirteen new songs, ones that he had been working on since soon after the release of *Rockit*, had been destroyed.

'All things change,' he said philosophically. 'Nothing remains the same. There's no way to put a value on it.' In the immediate aftermath he was undecided as to whether he would rebuild the studio, which was naturally covered by insurance. 'Too much else is going on,' he said. There was no obvious cause of the fire, although arson was ruled out and so an electrical fault seemed the most likely culprit.

Berry resumed his nomadic life of one-night stands, and one in August of that year is particularly of note. He returned to the Fox theatre in St Louis, where the concerts for the movie had been filmed, and Jerry Lee Lewis came to town – supporting him yet again. This would have been a big night in any case, but as Steve Pick of the *Post-Dispatch* was delighted to report in a long piece the following day, the old rivals really bent their backs and put on a memorable show. 'Lewis just may be the single most charismatic performer I've ever seen,' enthused Pick, and captured the light and shade of Lewis's piano technique: 'He could hit one key on the piano with such delicate force at such a perfect moment as to practically suspend time itself, and at another time bang out the most wonderfully dissonant, dirty and mean chords . . .'

Surprisingly, the reporter is of the opinion that Berry 'has always seemed like a nice guy on stage,' so nice that audiences 'let him get away with not remembering his own guitar licks'. Nice and lazy, in other words. With one or two lapses, however, this was one of those nights when Berry by and large paid respect both to the audience and to his own songs, and at the end 'he put all of his obvious excitement into one of the best guitar solos imaginable, which continued for chorus after chorus while the crowd stood and cheered.' Over the years, all Berry fans will have experienced such nights, and in a way they make the surly, out-of-tune gigs even less forgivable.

Meanwhile, Berry was getting no further with his application for a liquor licence for Southern Air. As with Club Bandstand, his ambitions as mine host were clearly being thwarted by his criminal record, and the forms were simply being allowed to sit in an official's in-tray. In September 1989 he announced that he was handing over operation of the restaurant to Francine, in the hope that her faultless past would help to produce the licence. The local aldermen were sympathetic, but William J. Torno, district head of the Division of Liquor Control, blocked the application. He knew perfectly well who actually owned the restaurant and was happy to recite his criminal record, including the 1974 raid on Berry Park when thirty arrests had been made. Officials like Torno were always going to frustrate Berry whenever they had the chance.

In December the problem of the liquor licence was instantly made irrelevant when Berry's videotape escapade became common knowledge. 'Chuck Berry Taped Women' headlined the *Post-Dispatch* two days after Christmas. 'A suit accuses rock 'n' roll pioneer Chuck Berry of videotaping women as they used the women's room at his Southern Air Restaurant in Wentzville. Hosana A. Huck of Wentzville, once a cook at Southern Air, filed the suit Tuesday in St Charles County Circuit Court.' In the UK, the *News of the World* slavered: 'Rock hero's disgusting dossier: Chuck Berry Peeping Tom shame.'

The videotapes, it was alleged, 'were created for the improper purpose of the entertainment and gratification' of Berry's 'sexual fetishes and sexual predilections'. Hidden cameras were installed in the women's 'rest rooms' — one rumour was that they were actually within the toilet bowls — and were connected to equipment in a second-floor office that Berry used for 'surreptitiously making or manufacturing videotapes depicting Huck undressing and dressing and using the toilet at the restaurant'. Other female members of staff and customers had also been taped. Huck's suit claimed emotional distress, embarrassment and humiliation, and sought unspecified damages. The gadget-obsessed Berry, as self-appointed chief electrician on the Southern Air project, had certainly had the opportunity to carry out the installation.

Berry's problems intensified when *High Society* magazine, a New York top-shelf publication owned by Drake Publishers Inc., printed eight photographs of him and young white women posing in the nude. The cover story was headed 'Johnny B Bad'. He sued for $10 million, alleging that the photos had been kept in a 'secure hiding place', and that the magazine had therefore acquired stolen property – from, it was alleged, Huck's husband Vincent. For once, it seems, Toddy lost her patience. Said an unnamed informant: 'She always knew Chuck wasn't exactly what you could call faithful – but it's one thing to know something and another thing to have it plastered all over the pages of a sleazy magazine.'

Following Hosana Huck's allegations Berry closed down the restaurant 'for three days or maybe longer', and it never reopened. The building was eventually bought by the local university. The law now had him in their sights again and while the Huck case rumbled on Associate Circuit Judge William T. Lohmar signed a search warrant for Berry Park. The affidavit used to obtain the warrant mentioned tapes 'of women urinating and defecating'. One of five informants whose allegations led to the affidavit was Vincent Huck, who had worked at Berry Park from October 1985 to January 1989. He claimed that an anonymous phone call led to his discovering the Southern Air tapes. After a dawn raid on Saturday 23 June 1990 it was stated that pornographic videos, hashish, marijuana, two .22-calibre rifles, a shotgun and $122,501 were seized. One unsubstantiated report also mentioned a box of 8mm films showing bestiality.

Berry's lawyer Wayne Schoeneberg said that in order to obtain the warrant the authorities had made ludicrous claims in their affidavit, notably that there were huge amounts of cocaine at Berry Park and that of Berry's $36 million in liquid assets, $9 million had been obtained by drug dealing. 'Where's the cocaine?' asked Schoeneberg after the raid. 'The affidavit says he has been suspected for some time of transporting cocaine. Why don't they follow him? He's the easiest man in the world to follow. He travels with one suitcase and his guitar. He gets on a plane, does his show, and he comes back.'

A report in *Rolling Stone* suggested that the authorities had indeed been trailing him, following a tip-off, and that on 12 March 1989 a sniffer dog got excited about Berry's guitar case and suitcase. However, nothing was found. Schoeneberg claimed that the firearms belonged to Berry's late father, and that the raid was clearly connected to the claims about Berry's alleged misdemeanours at Southern Air.

Within a week came the next development. A suit was now filed against Berry by an unspecified number of women making the same claim as Huck, that he taped them while they were undressing and sitting on the lavatory. The judge, Lester W. Duggan Jr, kept the identities of the women secret. 'The record speaks for itself,' he said. That would be Berry's criminal record, including juvenile armed robbery, that had been used as justification for fear of reprisals should the names be known. A staff bedroom was now mentioned as well as the rest rooms, and it was said that the plaintiffs had possession of the tapes.

Schoeneberg was indignant. 'This is the craziest thing I've ever heard of,' he said. 'He [Duggan] entertained a motion by one lawyer to a lawsuit, without any right for Charles Berry to be heard, for his attorney to be present . . . Has Charles Berry been stripped of all his rights? It seems to be open season on him.'

Hosana Huck's husband Vincent now got involved in the story once more. On 29 June, he alleged, Schoeneberg and another lawyer, Rex Burlison, picked a fight with him in a St Charles barroom. Schoeneberg immediately underwent a polygraph test and proclaimed: 'The results of that test are conclusive that I am telling the truth and that my accusers are lying.' 'It means nothing,' replied Assistant Prosecuting Attorney John Zimmerman. It was becoming clear that Vincent Huck was the instigator of both the scandal over the Southern Air tapes and the raid on Berry Park. 'He's got dollar signs in his eyes,' said one police source quoted in *Rolling Stone*. 'I don't think anybody at the Drug Enforcement Administration here in St Louis would admit that they even associate with him any more.'

The next development in the farce came when County Prosecutor William Hannah announced that neither he nor his staff would any longer discuss with the media any of the cases his office was involved with. With the Berry case in mind, he said: '[Attorneys] are bombarded by calls from the media for comments and information, taking time away from important duties.' Many of the callers, of course, wanted to know, in Schoeneberg's words, 'Where's the cocaine?' The police apparently went in to bust an international drug dealer and found a dirty old man instead.

This news blackout was in marked contrast to Hannah's hasty announcement of a press conference immediately after the raid, on 28 June, which to the surprise of many Berry attended. Hannah, in withdrawing cooperation with the press, was still bridling at the fact that Berry had upstaged him on that occasion. Once Hannah had given brief details of the police action Berry addressed the assembled press. 'I never used cocaine,' he insisted. 'And nobody in my band does either.' He also asserted that he would not be driven out of town by his enemies. 'I was born here. Thank God I can stay here.'

But a visit to Sweden removed him briefly from the firing line. Through his promoter he issued a statement saying: 'It must be a sting. Someone is out to get me.' And they were getting *to* him as well – at Stockholm airport he swung his shoulder bag at a television cameraman and knocked him to the ground. Back in St Louis, Schoeneberg confirmed that the charges included making pornographic movies of three young women, whose identities had been established by those who had seen the tapes. However, he added, there was no reason why Berry shouldn't complete his contracted tour of Sweden. On his return, said Schoeneberg, he would 'turn himself in, make bond, and then go on with business as usual'.

This is exactly what Berry did, in answer to charges that were now limited to possession of marijuana and indecent filming of minors, which was categorized as a form of child abuse under Missouri law. He denied both, and was released on a property bond of $20,000. The *Post-Dispatch* expressed its frustration at Prosecutor Hannah's withdrawal of cooperation. 'First he was criticized for holding a news conference about a search at Chuck Berry's home . . . that turned up little if anything of what it was supposed to find. Then, stung by negative reviews of that performance, he decided that he and his assistants won't discuss their business with the press . . . Responding to reporters' questions doesn't detract from a prosecutor's job; it is an important part of that job.'

At the time Hannah, a Republican, was campaigning to be his party's candidate for re-election to his post as Prosecuting Attorney. He was one of three Republicans seeking the post, and it had been nearly twenty years since an incumbent had been re-elected. One local lawyer said of him: 'I don't think he is capable of making a competent decision.' Retorted Hannah: 'Even the difficult cases, we don't shy away from. Including when a rock 'n' roll legend gets charged with a crime.'

The residents of Wentzville were split in their attitude towards the rock 'n' roll legend. Perhaps surprisingly, he still had many defenders. 'He's a good person,' said Clara Fortmann, who did his laundry. 'He gives me good tips and always sends Christmas presents.' Local garage owner George Ehll recalled Berry's efforts to assist racial integration in the town, when 'he held meetings with civic leaders and town officials . . . but he never got any thanks for it.' And a friend of Berry's, Theresa Schmitt, was convinced that he'd been framed. 'All he's ever done,' she said, 'is be a black man dating a lot of white girls.' The fact that he was a *married* black man did not seem to enter the equation.

On the other hand, the town elders seemed embarrassed by the presence of the errant Berry in their midst. There was no official acknowledgement of their resident celebrity, no use of his name to put the place on the map, and he was not mentioned in a booklet produced at the time by the Wentzville Chamber of Commerce. 'With all the trouble he's been in lately,' said the town's mayor Lee Barton, 'maybe it's a good thing.' Others claimed that Berry was simply irrelevant to the town's economic health.

In September the police returned the cash they had seized, tacitly admitting in doing so that it could not be the proceeds of drug dealing. 'I don't know if they are going to pay me interest on it,' said Berry with irony, but he claimed that he was far more concerned about his reputation. 'I don't think any of my friends, my colleagues or my associates – or even my enemies – think I'm involved with drugs.'

A month later Berry went on the offensive, shrewdly filing a $600,000 suit against Hannah for 'prosecutorial misconduct', and later in November got the result he had gambled on. The child abuse charges were dropped in return for a guilty plea to the misdemeanour of smoking marijuana, for which he was given two years' unsupervised probation. But the saga rolled on – Vincent Huck now sued Berry for libel, denying the accusation that he had stolen the photographs or videotapes.

'It's like a nuclear reaction,' said Richard Schwarz, one of Berry's lawyers. 'Huck sold the pictures and guaranteed he'd hold *High Society* harmless [i.e. confirm that the magazine bought the photographs in good faith]. Berry filed suit against the magazine and within days Huck's wife sues Berry.' The implication was clear – the theft of the photographs, the emergence of the underage videos, the Southern Air tapes and the drugs charges were all part of the same conspiracy against his client.

With the most serious charges against him now settled, Berry in turn dropped his suit against the beleaguered Hannah, whose attempt to secure re-election to his post was meanwhile roundly rejected by the electorate. Berry made a $5000 donation towards local drugs rehabilitation efforts. The 'lavatory tapes' were now the only threat to him.

In August 1991 he resumed his tactical battle against a local legal system that he was convinced was out to get him by fair or foul means. The gloves were off, said Schwarz. 'We're going to clear out the underbrush and get rid of these trashy people. A lot of the problem in St Charles County is that it acts like an old-time country machine when it's become an urban county.'

Berry filed a thirty-five-page complaint in the US District Court seeking that the civil suits still hanging over him be thrown out, and claiming that he should receive damages. He was unable to get a fair hearing, the complaint asserted, because 'a courthouse inflamed with racial animus [had] polluted the pool of potential jurors'. About the raid on Berry Park, he said: 'The search was fraudulent. There was no cocaine out there. There is no cocaine. There will be no cocaine.' In February 1992 Berry's complaint was rejected, on the grounds that his 'claims of civil rights violations fell short of Supreme Court standards allowing federal courts to take over cases filed first in state court'. It took another three long years for the videotape scandal to reach its conclusion.

'Most Women In Berry Settlement Will Get $5000,' announced the *Post-Dispatch* on 24 May 1995. Earlier in the year Berry had agreed to pay $830,000 into court as compensation to the women, who by now numbered seventy-four! According to the story the court apportioned the money, with the first-named victim, presumably Huck, due to receive $18,000, nine other named victims $17,000 each, two women whose children were taped $10,000 and the others $5000. Two days later the paper published a correction stating that Berry had paid a total of $1.2 million into court. Much of it, of course, was swallowed up in legal fees.

In the meantime, the proprietor of a video store and suntan saloon in Buffalo, some 200 miles from St Louis, had apparently been taping women clients as they lay naked on the sun beds. The store was shut down and the local newspaper editor went on record lamenting that the scandal had overshadowed the week's real news in Buffalo, the opening of a new gearbox-manufacturing plant. The accused proprietor complained that he didn't have the resources of a Chuck Berry to fight the charge.

Berry's overdeveloped sex drive has always been vigorously expressed in the rock star's conventional way, serial on-the-road adultery, as his autobiography confirms. In idle moments it seems to have spilled over not just into pornography, but in the notion of himself as the porn star. Not publicly, like the named performers who have established an alternative, above-ground Hollywood industry, but in home movies shot for his own entertainment – which, almost inevitably, have in fact become a matter of public record, presumably by theft. The boy who was fascinated by photography became the man with a fetish for young white girls, and the two hobbies were seamlessly combined. Unlike the ladies in the lavatory, his partners are clearly aware that they are being taped.

Someone who knows him well suggests that there is a strange symbolism involved in Berry's need to videotape himself having sex. 'It is as if it purifies the act by being captured on film, and makes him godlike. He has the power to do it, and the filming is a demonstration of his power.' Suddenly one is reminded of the monstrous businessman, bully, crook and giant ego Robert Maxwell, who was alleged sometimes to berate his minions while enthroned on his office lavatory. His ego had moved him beyond the trappings of dignity that we lower beings need to preserve our sense of self-worth. He could do anything, and what's more he could do it while having a crap. It is said that the American president Lyndon B. Johnson also held court in this way.

It is alleged that on one tape Berry urinates into a girl's mouth and when she responds by saying, as if on cue, 'Kiss me,' he replies, 'No, you smell of piss.' In an act of *soixante-neuf* on another occasion he farts in the girl's face, as if offering the fart as a gift. These bizarre curiosities must presumably be seen as exercises in power, not self-abasement. Such material as has surfaced shows no sign of masochism on Berry's part, just a lean and lengthy athleticism. And a full bladder.

A German company, Nobel Video, got hold of one eighty-minute tape and issued it as *Sweet Little Sexteen*. 'Chuck Berry: Die wilden SEX-ORGIEN mit seinen heiBesten Groupies!' promised the sleeve, which showed a shadowy Berry, seemingly in late middle age, posing with a young white girl, both naked apart from Berry's glinting wristwatch – one of the *High Society* pictures. 'When you've watched this film,' promises Nobel, 'you'll know all about Chuck Berry's ding-a-ling!' Meanwhile a 1993 edition of the American satirical investigative magazine *Spy* ran a lengthy piece about Berry's alleged enthusiasm for coprophilia as well as water sports. 'I never read the papers,' commented his wife.

# the oldest
# swinger in
# town

'TIME IS CATCHING up as Chuck Berry keeps on rockin'
and rollin',' read the strapline, while the piece was headed
'Golden oldie loses sparkle'. This happened to be a review
by Mike Priestley in the *Bradford Telegraph & Argus* dated 22 November
1991, but, alas, the comments could have applied to so many Berry gigs
of the past fifteen years. 'He's past it. He's just been going through the
motions,' said one middle-aged fan as she left the hall, after a lacklustre performance that naturally did not include an encore. The
microphone was set too high and the sound was wrong. 'When you're
old you want to have it right,' Berry told the audience. 'And if you want
to have it right, perhaps the best thing to do is turn up for a sound
check,' commented the reviewer.

The hits were paraded, as was Ingrid, and before his abrupt departure Berry got members of the audience up to dance to 'Reelin' and
Rockin''. The format of the show, the lazy attitude to the sound quality and Berry's willingness to blame anyone but himself – we
long-suffering fans know that by the late 1980s Berry was indeed going
through the motions. But with his investments secure, what else was he
to do? We keep turning up in the knowledge that there must be one

good gig left in him, unwilling to settle only for memories – and just occasionally, in the nick of time, he rewards our patience.

Apart from a couple of live recordings, one in Germany and one in Denmark, dated 1998, the only Berry recording to emerge in the 1990s – and the last studio effort to date – was a real curiosity. Shabba Ranks, real name Rexton Gordon, is a Jamaican reggae rapper and disc jockey, and in 1994 he released a track called 'Go Shabba Go' which purports to be a duet between the rapper and the rocker. The music is a painful collision of reggae and Berry's rock 'n' roll, over which the pair conduct a very stilted dialogue.

The musicians could include the legendary rhythm section of Sly Dunbar and Robbie Shakespeare, since Dunbar is one of several composer credits. The record was put together by producer Clifton Dillon, and either he or Ranks approached Berry for his contribution. According to Dave Torretta, it nearly didn't happen, for a familiar reason: 'Chuck wasn't going to perform until he had the money in his hand, so they were all waiting on him.' It seems unlikely that the pair ever met, and more likely that Berry's part was cut in New York before Dillon pieced together this unlikely collaboration. 'Chuck Berry keep the world merry, an' Shabba keep the girls happy.' Curiously, it was only included as a 'bonus' track on the European pressing of the CD *A Mi Shabba*, but this may be a comment on its quality.

Berry, though, continues to work on songs at Berry Park. There are persistent rumours of a forthcoming album. Jim Marsala, interviewed in 1984, said: 'He's making a double album . . . Johnnie and Chuck are laying the tracks now . . . it'll come out in '85.' By 1985 the date had moved on a year, to tie in with the sixtieth birthday celebrations. Still nothing happened. And it still hadn't appeared by the time of the fire in 1989.

Now he's back at work, always pushing back the deadline. 'He got serious about May [2001],' says Dave Torretta. 'He's always cutting stuff at his home studio, but he's usually not happy with it. We had the idea of getting it ready for his seventy-fifth birthday. Didn't make it. He's got "Big Boys" and "Dutchman". "Lady B Goode" – a great American Chuck Berry story. A couple of instrumentals. Maybe spring . . .' Very occasionally Berry has performed another new song, 'Loco Joe', at concerts, but his worries about being bootlegged have usually kept all this new material under wraps. And so far, just like the 1980s' compositions that presumably went up in smoke, that is where it remains at the time of writing.

Berry was back in the UK in February 1995 for a sixteen-date tour. One fanzine reviewer, Brian Smith, expected little when he attended the Bradford date. 'After many truly wonderful nights with the brown-eyed handsome man in the 60s and 70s, I've had to sit through too many achingly disappointing ones since to expect very much any more.' Compensation for those wasted nights came in the best Berry performance Smith had witnessed for twenty years. 'He paced the act well, interspersing rockers with a few blues, along with some jokes and patter . . . All in all, a cracking little show, all the more satisfying because of what's gone before.' Once in a while the enigmatic, unpredictable Berry could still produce the goods if he felt like it.

In May fans in Denmark inaugurated The European Chuck Berry Convention, a three-day event honouring someone who, as with many rock 'n' roll and blues originals, was probably more revered in the UK and mainland Europe than at home. However, in September the long-awaited opening of the Rock 'n' Roll Hall of Fame and Museum in Cleveland, Ohio, took place. As befits the man who was first on the list to be inducted, back in the days when the Hall of Fame was an idea awaiting a building, Berry starred in the inaugural concert. A capacity crowd of 57,000 in nearby Cleveland Stadium on the shore of Lake Eyrie heard him and Bruce Springsteen get a six-hour gig under way by duetting on 'Johnny B Goode'. John Mellencamp, Martha Reeves, Bon Jovi, Eric Burdon, Melissa Etheridge, Dr John, Al Green and Chrissie Hynde also performed.

In May 1996 Berry played one of his most unusual gigs. He was booked by the Civic Democratic Alliance in the Czech Republic to play in Dominican Square, Brno, at an all-day rally marking the first democratic elections since the split from Slovakia in 1993. He used some local backing musicians and was supported by three Czech bands and some lengthy political speeches. Berry had accepted the invitation on the understanding that he was not required to get involved in the political situation and, true to form, he cancelled an afternoon press conference before his appearance. The enthusiastic crowd, reportedly, struggled to follow his between-song patter but sang along with 'Roll Over Beethoven', 'Johnny B Goode' and the inevitable 'My Ding-a-Ling'.

October 1998 marked not just his seventy-second birthday but his golden wedding anniversary to Themetta, celebrated with a family party in a St Louis hotel, where his brother Henry – the Reverend Henry W. Berry – renewed their loosely observed wedding vows. And so Mrs Berry, having put up with his behaviour for half a century, signed on for another stint.

By the turn of the century Berry's most creative work was largely limited to his monthly gigs at local St Louis club Blueberry Hill, of which more later, but there were also creaking caravans like the Legends of Rock 'n' Roll tour of Europe in late summer 2000. The legends were Jerry Lee Lewis, Little Richard and Berry, and the rumour was that this was the last time that they would tour together – it was a repeat of similar European adventures in 1997 and 1998. The London venue was the bleak and vast ice-hockey shed of the London Arena in Docklands, as opposed to Wembley for the previous tour, and Berry won over the crowd – perhaps conscious that they were witnessing the passing of an era – with his familiar routine of known-by-heart hits, the casual collisions between one set of lyrics and another, and his sheer stage charisma.

The fourteen-song set began with 'Roll Over Beethoven' and included the familiar 'Mean Old World' and, curiously, 'I Do Really Love You' from *Chuck Berry in Memphis* among the hits, building up to a stretched-out version of 'Reelin' and Rockin''. Berry was sharp, good-humoured, and behaved in total contrast to the usual throwaway attitude of his later years. In the echoing cavern of the Arena, his guitar actually sounded in tune. Maybe that story about this being the last time the three cornerstones of rock 'n' roll would play together was just a promoter's pitch. If so, it worked – the place was comfortably full, and the crowd went home happy.

It took a lot of persuading on the part of Frances and many friends concerned about his best interests, but at last Johnnie Johnson agreed to do something about seeking acknowledgement for his part in Berry's music. There can be no doubt that Berry has always privately recognized the debt he owes to Johnson. Along Delmar Boulevard in St Louis there's a Walk of Fame, a series of brass stars and citations sunk into the pavement, honouring the celebrities associated with the city. In 1998 Johnson was included and, at the buffet party afterwards, Berry made a joking remark to the effect that, 'I got a song named after you.' He then got serious, and added, 'I got a *career* named after you.'

But Berry has never made any move towards financial recognition of this debt. Even when Johnson was at his lowest ebb, no help was forthcoming. Occasionally Berry would instruct Francine to call Johnson, offering him a gig, and afterwards Johnson would return to the hostel where he was staying. Otis Woodard, who employed Johnson as a bus driver for his food distribution charity at this time, once came across a picture of his employee in the local library, in a book paying tribute to St Louis musical heroes. He borrowed the book, rushed back to the charity office, and confronted Johnnie. 'Who *are* you?' 'Oh, yeh, I used to play piano a bit.'

But on 29 November 2000 Johnson filed a suit against Berry in a St Louis Federal District Court. It claimed that the two men were equal collaborators on fifty-two songs, including 'Roll Over Beethoven', 'No Particular Place To Go' (and hence 'School Day') and 'Sweet Little Sixteen'. Berry had been contacted before the action was started but refused to negotiate. 'On countless occasions beginning in 1955,' the suit alleges, 'Mr Berry failed to inform Mr Johnson that . . . because of his significant contributions to the creation of the Berry/Johnson songs, [Johnson] was entitled to a share in the copyright ownership and in the massive profits that were being generated by those copyrights.'

Berry's longtime agent, Dick Alen, was dismissive. 'If he hasn't filed the lawsuits for the forty years since the songs were written, I don't think it was true then, and I don't think it is true now.' Alen added that Berry was 'disappointed that Johnnie would do something like this'. The suit continued to say that Johnson let Berry assume leadership of the Trio 'in recognition of the fact that while Mr Berry was not of the same calibre as Mr Johnson as a musician and composer of music, Mr Berry was the superior lyricist, showman and . . . businessman'. It alleged that Berry took advantage of Johnson's alcoholism and naivety by concealing from him the fact that he was entitled to a share of the royalties. Unspecified damages were sought in settlement of the suit.

A publicist hired by Johnson's supporters to argue his case, Julie Doppelt, observed: 'He's a savant. He doesn't even know how to write music, he retains it in his head. And aside from having no sense of what the music business was, he would compose the music in his head and not realize that [by doing so] he composed the songs. Chuck would take advantage of this and register the copyright in his name.' Johnson's lawyer Mitch Margo said that his client 'was unable to appreciate the value of his contribution. Berry misled him into believing he was only entitled to a studio musician's fee.'

There is a three-year period in which a complainant can claim ownership of a copyright registered to someone else, and if this is deemed to apply then Johnson, if successful, would only be due a share of royalties for the period in the 1960s immediately after their regular collaboration ceased. On the other hand if this statute of limitation is deemed not to apply because of Berry's deliberate concealment of Johnson's rights, then Isalee, Berry's publishing company, stands to lose millions.

The process for recognition had begun in 1993 when Johnson was booked by a wealthy Houston businessman, George Turek, to play at his wedding. It was a mistake – Turek thought he was getting the blues guitarist Jimmy Johnson – but once he learned of Johnnie's story he decided to launch the effort to get his role acknowledged. He financed Johnson's biography – author Travis Fitzpatrick is his stepson. 'The more I learned about him the more I felt someone had to lead the way to make sure he gets all the accolades and honours he deserves before he passes on,' said Turek.

This crusade became entwined with another goal – to see Johnson inducted into the Rock 'n' Roll Hall of Fame. In May 1998 an advertisement in *Billboard*, featuring a photograph of Johnson and Berry, was addressed 'To The Nominating Committee'. 'Chuck wrote the words,' it said. 'Johnnie created the music.' And it asked the committee to 'Please do the right thing. Please place Johnnie's name on this year's ballot. He deserves to be recognized during his lifetime for the monumental contributions he made to rock 'n' roll. "But without Johnnie giving Chuck those riffs – Voilà! – no song, just a lot of words on paper." He created the music that started it all.'

On 13 January 1997 Berry sent a letter to Ahmet Ertegun at Atlantic Records. 'It has recently come to my attention that Johnnie

Johnson is being considered for nomination for the Rock & Roll Hall of Fame,' he wrote. 'I would like you to know that I am in full support of Johnnie's nomination. Johnnie and I have been friends and musical collaborators for over forty years. In my opinion, his membership into the Rock & Roll Hall of Fame would be of great value to the Foundation. His induction would round out the list of those musicians who made significant contributions during rock 'n' roll's infancy . . .'

The goal was achieved on 19 March 2001 following a campaign endorsed by Keith Richards, Dick Clark, Eric Clapton, Bo Diddley, Buddy Guy, John Lee Hooker, Etta James, Bob Weir (the ex-Grateful Dead guitarist with whom Johnson played in Weir's later band RatDog), Little Richard, Charles Brown, Jimmy Rogers, John Sebastian and Rod Stewart – and Chuck Berry. 'If I'm in the Hall of Fame and he's not, there is something wrong there,' Weir said. Rock Hall, as it is known to local cab-drivers, had to create a new 'Sideman' category to accommodate Johnson.

Before this, Berry received an honour of his own. In December 2000 he was at the John F. Kennedy Center in Washington to receive one of its prestigious Honors for services to the performing arts, along with dancer Mikhail Baryshnikov, actor–director Clint Eastwood, opera singer Placido Domingo and actress Angela Lansbury. Berry's tribute was delivered by a composer from a different discipline, Marvin Hamlisch, who said: 'I was taught the music of the three Bs, Bach, Beethoven and Brahms. But as a teenager I lived with the fourth B – Chuck Berry . . . I'm as proud of him as I am of George Gershwin and Leonard Bernstein.' 'Seated nearby with Mr and Mrs Chuck Berry Jr,' noted the *Washington Post*'s Ken Ringle, 'the duck-walking composer of "Johnny B Goode" looked touched and positively humbled.'

These days, inevitably, Berry packs his guitar case and heads for Lambert airport less often than in previous years. But he's still happy tinkering with the controls of his home studio, working towards that long-delayed album. 'He just does what he wants,' says Dave Torretta. 'It depends on his mood. But he's mellowed now – he used to get in your face, and he was particularly tough on drummers for some reason. No drummer was good enough. He just wants it simple – and perfect. His present drummer is excellent, and yet he still gives him the cold shoulder.

'Berry is his own man. He distrusts people. He's obstinate. And very painstaking, particularly with his lyrics. And yet in the last few years he's been a jewel. Really kind, in fact. In the work process he can get frustrated, of course. Difficult even. But generally he's a gem.'

# i found my
# thrill

O LIVER SAIN PLACES his fizzy drink down on the bar, and chuckles. He is sitting just inside the door of BB's Blues, Jazz and Soups, a blues bar in Soulard, south St Louis, where good music is still to be had for the price of a beer, a Coke, or for that matter a bowl of soup. Sain is a local legend, a mellow saxophonist now in his late sixties, a bandleader, songwriter, producer and engineer. He made hits for Chess Records in the 1960s, wrote songs like 'The Soul of a Man' for Fontella Bass and 'Walk Away' for Ann Peebles, and for years he has run his own studio on St Louis' Natural Bridge. Everyone knows Oliver, and he plays BB's every Thursday that his worrisome health permits.

Sain is a living example of the richness of St Louis music. In March 2001, at the Pageant concert hall on Delmar Boulevard, a show called *50 Years of Music: A Tribute to Oliver Sain* took place. Johnnie Johnson, Ike Turner and Little Milton, who arrived in town with Sain in 1959, were just three of the musicians who turned out to support Sain, while various civic dignitaries pressed awards and praise on him. It was a freezing night, the Pageant was full, and the modest, reserved Sain looked both delighted and a little overwhelmed.

Johnson played 'Kansas City', the Leiber and Stoller classic that has been part of his set for years, and returned later to support Little Milton. Turner showed his mastery of guitar and keyboards, nearly fifty years after his prodigious talent first hit town. Sometimes, as one observer remarked, he sounded like Link Wray, sometimes Jimi Hendrix. And after all his well-publicized troubles he looked as lean, as mean and as fit as ever, and a CD of new recordings released later in the year confirmed that time had not dimmed his talent. Tyrone Davis came on to sing his hits like 'Turn Back the Hands of Time' and 'Give It Up' before Little Milton, joined by his old friend Sain, topped the three-hour show.

Later in the year, when I caught up with him, Sain was wearing the same modest smile, but was clearly more comfortable back on his own turf down in Soulard. 'Chuck Berry?' he said. 'Hmm. He is a *strange* bird. Yes, sir. I tell you, though, he knows how to make a dollar. And how to keep it. A very good businessman, you get my meaning?' Too good-natured to be drawn further, Sain left the bar and climbed onto the stage, setting up a slinky riff on his electric keyboard. Later he threw in a Chuck Berry song, just for fun.

And now there are *new* Chuck Berry songs, and Dave Torretta insists that Berry seems serious about cutting the first album since 1979. But from the sixtieth birthday in 1986, the release of *Hail! Hail! Rock 'n' Roll* a year later, and most recently the seventy-fifth birthday in 2001, marked by a St Louis concert co-starring Little Richard, the possible 'pegs' for release have passed one by one. Berry is aware of this. He told *Billboard* in autumn 2001: 'It's laziness, or after you've had so much success, you get slack on the ability and the initiative, you know? And it's not right! It's my profession – it's what I should be doing.'

He enthused about his first extended experience of the computerized Pro Tools system that has replaced magnetic tape. 'I've done thirty hours there already,' he said, referring to local studio Four Seasons Media Productions. 'It's great, really up to date, and brand-new.' The unfinished material I was privileged to hear in St Louis certainly whetted the appetite, but I'm not holding my breath.

'Chuck? Yeh, Chucko I call him. I used to play guitar with him a lot. Round here, you know? He was awesome. "Play a guitar just like ringing a bell." That was him all right – I could take a solo fine, but then he'd just blow me away.'

Bob Friend and I have driven 30 miles west of St Louis, along a typically dreary motorscape, but as soon as you drop off Highway 70 into Wentzville you step back from urban America. Here, you feel, the price of cattle-cake or grain is more important than that of steel – only to learn that a car plant is second only to farming in the local economy. We drink beer in a bar that might have featured in a million dusty movies, before stepping outside to ask directions.

Paul Ross is loading his pick-up truck in the warm autumn sunshine. Just talk to someone in Wentzville, it seems, and they've played with Chuck Berry. 'Berry Park? Yeh, I used to go out there a lot when I was a kid,' says Paul. 'Back when it was open to the public. Then I used to play in the bars around here. But I've been sober for twelve years now. No reason to go into bars any more. Still play, though, me and my brother. As a matter of fact, Chuck owns that bar across the street. Or used to, any rate.' Paul points to another entry in Berry's property portfolio, an unprepossessing single-storey concrete building that seems to be very closed for business. 'If you see Chucko on the street around town he's just a regular guy. On stage, man, he's something else. Of course, he also had Southern Air, you know, on the way out of town. Until he screwed it all up.'

We follow Paul's directions out to Berry Park, along a straight, peaceful country road. The huge stone at the entrance – a tombstone, as Berry discovered once he'd bought it – announces that Berry Park is for the people. For a while it was indeed a brave experiment in interracial All-American leisure. Now, the stern 'No Trespassing' and 'Private – Keep Out' notices conflict sadly with the aspirations expressed on the stone. It looks locked, lonely and deserted.

Maybe Berry still harbours ambitions for his Park. But as a public leisure complex it had died on Independence Day 1974, when it was meant to host its third and last festival. Berry claims that an unidentified promoter was hired to put the event together, but failed to pay the star Leon Russell an agreed advance, as a result of which Russell did not appear. The promoter then disappeared without paying Berry Park or the other artists either. A disgruntled crowd, which Berry puts at 60,000, caused a huge amount of damage, and there were allegations of drug taking and thirty arrests. Berry's is the only available testimony to the fact that a third party, an outside promoter, was the cause of the trouble. He continued to work on improvements to landscaping and hard-standing areas, however, and so it seems likely that the dream died by degrees.

One of the liveliest places amid the sprawl of St Louis is a neon strip of the east–west Delmar Boulevard, six blocks long from Cicero's restaurant to the Pageant theatre. At its heart is Blueberry Hill, a bar, restaurant, music venue and memorabilia museum. This area is known as the Loop, where the trolley cars used to turn round. The revival of the area began when entrepreneur Joe Edwards opened Blueberry Hill in 1972.

'When my wife Linda and I bought the property it was just vacant space, used as a warehouse,' he says. 'I needed somewhere to display my collection of pop culture. At that time this neighbourhood was at a very low point, with a lot of properties boarded up. Now within the six blocks there are ten stages for live music, from an audience of seventy-five up to my new building The Pageant, which holds 2000-plus. With other people coming in I'd say this is now the liveliest neighbourhood in St Louis.'

No visiting Brit need feel homesick at Blueberry Hill, since one huge room is devoted to darts. 'In the first few weeks we were open,' says Edwards, 'a local reporter came in and offered me his dartboard if I'd put it up in the bar. At first I said no, but then the next day a different guy asked me where the dartboard was. He had a beer and left. On the third day the same thing, except that this time the guy didn't even buy a beer first. A few days later the reporter came back and I said, "Hey, let me have that board." I'd been conned, of course, by a darts fan. But it worked. It makes it a great social centre.' And it also adds to the nostalgic 'pub rock' feel of the place – beer, food, darts and Chuck Berry.

At the other end of this rambling property, past the booths and bars and Edwards's showcases and displays, which include 'the guitar that changed the world', a Chuck Berry blond Gibson, are the stairs leading down to the Duck Room. As well as a regular roster of local bands Edwards attracts some impressive names to his pub – 'John Mayall has been here several times, Leon Russell, Koko Taylor, Dave Davies from The Kinks . . .'

The basement room is named not for Berry's duck walk but for the huge metal beam supporting the ceiling. Until Edwards dug out 3ft of dirt to lower the floor, performers on the stage were in danger of decapitation, and the sightlines were poor. The room is wide but shallow from the stage to the bar at the back, the pillars are slender, and admission is restricted to a comfortable, breathable number. It is close to being the perfect pub-rock venue, and Chuck Berry plays here one Wednesday a month. Bar-owner Edwards is clearly a persuasive man, to seduce Berry into making a monthly Cadillac crawl from his luxury home in Indian Hills.

'I first met him in the mid-60s,' Edwards recalls, 'but that was just saying hello after a concert. In the mid-80s I started doing a rock 'n' roll beer at Blueberry Hill, just for fun. There was a series "Heroes of Rock 'n' Roll" on the can. Chuck had to be the first, of course. So that's how we got together. It was just one of those things – we realized we could trust each other. So we became friends over the years and one night he said it would be nice to have a place to play locally. Not necessarily the usual show with all the hits, maybe a little blues, just a family evening.

'We looked at each other and said, let's do it. He'd turn up and play unannounced, just sit in. Then in 1996 we began regular monthly advertised gigs. Obviously he plays for much less than his normal fee. He's very reasonable about it. Always punctual, always puts on a great concert. Sometimes his daughter Ingrid comes along, and his son Charles Jr is in the band. We keep it comfortable by limiting admission to 350, which is below capacity.'

'It's a whole different ball game playing here because of the warm relations between Joe and myself,' the *Post-Dispatch* reported Berry as saying in 1998. 'I didn't ask to be accepted here, but the acceptance has meant a lot.' Apart from these intimate home-town occasions, however, he admitted that 'the thrill has gone' after nearly fifty years of live performances, amounting to some 4600 gigs. As for why he stayed in his home town, he said: 'Fame didn't take me away because my family is here. One thing I found out is that almost every place is just about the same.'

During the same interview he explained his businesslike approach to gigs. 'Work on a flat guarantee and have it paid in advance. You can make more working on a percentage but if you do, you have to have somebody watch the box office. Then you have to have a couple of people watch them! And before you know it you've got an entourage . . .'

In the crowd for Berry's November 2001 appearance are a large group of dressed-down Italian businessmen, a Japanese party and at least two locals, my hosts Bob and Marilyn, who have never seen him perform before. Until now, I suggest, Berry has been their St Paul's Cathedral, since in all my years in London I have never made it beyond the front steps. Berry has always been available two miles from their home, but it took a tourist to prompt the visit. The Italians confirm that they are not here by accident. 'Chuck Berry is very famous in Italy. So when we heard that he was playing in a club we just had to make it part of our visit.'

The warm-up quartet, Kerry Hudson and the Mudbone Band, play spiky, energetic rockabilly, an ideal hors d'oeuvre. But Berry, of course, gave up trying years ago. At times he can clearly be so bored with the songs that have built his fortune that one wonders yet again why he bothers to strap on the Gibson for just another discordant, rushed, unrehearsed gig. Blueberry Hill could prove a waste of thousands of miles and a bloated credit card, but to see Chuck Berry play a pub room? I had yet to talk to Edwards and be assured that Berry always puts his back into this little monthly performance, but like the Italians, I thought it was worth the punt.

The presence of his longtime bass player Jim Marsala, his instrument cradled high on his chest, gives some reassurance of structure to the evening, and the giant of a man on keyboards, Bob Lohr, who has played with Berry for five years, will clearly take no nonsense from the star, and probably from nobody else either. He riffs stony-faced throughout, and when given the space rips out some perfect Johnnie Johnson solos. On drums there's Bob Kuban, whose 'northern soul' groove 'The Cheater' reached no. 12 in the *Billboard* charts in 1966, a trick repeated with lesser success by the follow-ups 'The Teaser' and 'Drive My Car'. A local star. Chuck Berry Jr, keeping a respectful eye on his father, completes the supporting cast on second guitar. When Dad gives him the nod at times during the evening and he eases into a solo the contrast in style is intriguing – he's a Berry all right, but his technique is filtered through the hard-rock sensibility of a forty-year-old. And physically, the stocky, shaven-headed Chuck Jr offers another contrast with his lean, dark-haired father.

Thankfully there is no endless sideshow riffing, no prolonged build-up to 'showtime, layze'n'gennelmen'. Berry is nothing if not businesslike, he's got a gig to do and this is one promoter he doesn't argue with, so soon he saunters on and plugs in. At seventy-five he is still stick-thin, stooping slightly now and methodical in his movements, as if he has to consider every rock 'n' roll pose before he does it. Although age has bent his shoulders, his height, still above 6 feet, makes him a commanding presence. The hair is as it ought to be, crinkled, greased back and jet black, maybe with a little artificial assistance. His two brief duck-walks late in the set may not get him safely under the family kitchen table these days, but they are essayed athletically enough to raise the roof. For his age he looks as fit as a whippet. I'm willing to forget the mucky videos, the sometimes mean-spirited attitude to life, the years of evil-eyed confrontations with the world, as long as he doesn't ruin my evening.

Will he be in tune? His former bass player Dave Torretta tells me: 'When I was in his band with Billy Peek on guitar we used to take it in turns to distract Chuck backstage before we went on. Ask him about anything, it didn't matter. Then the other one could get a hold of his guitar and check the tuning.' *Nobody* touches Chuck Berry's guitar and too often it seems that this rule covers the great man himself, lazily ignoring the slipped strings and riffing on regardless. He favours a very light-gauge string suited to his style, more likely to stretch and slacken than a heavier-duty wire.

But on this night he is in tune, almost, and he's ripping into 'Rock 'n' Roll Music' just 10 feet away from me. Yes, worth the gamble. After a sketched-in version of 'Let It Rock' the liberties taken with 'Memphis' cannot disguise its individuality. 'Beethoven', 'School Days' and 'Sweet Little Sixteen' are lingered over, and when he makes his familiar stab at Elmore James's 'It Hurts Me Too' he does us the courtesy of treating those despairing lyrics with respect. 'Reelin' and Rockin'' is always a dodgy moment, too often endless and lavatorial, and Mr Berry is indeed a connoisseur of lavatories. But tonight's treatment is briefer and straightforward, a reminder that in its simplest incarnation it was one of his most rousing chorus songs.

Those 'Nadine' rhymes and complex lyric lines are still jaw-dropping, followed by a pleasant walk through Jimmy Reed's 'Honest I Do'. Suddenly he shouts: 'Is Schoeneberg here? I just wanna know if my attorney's here. Could get served any time!' One can only guess what he might have been up to behind the back wall of the Duck Room.

After another stalwart, his rude and rather tedious take on 'South of the Border', he hits a familiar guitar introduction and stops dead. 'Oh, no. That's "Nadine". We've done that.' When he finds the right groove, 'Maybellene', it is the highlight of the evening, a frantic chase but with every familiar word still as clear as a bell. The inevitable 'My Ding-a-Ling' follows, but the crowd are in enthusiastic voice, and there's room to get a refill at the bar while he runs through his creaking willy puns.

A contemplative 'Mean Old World' leads into 'Johnny B Goode', and so it's time to get the girls up on stage. As Berry riffs on he is suddenly surrounded on cue by twisting women half a century his junior, just as he likes it, and he climbs into the audience to admire them from a lower angle. Suddenly we're in a 1960s 'beat group' movie, except that the girls' hair swishes in time to the music rather than swinging stiffly in aerosol-sprayed helmets. Berry mounts the stage again unassisted, and asks the tiresome question about whether we really want him to play all night. As always, with the affirmative answer billowing from the crowd, he disappears for good, clanging his Gibson like a steam-train siren as he jigs carefully backwards towards the stage door.

Maybe he knows that these days such intimate little pub gigs are his most flattering showcase, the most enjoyable way of maintaining the adulation-feed. His voice was never a technical phenomenon – it was always simply, delightfully, Chuck Berry's voice – and for it to be miked up in echoing stadiums inevitably confirms its decline in old age, with the edges cracked and the pitch often uncertain. But in a small room he knows he doesn't have to strain. As for his guitar, for many years he has so often tended just to sketch in those wonderful original solos knowing that his audience are replaying the real thing in their heads.

So at Blueberry Hill we've had the songs, the strut, the facial mugging, the time-honed backchat, and reminders of the greatest guitar in rock 'n' roll. From a distance of 10 feet. It was a night to savour, a pilgrimage undertaken more than thirty-seven years after I had first seen him at the Colston Hall in Bristol. When Carl Belz wrote in 1969 that Berry's music had failed to develop because it didn't need to, he was of course quite correct – although *San Francisco Dues* did expand the frame of reference slightly three years after he gave that verdict. But once you've written 'Johnny B Goode' it isn't possible to top it. Maybe Belz was in fact complimenting Berry, saluting the fact that he had created rock 'n' roll perfection. Because once you've done that, all you can do is repeat it.

# acknowledgements

My first vote of thanks must go to Fred Rothwell, author of *Long Distance Information: Chuck Berry's Recorded Legacy*. This assiduous and entertaining piece of detective work is an account of every Chuck Berry recording session, and as such was an invaluable reference source. It was always my intention to make this biography run parallel to Fred's book, as a companion piece, but inevitably I swerve into it regularly – after all, an artist's recordings provide a useful chronological spine to his career, and are indeed his legacy.

Having finished his own book, Fred turned over to me on very extended loan his bulging cuttings files and other reference material. This was a remarkable act of generosity, enriching my own library, which I can only repay by wholeheartedly recommending his book. John Tracy, of Perennial Music, also kindly filled in some gaps in my references from his own archive.

My first contact in St Louis, Berry's home town, was an old pub-rock chum Roy St John, who once fronted such London-based outfits as Klondike Pete and the Huskies. I particularly recall one Saturday night gig in a Kilburn pub where the women, as well as the men, were fighting, seemingly oblivious to Roy's unique combination of laid-back American cool and English irony. He is now back in his native city as one of its top radio presenters, and was my guide to St Louis.

But he doesn't have a spare room, so I will be forever grateful to Marilyn Andrew, her partner Bob Friend and her daughter Erin Eckstein, whose comfortable house off Delmar Boulevard proved to be a home from home to an unknown Englishman who turned up late one evening and refused to leave. And just as Tony Bennett left his heart in San Francisco, so I left two pairs of jeans in St Louis – thanks for sending them on.

It was, of course, a particular privilege to meet the legendary Johnnie Johnson and his charming wife Frances, and also to talk to such local luminaries as Oliver Sain, Otis Woodard and Joe Edwards, as well as visiting Dave Torretta's basement studio. Dave and his wife Connie play in soul band Fairchild, and to sit in a bar with a bottle of wine listening to music of Fairchild's quality being played a few feet away was to be taken back to the heady days when Peter Green's Fleetwood Mac, John Mayall's Bluesbreakers and The Spencer Davis Group worked in such north London pubs as The Manor House and The Fishmongers' Arms.

I am very grateful to Bob Baldori for his insights into Chuck Berry's music. Bob still plays with Berry and he is an advocate for the positive sides of the great man, which of course are many – I write this book primarily as a fan. Neither Bob nor Dave Torretta, who is engineering Berry's current material, are responsible for any of the darker stuff in the book, and as for Johnnie Johnson – he is incapable of thinking ill of anybody. He has a Mandela-like immunity to bitterness which is utterly admirable.

Finally, thanks to my editor at Aurum Press, Graham Coster, who shares my passion for the blues, rock 'n' roll, Chuck Berry – and cricket.

# bibliography

*The Autobiography* by Chuck Berry (Faber and Faber Limited, 1988)

*Long Distance Information: Chuck Berry's Recorded Legacy* by Fred Rothwell (Music Mentor Books, 2001)

*Chuck Berry: Mr Rock 'n' Roll* by Krista Reese (Proteus Books, 1982)

*Chuck Berry: Rock 'n' Roll Music* by Howard A. DeWitt (Pierian Press, 1985)

*Father of Rock 'n' Roll: the Story of Johnnie 'B Goode' Johnson* by Travis Fitzpatrick (Thomas, Cooke & Company, 1999)

*The Story of Chess Records* by John Collis (Bloomsbury, 1998)

*Spinning Blues Into Gold* by Nadine Cohodas (Aurum Press Limited, 2001)

*Top Pop Records 1955–1972* by Joel Whitburn (Record Research, 1973)

*Top Rhythm & Blues Records 1949–1971* by Joel Whitburn (Record Research, 1973)

*Top Country & Western Records 1949–1971* by Joel Whitburn (Record Research, 1972)

*British Hit Singles*, Ninth Edition by Paul Gambaccini, Jonathan Rice and Tim Rice (Guinness Publishing, 1993)

*Record Hits* compiled by Clive Solomon (Omnibus Press, 1977)

*British Hit Albums*, Fourth Edition by Paul Gambaccini, Jonathan Rice and Tim Rice (Guinness Publishing, 1990)

*The Rolling Stone Interviews* (Straight Arrow Publishers, Inc., 1971)

*The Sound of the City* by Charlie Gillett (Sphere Books, 1971)

*Lillian Roxon's Rock Encyclopedia* by Lillian Roxon (Grosset & Dunlap's Universal Library, 1971)

*The Story of Rock* by Carl Belz (Oxford University Press, 1969)

*The Poetry of Rock* by Richard Goldstein (1969)

*Times of Our Lives* by Orick Johns (1973)

*The Rockin' 50s* by Arnold Shaw (Hawthorn Books, Inc., 1974)

*Bo Diddley: Living Legend* by George R. White (Castle Communications, 1995)

*I Am the Blues: the Willie Dixon Story* by Willie Dixon with Don Snowden (Quartet Books Limited, 1989)

*Buddy Holly: a Biography* by Ellis Amburn (St Martin's Press, 1995)

*Remembering Buddy* by John Goldrosen and John Beecher (GRR/Pavilion, 1987)

*Muddy Waters: the Mojo Man* by Sandra B. Tooze (ECW Press, 1997)

*Rock, Roll and Remember* by Dick Clark with Richard Robinson (Popular Library, 1978)

*The Life and Times of Little Richard* by Charles White (Harmony Books, 1984)

*Hellfire: The Jerry Lee Lewis Story* by Nick Tosches (Plexus, 1982)

*Great Balls of Fire: The True Story of Jerry Lee Lewis* by Myra Lewis with Murray Silver (Virgin, 1982)

*Jimi* by Curtis Knight (W.H. Allen, 1974)

*Stone Alone* by Bill Wyman

*No Direction Home: the Life and Music of Bob Dylan* by Robert Shelton (New English Library, 1986)

*Urban Blues* by Charles Keil (The University of Chicago Press, 1966)

*Coast to Coast: a Rock Fan's US Tour* by Andy Bull (Black Swan, 1993)

*Making Tracks* by Charlie Gillett (W.H. Allen, 1975)

*Blues Who's Who* by Sheldon Harris (Da Capo, 1981)

*The Story of the Blues* by Paul Oliver (Penguin, 1972)

*Conversation with the Blues* by Paul Oliver (Cassell, 1965)

*The Guinness Who's Who of Blues* edited by Colin Larkin (Guinness Publishing, 1993)

*The Penguin Encyclopedia of Popular Music,* Second Edition edited by Donald Clarke (Penguin, 1998)

*Reading Jazz* edited by Robert Gottlieb (Bloomsbury, 1997)

*Combo: USA* by Rudi Blesh (1971)

*Encyclopedia Britannica*

*Rolling Stone*: various

*St Louis Post-Dispatch*: various

*Melody Maker*: various

*New Musical Express*: various

*Record Mirror*: various

*DISCoveries*: December 1988

*Music Now*: date unknown

*Guitar Player*: February 1971

*Blues & Soul*: various

*Living Blues*: July–August 1977

*Blues Unlimited*: various
*Cream*: March 1972
*Sounds*: various
*Disc*: 16 January 1965
*Sunday Express*: date unknown
*Trouser Press*: date unknown
*Musician*: October 1988
*Riverfront Times*: 22–28 October 1986
*The Age*: 26 March 1988
*News of the World*: various
*Bradford Telegraph & Argus*: 22 November 1991
*Washington Post*: date unknown
*Jazz Journal*: various
*Billboard*: various
*Cash Box*: various
*Goldmine*: various
*Let It Rock*: various
*Now Dig This*: September 2000
*Jazzbeat*: April 1964
*Mojo*: September 2000
*The Mail on Sunday*: 4 March 2001
*The Observer*: 4 March 2001
Booklet accompanying box set *Chuck Berry: The Chess Years* (Charly) by
   Adam Komorowski
Essay by Colin Escott intended for (unissued) Bear Family box set
*The Chuck Berry Story: Long Live Rock 'n' Roll!* by Ralph M. Newman (TBE,
   April–May 1980)

# index